STOCK MARKET DEVELOPMENTS IN THE COUNTRIES OF THE GULF COOPERATION COUNCIL

Finance and Capital Markets Series
For a full list of all titles in the series please go to www.fcmseries.net

Stock Market Developments in the Countries of the Gulf Cooperation Council

EDITED BY
AHSAN MANSUR
AND
FERNANDO DELGADO

First published 2008 by
PALGRAVE MACMILLAN

Palgrave Macmillan in the UK is an imprint of Macmillan Publishers Limited, registered in England, company number 785998, of Houndmills, Basingstoke, Hampshire RG21 6XS.

Palgrave Macmillan in the US is a division of St Martin's Press LLC, 175 Fifth Avenue, New York, NY 10010.

Palgrave Macmillan is the global academic imprint of the above companies and has companies and representatives throughout the world.

Palgrave® and Macmillan® are registered trademarks in the United States, the United Kingdom, Europe and other countries.

ISBN-13: 978–0–230–20670–0 hardback
ISBN-10: 0–230–20670–0 hardback

This book is printed on paper suitable for recycling and made from fully managed and sustained forest sources. Logging, pulping and manufacturing processes are expected to conform to the environmental regulations of the country of origin.

A catalogue record for this book is available from the British Library.

Library of Congress Cataloging-in-Publication Data

    Stock market developments in the countries of the Gulf Cooperation Council / edited by Ahsan Mansur and Fernando Delgado.
      p. cm.—(Finance and capital markets series)
    Includes index.
    ISBN 978–0–230–20670–0 (alk. paper)
     1. Stock exchanges – Persian Gulf States. 2. Finance – Persian Gulf States. I. Mansur, Ahsan S., 1951–

HG5712.A3S76 2008
332.64′2536—dc22   2008021568

10 9 8 7 6 5 4 3 2 1
17 16 15 14 13 12 11 10 09 08

Printed and bound in Great Britain by
CPI Antony Rowe, Chippenham and Eastbourne

Contents

List of Figures

List of Tables

List of Boxes

Notes on Contributors

THE EDITORS

Ahsan Mansur, a national of Bangladesh, is a Division Chief at the Middle East and Central Asia Department of the International Monetary Fund. He obtained his BA (Hon.) in Economics from the University of Dhaka, Bangladesh and his PhD from the University of Western Ontario, Canada. During his long career at the IMF, Mr. Mansur has worked on Middle Eastern, Asian, African and Central American countries. He also served as the IMF Senior Resident Representative to Pakistan during 1998–01 and as the Fiscal Advisor to the Minister of Finance, government of Bangladesh (1989–91). Most recently, he served as the Division Chief for the Gulf Cooperation Council (GCC) Division, when he also headed the team working on recent stock market developments in the GCC region. Mr. Mansur has published extensively in various journals (including Econometrica, journal of Economic Theory and the INF Staff Papers), in edited books on special economic topics and in the IMF Occasional Paper and Working Paper series.

Fernando Delgado has a PhD in Economics by the Universidad Complutense (Madrid-Spain); a MBA by the IADE-Universidad Autónoma de Madrid and a Master in Banking Management by the IESE (Spain). Currently, he is a Deputy Division Chief at the Middle East and Central Asia Department of the IMF, where he leads missions to Bahrain, Djibouti and Syria. As mission chief with the Money and Capital Markets department of the IMF he headed the technical assistance teams during the banking crisis in Ecuador, Nicaragua, Paraguay and Dominican Republic. Previously he was General Manager of the International Division of Caja de Madrid, the fourth largest Spanish financial group, member of the Board of Caymadrid Ltd., Chairman of the Economic and Monetary Policy Committee of the European Savings

Banks Group and Associate Professor in the Applied Economics Department of the Universidad Complutense de Madrid. He has published a number of articles and working papers, mainly in the field of industrial organization applied to the financial system.

THE CONTRIBUTORS

Mitra Farahbaksh is a senior Economist at the International Monetary Fund. Some of her publications include: (i) Issues in prudential Regulation and Supervision of Islamic Banks, IMF Working Paper No. 98/30; and (ii) Bank-by-Bank Credit Ceilings in *Instruments of Monetary Management: Issues and Country Experiences*, edited by Balino and Zamalloa, IMF 1997. Mitra holds a PhD in Economics from New York University.

Maher Hasan gained a PhD in economics from Washington State University in 2001. He joined the IMF in 2005 and is currently Desk Economist for several countries including GCC. Dr. Hasan has written several research papers on issues related to GCC stock markets and the MENA regional financial sector. He served as a Director of the Governor's Office and Assistant Director for the Banking Supervision Department of the Central Bank of Jordan before joining the Fund.

Dima Jardaneh is an Economist in the Middle East and Central Asia Department at the International Monetary Fund. Dima previously worked in banking and served as an Equity Research Analyst with a focus on financial institutions in the MENA region. Dima holds an MA in Economics from New York University.

Mohammed Omran is the Vice Chairman of Cairo and Alexandria Stock Exchange and Professor of Finance at the Arab Academy for Science and Technology. Professor Omran was a Visiting Professor in several research and academic institutions. He served several years as an Economist at both the Arab Monetary Fund in Abu Dhabi and the International Monetary Fund in Washington DC. He was an advisor to the Minister of Investment and an Acting Executive Director to the Egyptian Institute of Directors. Professor Omran has been awarded several research grants and prizes, was a Fulbright Scholar and is a Research Fellow at the Economic Research Forum. He specializes in financial markets, corporate governance, corporate finance and privatization, concentrating on the MENA region. He has over 30 published papers in various international Economics and Finance journals.

Lema Zekrya has worked on public finance and debt issues in Africa and Asia (Afghanistan, C.A.R., Côte d'Ivoire, India, Lao PDR) and is currently working at the World Bank on the Heavily Indebted Poor Countries (HIPC) Initiative. She studied at the London School of Economics and Harvard University (MPA/IFD).

Preface

Powered by the region's massive oil earnings, Gulf Cooperation Council (GCC) economies grew dramatically, with positive fiscal and external current account positions, and rapidly expanding banking systems. The GCC corporate sector had explosive profitability and earnings growth relative to its global peers, supported by expansionary fiscal spending and massive investment programs throughout the region. These conditions, coupled with rosy economic prospects, fuelled the unprecedented boom in most GCC equity markets beginning in 2003. The GCC markets surpassed the gains in stock price indices recorded during the NASDAQ dot.com bubble and the Japanese asset price bubble of the late 1980s. However, despite the strong fundamentals, most characteristics of a stock market bubble were also observed during the GCC boom.

Amid surging stock prices and growing concerns about the impact of a major market correction on the domestic financial system and the real economy, the GCC authorities requested that an International Monetary Fund staff team undertake this study. The staff team, led by Ahsan Mansur, comprised Messrs. Fernando Delgado, Maher Hasan, Mohammed Omran, and Mses. Mitra Farahbaksh, Dima Jardaneh, and Lema Zekrya. An earlier version of this study was presented to the GCC Secretariat and to all GCC country authorities in October 2006. All chapters have since been revised, in light of comments received from the relevant GCC authorities and also to reflect developments in GCC markets through June 2007.

This book analyzes the factors contributing to the rapid increase in GCC stock prices during 2003–05 and the subsequent correction that began in late 2005 and intensified further in early 2006. It analyzes the similarities and differences in the markets' performance, the reactions of the national authorities during the boom and bust cycle, and the impact of the correction on domestic economic activity. The book has eight chapters: an overview chapter that examines the issues in a regional context, six separate country chapters that analyze stock market behavior in each of the six GCC countries, and a final chapter on the GCC countries' capital market institutional and legal frameworks.

The first paper by Messrs. Mansur, Delgado, and Hasan, provides an overview of GCC market developments drawing on the findings of the country specific chapters. It analyzes the factors contributing to the boom and bust cycles in four GCC countries from a regional perspective and why the remaining two countries had such a different experience. Some lessons and policy recommendations that aim to reduce the vulnerability of the equity market and the banking sector are also presented. The analysis concludes that, although stock price indices increased broadly in line with economic fundamentals during 2002–04, speculative pressures led to a substantial overvaluation in the fast-growing GCC markets in 2005. Market valuations declined to historical average levels in relation to earnings following the correction, and as of end-June 2007, prices were back in line with fundamentals. However, structural weaknesses and geopolitical risks have contributed to continued price volatility. The paper observes that the stock market correction had a limited impact on financial stability and economic growth, due to the soundness of the region's banking systems, the retention of capital gains by most household investors, and the preventive and remedial measures taken by the authorities. The authors recommend continued oversight to limit financial exposure to stock market risk, including regional coordination to address contagion effects. Reforms to address the capital markets' structural weaknesses should also continue.

The chapter on Bahrain by Ms. Jardaneh and Mr. Omran discusses the wide performance gap between the Bahrain Stock Exchange (BSE) and other GCC stock markets. It finds that although the BSE's performance during 2002–05 was broadly in line with fundamentals and exceeded returns in other emerging markets, the gains were well below those recorded in the booming GCC markets. The correction experienced by the BSE was also relatively modest compared with the large corrections in some of the other regional markets. The authors argue that the BSE's divergent behavior is rooted in factors that differentiate Bahraini stocks from the rest of the region. These factors include important differences in Bahrain's macroeconomic, market specific and regulatory characteristics; the country's lesser dependence on oil; the limited privatization schedule and few initial public offerings (IPOs) in recent years; greater opportunities for private sector investment and funding; and well-established regulatory standards in the capital market. Deepening of the stock market in Bahrain will require measures to activate listings through share issue privatization; to strengthen the role of small and medium-sized enterprises and venture capitalists to broaden the investor base; to develop advanced financial instruments; and to ensure that the regulatory environment keeps pace with developments in capital markets.

The chapter on Kuwait by Mr. Hasan examines the developments in the Kuwait Stock Exchange (KSE) over the last three years, including the improvement in fundamentals; exuberant demand; the authorities' policy response; and structural weaknesses that make the market prone to boom and bust cycles. The chapter also includes a set of warning signals to assess market developments. The analysis concludes that the 2006 correction brought market valuation closer to market fundamentals and it is unlikely that the recent moderate correction – or a slightly sharper one – would have a significant adverse impact on private sector demand or on banking system soundness. The profitability of non-bank financial institutions is however very sensitive to market developments and should be monitored closely. Furthermore, the stock market has important structural weaknesses that could increase the depth and the length of any correction. The authorities' future policies should focus on measures to strengthen the market's resilience to the development of speculative bubbles.

The chapter on Oman by Ms. Farabaksh finds that during 2002–05 the Muscat Stock Market (MSM) witnessed relatively smaller gains than the boom experienced by the other regional stock markets and had a more modest correction in the latter part of 2005 than those same markets. Also, the MSM, along with the BSE, was one of the two markets in the region where the price index rose in 2006. The chapter analyzes the factors that explain the observed differences in the development of Omani stock prices relative to other GCC markets, and the specific characteristics that have set its market apart from those of the rest of the region. It concludes that the market's performance reflected the underlying strong economic fundamentals and the specific characteristics of the Omani market, including significant market depth and a strong legal framework. The relatively moderate increase in stock prices in Oman compared to other GCC countries reflected market-based factors such as the small impact of IPOs, macroeconomic developments, and well-established regulatory standards and structural reforms.

The chapter on Qatar by Mr. Delgado and Ms. Zekrya finds that the Doha Securities Market (DSM) was one of the most exuberant in the region, reflecting improved economic fundamentals (namely, the increase in oil prices and the planned expansion of the Qatari gas industry and associated services) that supported the valuation of Qatari companies. However, the market was also propelled by rising speculative demand. The chapter analyzes the factors that contributed to the surge in the DSM price index beyond what was justified by the strengthening of fundamentals during 2002–05. The chapter also examines the correction that followed the index's September 2005 peak. The chapter concludes that the recent market correction has brought prices broadly in line with economic fundamentals, as most indicators of stock overvaluation have disappeared. Much of the remaining gains are likely to be retained since such valuation can be largely explained by Qatar's strong economic fundamentals and specific economic characteristics. The Qatari economy endured the correction well, and economic growth and financial stability were not affected. Strengthening the capital market regulatory framework will foster market stability and prevent the recurrence of another boom and bust cycle.

The chapter on Saudi Arabia by Messrs. Delgado and Hasan analyzes the factors that contributed to surging stock prices on the Saudi Arabian stock market (Tadawul) beyond what was justified by the strengthening of fundamentals and thereby precipitating a major market correction in early 2006. The recent oil boom greatly impacted the value and profitability of the Saudi corporate sector in general, and firms associated with oil and petrochemical services and products in particular. As investors were persuaded that oil prices would remain high for the medium term and that prospects for profit growth were sound, the stock prices of Saudi firms began a startling upward trend. Eventually, the euphoria generated among small investors by quick and easy gains accelerated the increase in prices at a time when firms' profit growth rates were starting to slow. The resulting price bubble finally burst on February 25, 2006, leading to a strong market correction. The chapter finds that the market correction, which continued through the first half of 2007, has reduced prices to levels broadly in line with fundamentals; the impact of the correction on financial stability and economic growth is expected to be negligible; and a number of measures can be taken to prevent another boom and bust cycle in the future.

The chapter on the United Arab Emirates (UAE) by Mr. Omran examines stock price behavior during the period leading up to and immediately following the stock market correction of 2005. Both the Abu Dhabi Securities Market (ADSM) and the Dubai Financial Market (DFM) experienced unprecedented stock price increases during 2003–05, due largely to improved economic fundamentals, intensified speculative activities, and market specific factors. However, this stellar performance was followed by a sharp correction – by June 2007, the ADSM and the DFM had declined by about 43 percent and 48 percent from their peaks in May and November 2005, respectively. The paper concludes that although the market correction has adversely affected a large number of individual investors, the UAE economy has weathered the turbulence in equity markets very well, largely due to a resilient financial sector, historically high oil prices, and robust government finances. To reduce the risk of asset price volatility in the future, further efforts are needed to strengthen the regulatory framework governing capital markets and develop the authorities' supervisory capabilities; expand the role of institutional investors; encourage the development of a bond market; and facilitate the introduction of new financial instruments leading to greater efficiency in the pricing and distribution of risk among investors.

The final chapter by Ms. Farahbaksh discusses the evolution of the securities regulatory framework across the region over the last few years. It identifies the similarities and differences between the institutional set-ups and regulatory frameworks in GCC countries, with the International Organization of Securities Commissions' (IOSCO) best practices taken as benchmarks. Finally, the chapter provides a number of recommendations that could form the basis for a future reform agenda.

This book is the outcome of the strong support and encouragement we received from many of our senior colleagues in the Middle East and Central Asia Department of the International Monetary Fund. We would like to give special thanks to Messrs. Mohsin Khan, Amor Tahari, Lorenzo Perez, and Juan Carlos Di Tata for their continuous support, without which this project could not have been completed. Special thanks also to Mses. Ai Kato-Ilagan, Sheila Tomilloso, and Ana Franco for word processing, to Messrs. Kazuta Sakamoto and Arthur Ribeiro da Silva for research assistance, and to Ms. Luisa LaFleur for valuable editorial support. The country specific chapters also significantly benefited from comments from Mr. Al-Raisi, Senior Manager, Central Bank of Oman, and representatives of the capital market authorities in Doha, Oman and Saudi Arabia. The views expressed in the various chapters, and any errors, are entirely the responsibility of the authors, and should not be attributed to the International Monetary Fund.

CHAPTER 1

GCC Equity Market Developments: An Overview

Ahsan Mansur, Fernando Delgado, and Maher Hasan

1.1 INTRODUCTION

The equity markets of several Gulf Cooperation Council (GCC)[1] countries underwent a major correction in 2006 that wiped out much of the gains accumulated during a spectacular three-year bull run. This chapter analyzes the rapid increase in stock prices from 2003 to 2005, and the subsequent correction in 2006, the different behaviors of the various regional markets, as well as the conduct of the national authorities during the price increase and correction phases. Based on this analysis, the chapter explores the correction's effect on financial stability and economic growth and analyzes whether the correction has brought stock prices in line with fundamentals. Finally, some lessons are drawn and policy changes are recommended to reduce equity market and banking sector vulnerability.

Although stock price indices increased broadly in line with economic fundamentals during 2002–04, substantial overvaluation took place in the fast-growing markets[2] in 2005. Market overvaluation diminished significantly following a sharp correction in 2006 and, as of end-June 2007, prices are broadly in line with fundamentals. However, some factors, including structural weaknesses and geopolitical risk, explain the continued high price volatility. Under these circumstances, further corrections affecting mainly speculative stocks cannot be ruled out, but a substantial part of equity valuation gains is likely to be retained across the region as long as fundamentals remain strong. On the other hand, further sharp price increases beyond the improvement of fundamentals will raise the risk of overvaluation and thus the risk of severe future corrections. The bursting of the bubble has had limited impact on financial stability and economic growth due to the soundness of the region's banking systems, the retention of capital gains for buy-and-hold household investors, and the preventive and remedial measures taken by the authorities. Continuous intensified oversight is needed to limit financial exposure to stock market risk, including regional coordination to address contagion effects. The implementation of structural reforms to firm up the capital markets' structural weaknesses should also continue.

The remainder of this chapter is organized as follows: Section 1.2 provides a brief background of the recent evolution of the GCC equity markets. Section 1.3 explores why stock prices rose during the 2003–05 period. Section 1.4 analyzes the causes of the 2006 market correction, and the role of the national authorities. Section 1.5 examines the markets after the 2007 recovery and whether the correction has run its course. Section 1.6 describes the effect of the correction on financial stability and economic growth. Finally, Section 1.7 provides some policy recommendations.

1.2   BACKGROUND

Since their inception over the past two decades (Table 1.1), GCC equity markets have generally underperformed vis-à-vis the equity markets in

Table 1.1   GCC stock markets

Country	Market	Year of establishment
Bahrain	Bahrain Stock Exchange (BSE)	1987
Kuwait	Kuwait Stock Exchange (KSE)	1977
Oman	Muscat Securities Market (MSM)	1988
Qatar[a]	Doha Securities Market (DSM)	1995
Saudi Arabia[b]	Tadawul	1984
UAE	Abu Dhabi Security Market (ADSM)	2000
UAE	Dubai Financial Market (DFM)	2000

Notes:
[a] Activities started in May 1997.
[b] Although the Tadawul platform was launched in October 2001, an organized stock market has existed since 1984.

Source: BSE; KSE; MSM; DSM; Tadawul; ADSM and DFM.

industrial countries and some large emerging markets. Except for short-lived and isolated speculative outbursts, their growth and profitability have been well below major equity markets and only marginally above the Morgan Stanley Emerging Markets Index (MSCI). These boom and bust episodes included the 1982 *Al-Mannak* bubble in Kuwait, mainly due to the lack of effective regulation for over-the-counter trade; the 1991 Saudi Arabian bubble, prompted by the repatriation of funds after the Kuwaiti invasion; and the 1998 Omani bubble after the market was opened to foreign investors.

In early 2003, stock prices in most GCC markets began to increase rapidly. Excluding Oman and Bahrain, whose markets kept a moderate growth path, the GCC weighted price index[3] increased by 480 percent on average in the three-year period of 2003–05. This was an exceptional performance by any measure, particularly at a time of low interest rates and a declining trend in the global rate of return on financial assets. The GCC outperformed the MSCI, which grew by 140 percent in the same period, and only other Middle East markets with some similar characteristics, such as Egypt and Jordan, were able to surpass the GCC markets.[4]

The size and depth of the GCC markets increased dramatically during the same period, well beyond other Middle East and North Africa (MENA) markets and the average in emerging markets and industrial countries. For instance, Saudi market capitalization jumped from 22 percent of the entire MENA region in 2000 to 41 percent in 2005. The increase in the value of

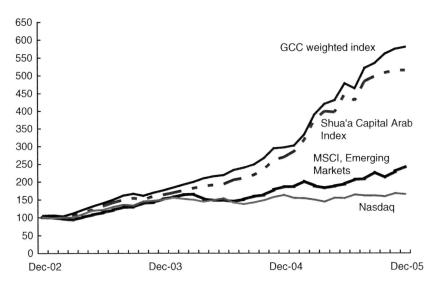

Figure 1.1 Performance of GCC stock price indices, 2002–05 (December 31, 2002 = 100)

Sources: Bloomberg; and Fund staff estimates.

Table 1.2   Equity markets in selected MENA countries: selected indicators, 2000 and 2005

Market	Market cap. ($ billions)		Market cap. (% GDP)		Value traded ($ billions)		Turnover ratio (%)	
	2000	2005	2000	2005	2000	2005	2000	2005
Egypt	28.5	79.5	30.7	72.4	11.8	27.7	34.7	34.8
Jordan	4.9	37.6	58.5	289.1	0.4	23.8	7.7	63.3
Kuwait	19.8	141.5	56.1	190.0	4.4	97.3	22.2	78.5
Qatar	8.2	87.1	46.2	253.6	0.4	28.3	4.5	32.4
Saudi Arabia	67.9	646.0	36.0	210.0	17.4	1,103.7	25.6	170.8
UAE	11.0	231.4	15.7	178.5	0.1	140.6	1.0	60.8
GCC	117.0	1,135.5	34.2	191.6	23.03	1,373.9	19.7	121.0
MENA	312.0	1,594.6	33.0	106.2	232.0	1,675.0	75.0	106.0

Sources: Arab Monetary Fund (AMF); Emerging Markets Database (EMDB); Federation of Euro-Asian Stock Exchanges (FEAS); International Financial Statistics (IFS) and World Development Indicators (WDI).

trade was even higher, with the total value of Saudi shares traded in the MENA region increasing from 7.5 percent in 2000 to around 66 percent in 2005. Total GCC market capitalization jumped from $107 billion (38 percent of the entire MENA region in 2000) to $1.1 trillion (69 percent of the MENA region in 2005).

Although all GCC markets registered gains during the period, there were wide performance differences between them. Stock prices in two of the seven regional equity markets,[5] Bahrain Stock Exchange (BSE) and Muscat Securities Market (MSM), grew at a relatively moderate pace during the booming years of 2003–05. The remaining five markets (Dubai Financial Market [DFM], Tadawul, Doha Securities Market [DSM] and, to a lesser extent, the Kuwait Stock Exchange [KSE] and the Abu Dhabi Securities Market [ADSM]), registered price increases that rapidly outpaced the growth in economic activity. Similarly, the volume and value of trade on the BSE and the MSM fell behind the extraordinary growth of the other GCC markets.

Market sentiment began to change in late 2005, and a sharp correction swept through most markets in early 2006. The widening gap between the increase in stock prices and economic fundamentals and the growing perception of overvaluation resulted in a price correction in the region's major markets (Qatar, Saudi Arabia, United Arab Emirates, and, to a lesser extent, Kuwait). The triggers for the correction were related to market-specific factors and explain why prices started to decline on different dates, beginning with the Qatari market in September 2005. Driven mainly by the bullish Saudi market, the GCC weighted price index continued to increase until February 2006, when it reached its peak of over 530 percent above the end-2002 level.

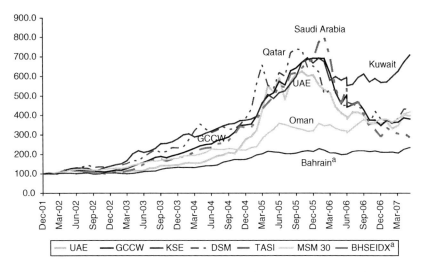

Figure 1.2 GCC stock market indices and weighted average GCC index, December 2001–March 2007

Note: [a] Bahrain Stock Price Index (BHSEIND) for 2005 was calculated based on the monthly growth rate in the new BHSEASI index.

Sources: Bloomberg; Stock market authorities; Fund Staff estimates; and Global Financial House.

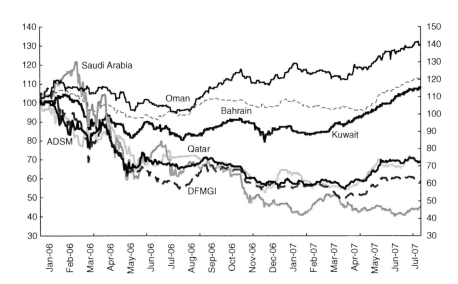

Figure 1.3 Performance of stock price indices, January 2006–July 26, 2007 (January 2006 = 100)

Sources: Bloomberg and Dubai Financial Markets.

The correction was across the board and accelerated sharply in the following three-month period through end-May 2006, with the cumulative losses amounting to 40–60 percent from the indices' peak values.[6] Prices remained volatile but began to stabilize in most markets during the second half of 2006, and upward price movements resumed in most markets by end-June 2007.

1.3   THE BOOMING YEARS: 2003–05

Rising GCC equity prices were initially due to strengthening economic fundamentals. Higher corporate profits resulting directly or indirectly from increasing oil prices and the associated boom induced by heightened public sector demand and the implementation of structural reforms,[7] fuelled the take-off in stock prices across the region in 2003. Other factors that directly explain the increase in stock prices were the Initial Public Offering (IPO) policy followed in some GCC countries and the shift in regional investors' preferences regarding the allocation of financial resources. Stock valuation indicators and the increase in price volatility pointed to a speculative bubble beginning in late 2004. Narrow market leadership and ample liquidity and credit contributed to the increase in speculative demand. Also, structural weaknesses affecting the GCC equity markets played an important role in the market boom and subsequent correction.[8] This section analyzes why GCC equity prices increased and the differences between the rapidly growing and less-buoyant GCC markets.

1.3.1   The strengthening of economic fundamentals

There is a strong correlation between the performance of all GCC stock price indices and oil prices. Although oil revenues have not been directly invested in domestic stock markets, oil wealth has found its way to the regional equity markets through several channels. The share prices of listed hydrocarbon-related companies have skyrocketed along with profits, boosted by higher unit prices, strong international demand, revaluation of inventories and reserves, and, in some cases, feedstock prices remaining below international prices (see Table 1.3 below). Despite the relatively high rate of savings of additional oil revenue, GCC authorities have increased expenditure, including in infrastructure and social projects. The fiscal stimulus increased liquidity and disposable income, contributing to the bull market. With oil prices projected to remain high in the medium term, the market has a solid basis to maintain a large part of the price gains made since 2002.

Corporate profitability grew markedly due to strong economic activity and private sector development was spurred by structural reforms.

Table 1.3 Companies listed in GCC stock markets: average profit growth

Stock market	Percentage growth	Period
BSE[a]	15.0	2000–05
MSM	22.5	2004–05
KSE	51.8	2000–05
ADSM[b]	41.7	2002–05
DFM[c]	71.4	2003–05
DSM	34.7	2000–05
Tadawul	52.0	2000–05

Notes:
[a] Sample of 4 companies representing 50.2 percent of total market capitalization as of end-2005.
[b] Sample of 5 companies representing 64 percent of total market capitalization as of end-2005.
[c] Sample of 7 companies representing 73.9 percent of total market capitalization as of end-2005.

Sources: BSE; KSE; ADSM; DFM; DSM; Tadawul and Fund staff estimates.

Table 1.4 Market share of Hydrocarbon-related companies (In % of total market share as of end-2005)

BSE	0.0
MSM	0.0
KSE	2.2
ADSM	5.4
DFM	0.0
DSM	33.0
Tadawul	27.3

Sources: National authorities and Fund staff estimates.

Companies listed in the GCC stock markets registered remarkable rates of profitability growth during the last five years, ranging from 40 to over 70 percent per year, except in the relatively slow Bahraini and Omani markets.[9] Although it is unlikely that these high rates of profitability growth are sustainable in the medium term (and this is one of the reasons for the 2006 market correction), the expected average profits of GCC-listed companies are still high compared with industrial and emerging markets. High oil prices (and the induced effects on economic activity) have resulted in larger stock price index gains in the leading oil-exporting countries, due in part to the larger share of hydrocarbon-related companies in total market capitalization. For instance, in the case of Saudi Arabia, the domestic price structure for petrochemicals feedstock could explain a large part of Saudi Basic Industries Corporation's (SABIC) competitive advantage, and the increase of SABIC's share price explains one half of the gains in the Tadawul All-Shares Index (TASI). Other factors not reflected in the firms' financial statements also influence the market valuation of GCC firms and could explain their higher Price-Earning Ratio (PER) and Price-To-Book Value ratio (PBV) ratios. These factors include the low tariffs on production inputs; free or very low cost land and infrastructure; very low costs of electricity, water, fuel, and feedstock (particularly for the petrochemicals sector); and a low tax rate (including for foreign investors).

Privatization, market liberalization, and listing regulations also positively impacted the rising price indices. The use of IPOs as the preferred privatization channel, and the generalized policy to price IPOs below their market value as a means to distribute wealth among the population at large, have also had an impact on price gains. Although speculative demand may have been responsible for some of the differential between the IPOs' offering price and the level at which prices plateaued, the policies in some markets (particularly Qatar, Saudi Arabia, and the United Arab Emirates) requiring that offering prices be related to the nominal value of the shares and not to their economic value is deemed to be responsible for most of the price gain. This factor alone could explain up to two-thirds of the Qatari stock price index gains during 2003–05, and up to one-third of the Tadawul and ADSM gains during the same period (see Tables 1.5 and 1.6).

Improvements in the stock markets' legal, regulatory, and supervisory frameworks may have also contributed to rising stock prices in some markets. For instance, in the United Arab Emirates, the Emirate Securities and Commodities Authority (ESCA) was established in 2000 to improve transparency and discourage unsound practices in the capital market. In Saudi Arabia, the authorities strengthened the equity market legal and regulatory framework by approving a new capital market law in 2003 and creating the Capital Market Authority (CMA) in 2004. These improvements, however, have not been homogeneous in the region, as explained in the chapter on Institutional and Legal Aspects of Capital Markets in the GCC Countries. In fact, some of the differences in performance among the regional markets can be explained by the uneven improvements in transparency, which have a real (but unquantifiable) impact on investors' confidence.

The shift in the regional allocation of Arab capital flows also explains a part of the gains. The perceived increase in political risks associated with foreign assets for domestic investors, and the global search for yield at a time of record low interest rates, have attracted a large amount of capital to regional stocks. The broad range of legal, regulatory, and supervisory changes and the ensuing increase in market transparency has further strengthened investor confidence in the region. Due to the relative scarcity

Table 1.5 Impact of IPOs on TASI, 2003–05

Issuer	Market capitalization[a] (%)	Date of listing	First day price increase			"Plateau" initial price increase[b]			First year price increase[c]		
			TASI (%)	Stock (%)	Percentage contribution[d]	TASI (%)	Stock (%)	Percentage contribution[d]	TASI (%)	Stock (%)	Percentage contribution[d]
Saudi Telecom	21.5	1/25/2003	5.6	39.4	8.5	3.01	30.1	6.5	69.7	148.7	32.0
Total 2003									76.2		32.0
Sahara	0.5	7/7/2004	0.9	200.0	1.0	4.9	250.5	1.2	76.2	277.5	1.4
Ettihad Etisalat	2.9	12/20/2004	-2.1	500.0	14.4	-2.3	650.0	18.7	-1.5	652.0	18.7
Total 2004									84.9		20.1
NCCI	0.3	1/17/2005	0.1	81.2	0.2	2.0	76.6	0.2	110.0	242.4	0.7
Bank Al Bilad	2.1	4/30/2005	-2.6	1,430.0	29.9	-2.5	1,388.0	29.0	44.8	1,596.0	33.4
SADAFCO	0.2	5/23/2005	-1.5	94.4	0.2	0.6	123.2	0.2	31.3	159.3	0.3
Almarai	0.7	8/17/2005	0.4	14.6	0.1	0.4	14.6	0.1	18.0	65.0	0.5
Total 2005									103.7		34.8

Notes:

[a] Market capitalization as of end of the first year of listing or closest end-of-year date.

[b] Includes the price increase during the first few days of listing, until a "plateau" price was established.

[c] Price increase from the date of listing to end-December of the IPO year.

[d] Stock price increase weighted by its market capitalization.

Sources: Bakheet Financial Advisors and Fund staff estimates.

Table 1.6 Impact of IPOs on DSM, 2003–05

Issuer	Market capitalization[a] (%)	Date of listing	First day price increase			"Plateau" initial price increase[b]			First year price increase[c]		
			DSM (%)	Stock (%)	Percentage contribution[d]	DSM (%)	Stock (%)	Percentage contribution[d]	DSM (%)	Stock (%)	Percentage contribution[d]
Industries Qatar	31.9	8/4/2003	1.0	521.0	166.2	8.80	567.0	180.9	12.8	499.0	159.2
		Total 2003							69.8		159.2
Qatar Meat and Livestock	0.2	1/21/2004	−0.2	109.0	0.2	2.5	113.0	0.2	61.0	110.0	0.2
		Total 2004							64.5		159.2
Qatar Gas Transport	6.8	10/4/2005	−1.8	609.0	41.2	−5.7	278.0	18.8	11.3	387.0	26.2
Dlala	0.4	5/9/2005	0.3	1,031.0	4.1	1.3	1,150.0	4.6	−16.0	1,111.0	4.4
		Total 2005							70.2		30.6

Notes:
[a] Market capitalization as of end of the first year of listing or closest end-of-year date.
[b] Includes the price increase during the first few days of listing, until a "plateau" price was established.
[c] Price increase from the date of listing to end-December of the IPO year.
[d] Stock price increase weighted by its market capitalization.

Sources: Zawya; Authorities and Fund staff estimates.

of available regional assets, these flows have been pushing up local stock and real estate prices. Since the increase in regional liquidity responded in part to this shift in investors' preferences toward regional assets, it provided an additional source of stable demand for regional stocks and an opportunity to deepen the market and diversify the product range.

1.3.2 Emergence of bubbles

This sub-section analyzes the potential development of bubbles in the booming GCC markets, based on warning signals derived from previous bubble episodes. Although several methodologies can be found in the current literature to assess whether stock price levels are due to the existence of equity market bubbles, none of them could be effectively applied to the GCC equity markets, as discussed in Appendix I. Limitations on model specification, the need for long data series, and the lack of available indices are among the factors that made these methodologies unsuitable. Alternatively, this chapter provides a descriptive analysis of the most common warning signals of speculative behavior, including the relatively high increase in the price index vs. other economic variables linked to fundamentals; the weak correlation between the price and economic value of stocks; high price volatility; a sizable acceleration in money and credit expansion including heavy use of margin lending; and an increasingly narrow market leadership.

Speculative demand surged in late 2004, resulting in an acceleration of stock prices beyond what could be justified by the improvement in economic fundamentals and other economic factors. The overheating of the markets, which was progressively apparent to professional investors, showed in a substantial acceleration of price increases and deterioration of valuation ratios. For instance, in Saudi Arabia, the PER broke its historical upper boundary of 20 in November 2004, and started a sharp take-off that propelled it to almost 50 at the peak of the stock price index at end-February 2006. Also, the PER for the most actively traded companies in the ADSM and DFM reached 45 and 66 times, respectively. The increase in price volatility pointed to the proximity of a correction. The speculative boom was enabled by abundant liquidity and credit in all markets, and was intensified in some cases by narrow market leadership in a limited, but highly active, group of speculative stocks (see Figure 1.4).

Professional investors and other insiders identified the emergence of a bubble early on. A March 2005 survey[10] of 740 business leaders in the GCC region revealed that more than 45 percent of them believed that a price bubble was developing in the booming markets, while more than 50 percent of them estimated that the markets were overvalued by at least 20 percent (see Tables 1.7 and 1.8).[11] The continued rapid increase in market indices after March 2005 further accentuated the perception of overvaluation.

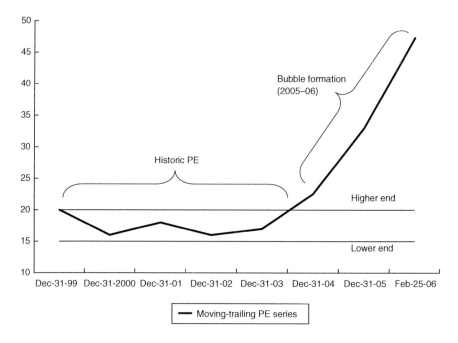

Figure 1.4 Saudi Arabia – PER, December 1999–February 2006
Sources: Shua'a Capital and Bakheet Investment Group.

Rapidly increasing price indices were the most obvious indicators that bubbles were developing in several GCC markets. As outlined in Section 1.2, the stock markets' performance exceeded their average historical performance during this period. The sheer size of the increase in stock price indices is daunting when compared with the gains in preceding major stock market bubbles, such as the dot.com bubble in 2000 or the Nikkei bubble in the late 1980s. Since the beginning of their acceleration, during the first quarter of 2003, the best performing equity markets in the region have accumulated gains well over those of the National Association of Securities Dealers Automated Quotation System (NASDAQ) and Nikkei markets during their bubble episodes (see Figure 1.5).[12]

The valuation indicators showed a progressively weaker correlation between stock prices and economic value. The price of a stock should theoretically reflect its economic value. One of the most common ways to calculate the economic value of a stock is through the present value of the dividends the investor will receive. Thus, the increase in the PER beyond what could be justified by an expected increase in future earnings is considered a clear sign of overvaluation. By the end of 2005, the markets' gains (with the exception of the KSE)[13] outpaced corporate earnings growth significantly resulting in the PER and PBV[14] exceeding their historical levels

Table 1.7 Business leaders' assessment of overpricing in the stock market (March 2005)

Stock markets					Real estate markets				
Has a price bubble formed in the stock market in:					Has a price bubble formed in the real estate market in:				
	Kuwait	Saudi Arabia	UAE	Qatar		Kuwait	Saudi Arabia	UAE	Qatar
Yes (%)	45.2	62.7	50.0	59.3	Yes (%)	80.6	55.3	83.3	81.5
No (%)	54.8	37.3	50.0	40.7	No (%)	19.4	44.7	16.7	18.5
To what extent is the market overpriced?					To what extent is the market overpriced?				
	Kuwait	Saudi Arabia	UAE	Qatar		Kuwait	Saudi Arabia	UAE	Qatar
By 0 to 10%	21.4	16.0	7.2	0.0	By 0 to 10%	12.0	9.6	4.9	0.0
By 11 to 19%	14.3	26.6	18.9	43.8	By 11 to 19%	16.0	30.1	18.9	9.1
By 20 to 29%	14.3	18.1	36.0	25.0	By 20 to 29%	32.0	31.3	28.6	31.8
By 30 to 39%	35.7	20.2	23.4	12.5	By 30 to 39%	12.0	12.0	25.4	18.2
More than 40%	14.3	19.1	14.4	18.8	More than 40%	28.0	16.9	22.2	40.9

Source: HSBC-MEED Middle East Business Confidence Survey.

Table 1.8 GCC, United States and Japan: developments in equity valuations
(Equity indices rebased to 100 at peak price date)

	−2 years	−1 year	−2 months	−1 month	Peak	+1 month	+2 months	+3 months	+4 months	+1 year	+19 months	+2 years
Japan (Nikkei)	55.4	77.5	91.3	95.1	100.0	95.5	88.9	84.1	86.6	61.3	62.0	57.7
US (Nasdaq)	34.6	47.7	80.2	88.8	100.0	83.0	67.0	76.8	78.8	40.7	32.2	38.2
Saudi Arabia	22.9	43.0	80.5	90.5	100.0	74.0	66.1	50.3	62.7	40.6	38.1	–
UAE (NBAD)	22.0	32.2	91.2	91.8	100.0	95.5	96.6	80.6	76.9	56.9	56.6	–
Qatar	29.0	42.5	79.2	93.9	100.0	96.3	86.6	79.1	71.6	59.3	48.5	–
Kuwait (KSE)	42.8	53.9	97.7	95.7	100.0	90.9	87.2	81.2	85.8	79.9	107.0	–
Bahrain	56.8	79.8	95.5	93.7	100.0	96.6	90.3	90.0	88.2	91.3	92.2	–
Oman	41.8	59.7	79.5	81.4	100.0	94.2	90.0	88.6	88.4	86.1	104.5	–

Notes: Equity Peaks: Japan (12/29/1989), US (3/10/2000), Bahrain (11/16/2005), Kuwait (7/2/2006), Oman (6/20/2006), Qatar (9/20/2005), Saudi Arabia (2/25/2006), UAE (11/12/2005).

Source: Bloomberg.

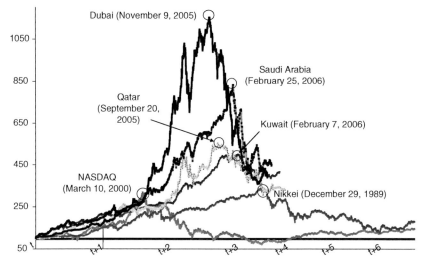

Figure 1.5   Stock price indices in selected GCC countries compared with the "Dot.Com" and Nikkei Bubbles (Normalized to 100 at the start of the acceleration of price increases "t")

Source: Bloomberg.

and the average levels for the emerging and developed markets. Similarly, the Dividend Yield ratios (DY) compared less favorably with historical and other markets' levels (see Table 1.9).[15] At their peaks, the average PER of the Tadawul (47.3), DSM (42), and DFM (43) were close to the average PERs of 61 and 50 for NASDAQ[16] and the S&P 500, respectively at the peak of the dot.com bubble. They were also close to the peak level of 49 achieved during the short-lived first Saudi market bubble between January 1991 and June 1992, when the price index increased by 83 percent in 1991 and by an additional 25 percent in the first six months of 1992 before losing all its gains in the following three years.

Volatility in the GCC stock markets rose substantially, as measured by the monthly coefficient of variation of the price indices. A sizable increase in price volatility, frequently associated with the bursting of speculative price bubbles,[17] was observed just prior to the start of the market corrections. The hike in the coefficients of variation ranged from 95 percent in the DSM to 380 percent in the Qatari market. These increases in price volatility were large when compared with the spike in the NASDAQ coefficient of variation during the dot.com bubble (224 percent in April 2000). The volatility in the overheated GCC price indices was also well above that observed in some previous bubbles in the region (see Figures 1.6 and 1.7).[18]

Table 1.9   Key stock market valuation indicators[a]

	PER	PBV	Dividend yield (percent)
Bahrain Stock Exchange	12.78	2.13	3.06
Kuwait Stock Exchange	16.38	4.14	2.52
Muscat Stock Market	18.12	2.59	2.63
Doha Stock Market	30.20	6.50	1.30
Tadawul All Shares Index (Saudi Arabia)	39.80	9.00	1.40
Dubai Financial Market	43.60	5.43	1.30
Abu Dhabi Stock Market	33.70	6.15	1.01
Bombay Sensex	20.33	4.45	1.28
Korea Stock Exchange	11.68	1.60	0.55
Russia Trading System	10.05	1.41	1.88
Brazil Stock Market	10.45	1.47	5.70
Taiwan Stock Exchange	13.81	1.79	3.83
South Africa Top 40	10.90	1.82	2.62
Mexico Bol	11.35	3.04	1.78
Shanghai Composite	18.31	1.80	2.65
Kuala Lumpur Composite	14.10	1.70	4.81
Average Emerging[b]	19.72	3.44	2.40
Nasdaq Composite	35.38	2.56	0.67
S&P 500	18.23	2.82	1.80

Notes:
[a] Data as of end-2005.
[b] Simple average.

Sources: Bloomberg; stockselector.com; Bakheet Financial Advisor; KAMCO and Fund staff estimates.

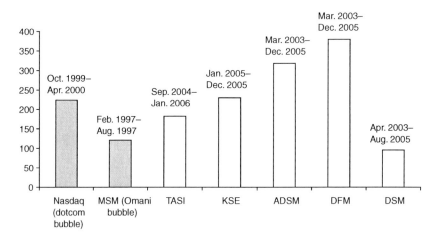

Figure 1.6   Increase in coefficient of variation during the Dot.com and Omani Bubbles and the booming GCC markets (In percent)

Sources: Bloomberg and Fund staff estimates.

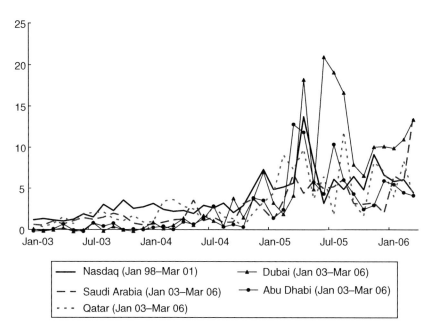

Figure 1.7   Recent volatility of selected GCC stock markets vs. NASDAQ's Dot. com Bubble

Sources: Bloomberg and Fund staff estimates.

A rapid increase in money growth may have contributed substantially to the spike in stock prices. Markets in countries with higher rates of money (M2) growth tend to outperform those with lower money growth rates (see Figure 1.8).[19] The acceleration in money growth in most countries is attributed mainly to the strong rate of increase in credit to the private sector, ranging from a compound annual rate of 21.0 percent in Kuwait to 36.5 percent in Qatar, during 2003–05.[20] These rates of credit growth are substantially above those observed in the two years preceding the bursting of the NASDAQ bubble (10.8 percent) or the five-year boom period preceding the Nikkei bubble (15.5 percent). An important part of the increase in credit was channeled to finance speculative demand in the stock market, as hinted at by the heavy use of margin lending and personal facilities.[21]

The strong growth in margin lending and personal loans also points to the development of a speculative bubble. Margin lending increased substantially in some of the GCC countries in 2003–05. For instance, in Kuwait it increased from 6 percent to 9 percent of total private sector credit, while the corresponding increase in Saudi Arabia was from 2 percent to 8 percent during 2003–04. The market indices moved in tandem with the level of margin loans in many countries.[22] Furthermore, a substantial part of personal loans, which have been the fastest growing

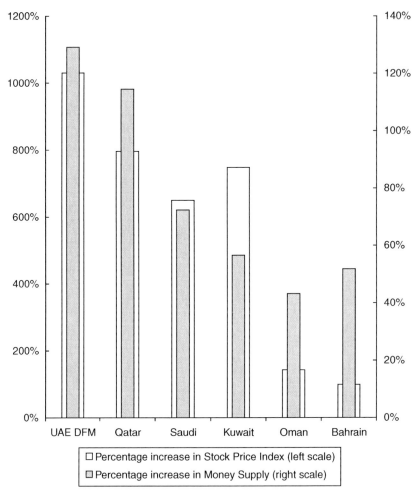

Figure 1.8 Cumulative percentage increase in money supply and stock indices in GCC December 2000–December 2005

Sources: Bloomberg; and IMF Statistical Databases.

component of credit to the private sector in most GCC countries during the period, were likely channeled to the stock exchange. The heavy use of margin lending could also be assessed by the relatively high percentage of market capitalization that was financed by leveraged positions. As of end-2005, margin loans represented about 3 percent of the Kuwaiti and Saudi[23] markets' total market capitalization, well above the 2.3 percent of market capitalization in the case of the New York Stock Exchange (NYSE) and the NASDAQ at the peak of the dot.com bubble, and close to the peak levels achieved at the time of the 1929 NYSE crash. In light of the relatively low free-float ratio in GCC stock markets (as commented below), the effective leveraged positions were even higher.

The development of a speculative bubble was also apparent because of the appearance of narrow market leadership[24] in some GCC markets. This phenomenon, which was observed in the dot.com bubble when the prices of technology stocks (predominantly quoted in NASDAQ) soared while the prices of most other groups of stocks (such as the mainstream stocks included in the S&P 500) lagged or fell, reflects the existence of a high degree of speculative demand in the market. Stock markets in Qatar, Saudi Arabia, and the United Arab Emirates experienced this phenomenon. In Saudi Arabia, a group of 20 speculative stocks[25] showed recurrent rises since 2004,[26] well above the increase in the TASI, and sudden sharp falls. Similarly, groups of relatively small stocks have attracted disproportionate volumes of trade and valuation gains in the DFM, ADSM, and DSM, pointing to the existence of an increasingly narrow market leadership associated with speculative demand (see Figure 1.9).[27]

1.3.3 Structural weakness and its role in the development of the bubble

Several common weaknesses in the GCC equity markets contributed to the development of strong speculative demand and later to the severity of the correction and the persistence of high volatility in stock prices. These weaknesses can be classified as supply factors (market and sector concentration, limited supply of stocks, and lack of alternative domestic financial

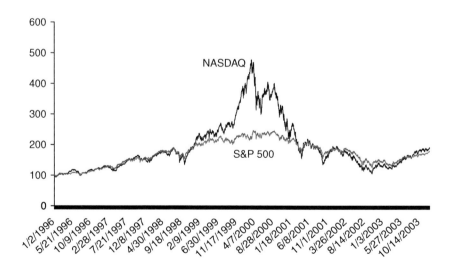

Figure 1.9 NASDAQ and S&P 500 indices (January 2, 1996–December 31, 2003)

Source: Bloomberg.

Table 1.10   GCC market capitalizations (in billions of US dollars), Free-Float[a], GCC and Non-GCC nationals ownership limitations, end-2005 (%)

	Market cap.	Free-Float	GCC limitations	Non-GCC limitations
Bahrain	17.40	35.46	35.46	33.42
Kuwait	142.10	65.56	44.62	44.62
Oman	12.70	38.23	29.62	29.62
Qatar	87.10	58.44	21.54	21.46
Saudi Arabia	646.00	46.78	23.75	0.00
United Arab Emirates	231.40	51.45	22.63	22.63
Total/Percent of full capitalization	1,136.70	49.89	25.45	9.29

Note: [a] Calculated based on a sample of listed companies.

Sources: Global Investment House (GCC Market Review); Credit Suisse (Gulf Equity Markets) and Fund staff estimates.

assets) and demand factors (role of small investors, underdevelopment of institutional investors, and cross holdings of listed companies). In addition, important legal and regulatory weaknesses remain in some GCC markets. This section analyzes the role of these weaknesses in the development of the speculative bubble.

Most GCC capital markets are characterized by a limited supply of stocks and lack of alternative financial instruments in domestic currency. The limited supply of stocks is related to the small number of companies listed relative to the large size of the markets, and to the reduced free-float of shares. As of end-2005, Tadawul had the largest market capitalization ($650 billion) among Arab stock exchanges, followed by the United Arab Emirates ($244 billion); and the GCC markets combined ($1.1 trillion) were comparable with Hong Kong, the largest emerging market in the world ($1.1 trillion in market capitalization). However, the number of companies listed in the GCC markets is relatively small. Thus, the average market value of the listed companies is very high by both emerging and industrial market standards,[28] pointing toward high market concentration. Also, there is generally a high degree of sectoral concentration.[29] Furthermore, the free-float of shares (amount available for trade) is very limited, due to the large percentages held by the government and large strategic stockholders, which further contributes to price volatility.[30] Finally, the lack of alternative domestic financial instruments[31] puts further upward pressure on stock prices.

On the demand side, the underdevelopment of institutional investors and the entry of a large number of relatively inexperienced and uninformed small

Table 1.11 Equity markets in selected emerging economies, April 2007

Market	Number of companies	Market capitalization (millions of US dollars)	Market capitalization[a] (% of GDP)	Value traded (millions of US dollars)	Turnover ratio	Average company's market value (millions of US dollars)
Bahrain	44	21,036.5	130.9	73.1	0.4	478.1
Brazil	408	846,002.7	79.2	38,765.5	4.7	2,073.5
Chile	246	202,250.1	139.3	2,767.5	1.4	822.2
China	1,478	3,428,617.6	130.4	707,918.0	22.4	2,319.8
Egypt	558	97,662.6	91.0	2,319.9	2.4	175.0
India	4,826	929,433.6	104.8	60,029.0	6.7	192.6
Israel	626	199,369.7	142.2	9,633.8	4.8	318.5
Jordan	230	32,362.0	226.0	1,069.2	3.3	140.7
Korea	1,703	904,248.4	101.8	152,329.2	17.4	531.0
Morocco	65	64,857.9	113.0	1,519.3	2.4	997.8
Nigeria	202	52,927.0	45.9	1,096.2	2.2	262.0
Oman	127	13,759.1	38.2	337.1	2.2	108.3
Russia	311	1,112,458.9	113.6	54,253.7	4.8	3,577.0
Saudi Arabia	88	308,555.7	88.5	70,253.0	22.4	3,506.3
South Africa	388	812,064.8	318.3	25,585.1	3.1	2,093.0
Taiwan	1,214	648,653.9	n.a.	82,780.4	12.8	534.3
Turkey	314	192,516.7	49.1	22,985.7	12.1	613.1

Note: [a] GDP is end-2006 value.

Sources: World Bank Emerging Markets Database (EMDB); World Economic Outlook (WEO) and Fund staff estimates.

investors affected the price discovery function of the market. Traditional institutional investors in the GCC countries are relatively small, other than public pension and investment funds. Excluding government institutions, the market share of private institutional investors ranges from 2–3 percent in Saudi Arabia and Qatar to about 10 percent in Abu Dhabi, well below the emerging markets average.[32] The two largest types of investors in GCC equity markets are governments (either directly or through autonomous institutions) and individuals. While the market has been long dominated by a few large individual investors, a rapidly growing number of small and usually poorly informed households have entered the stock market since 2003, mainly attracted by the state-sponsored IPOs in the region. Market transparency and advisory financial services provided to small investors were generally lacking, and small investors' decisions were mainly guided by rumors and, in some cases, market manipulators. Also, the relatively large cross holdings of nonfinancial companies in some markets helped to fuel the speculative bubble.

Despite significant progress in some countries, important weaknesses remained in the legal, regulatory, and supervisory frameworks governing the regional capital markets. The legal framework was particularly inadequate in Kuwait and Qatar, where there were no capital market authorities, and the KSE and DSM were regulated by a number of institutions, creating supervisory gaps and overlaps. Even countries that already enforce best international practices in the areas of regulation and supervision of capital markets presented some weaknesses in corporate governance, accounting practices, and the general legal and judicial framework applied to the corporate sector. These shortcomings affected the ability of investors to make sound assessments on the fair price of stocks, and created incentives for insider trading and market manipulation that contributed to the size of the speculative bubble.

1.3.4 What was going on in the less-buoyant GCC markets?

Several reasons explain the differential behavior of the BSE and the MSM, including the use of IPOs by the public sector, development of the domestic financial markets, and legal and regulatory frameworks. The most important factor setting these two markets apart seems to be the relevance of the oil sector in the economy. Market participants generally overlooked these two markets largely because of the lesser weight of companies in the hydrocarbon sector in these markets, and the relatively lower relevance of high oil prices in their nominal GDP growth. As a result, although the BSE and the MSM accounted for 7.8 percent of total market capitalization in the GCC at end-2002, their share had dropped to 2.6 percent at end-2005 because of the rapid growth of the other five regional markets. Because the developments

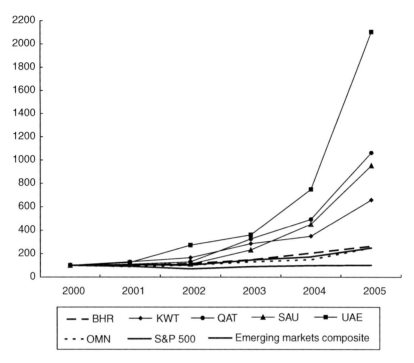

Figure 1.10   Market capitalization increase in the GCC, other emerging
markets, and the US (S&P) 2000 =100

Sources: Global Investment House; Bloomberg; and S&P Emerging Markets Database.

in Bahrain and Oman followed a more traditional pattern – prices on these
markets increased broadly in line with the increase in corporate profitability and economic activity, and did not seem to share the development of a
speculative bubble – the remainder of this chapter focuses on the markets
that underwent a rapid price increase and subsequent strong correction.

1.4   THE 2006 PRICE CORRECTION

1.4.1   Causes of the price fall

The market correction was mainly a consequence of the growing gap between
stock prices and economic fundamentals. The speculative demand generated
by the factors discussed in the previous section resulted in an increase in
stock prices far beyond what could be justified by the improvement in economic fundamentals, particularly since the last months of 2004. From the
beginning of 2003 to its peak in February 2006, the weighted GCC index
had accumulated a gain of over 760 percent. The increase in international oil

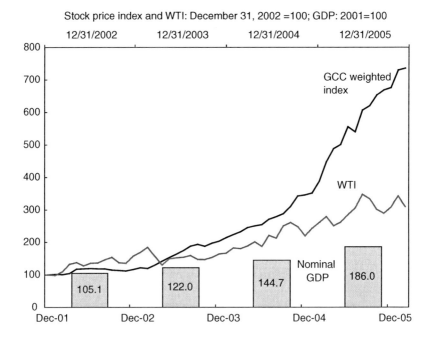

Figure 1.11   Performance of the GCC weighted price index vs. selected variables, 2000–06

Sources: National authorities; Bloomberg; and IMF staff estimates.

prices, some of the main economic variables (nominal GDP, current account balance, oil revenues, and overall fiscal surplus), and a favorable profit outlook underpinnned the strong growth of stock prices during 2003 and most of 2004. Toward the end of 2004, stock prices initiated a speculative climb that opened a substantial gap between prices and economic fundamentals.

The same structural weaknesses that fuelled the increase in speculative demand contributed to the severity of the market correction. The high concentration implied a strong correlation between stocks and, thus, insufficient diversification of portfolios to compensate for losses in sectors or companies with gains in other segments of the market. The reliance of small investors on rumors, and the lack of well-developed traditional investors which could profit from underpriced stocks, prompted overshooting of the price correction in some stocks. The lack of institutional investors and transparency on the sources of earnings of listed companies also exacerbated the decline in prices and their volatility. Finally, the legal, regulatory, and supervisory weaknesses mentioned above have greatly reduced the potential positive impact of the authorities' measures to open the markets to foreign investment.

The announcement of lower-than-expected 2005 profits for many listed companies triggered the subsequent region-wide correction, which came as a manifestation of the existing gap between stock prices and fundamentals. As mentioned in Section 1.3, corporate profits grew at cumulative annual rates of 40 to 50 percent during 2000–04. Market valuations at end-2005 suggested that market participants expected rates of profit growth to continue in the same range or even slightly higher (for instance, in the range of 50–60 percent for Saudi Arabia). However, average profit growth was substantially lower for 2005 (37 percent in Saudi Arabia), and some blue chip companies performed well below expectations. In the KSE, the low dividend distribution made investors skeptical about the quality and sustainability of profits. The slower growth in profits further underlined the overvaluation of stocks, prompting a massive withdrawal by large investors first, followed by the bulk of small household investors once the bubble had already been breached.

The correction was also triggered by various market-specific factors, explaining the different start dates. For instance, the simultaneous capital increases and issuance of a large number of IPOs with high oversubscriptions that drained liquidity from the market, seem to have had a particularly important impact on the UAE markets. Concerns that high profits reported by some listed companies were a result of equity trading rather than their core operations weighed heavily on Kuwaiti investors. In Saudi Arabia, the unfortunate timing of the tightening of some operational regulations and supervisory measures contributed to the market correction. Coinciding with the reporting of lower corporate profits, the Saudi CMA introduced regulations to limit speculation, fined three stock traders a record SRls 169 million ($45 million), and banned them for three years for market manipulation. These actions, which are positive in terms of market strengthening, may have created further unrest among investors at a particularly delicate juncture.

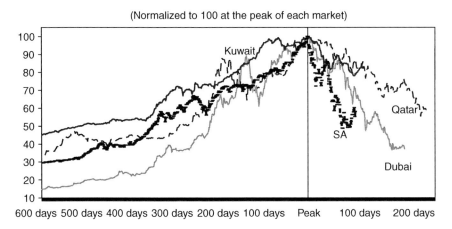

Figure 1.12   Stock price indices in selected GCC countries

The high degree of price correlation among GCC equity markets gave rise to an expected contagion effect. In addition to the market-specific factors triggering the corrections, it was the decline in the Saudi market that accentuated the fall in stock prices in the rest of the GCC. The large amount of cross-country investments, predominantly held by Saudi investors, was the main contagion channel. Margin calls on Saudi and other GCC investors exacerbated selling pressures. As a result, the decline in the Qatar and Abu Dhabi price indices rapidly matched that of Saudi Arabia at about 40 percent in the first half of 2006. The decline in Dubai, with no hydrocarbon-related companies listed and a higher proportion of real estate companies in its composition, was about 60 percent.[33]

1.4.2   The role of the national authorities

The national authorities emphasized asset inflation containment measures and prudential oversight during the markets' boom period. The strengthening of the capital market regulatory and supervisory frameworks and the tightening of prudential regulations over the past two years have clearly helped to contain the impact of the declining stock markets on the region's financial sectors. Some countries in the region have introduced new capital market laws and regulations and streamlined the institutional setting for the oversight of equity market intermediaries (Box 1.1 as below).

Despite the sharp correction, the authorities have refrained from direct intervention in most cases. In all cases, GCC authorities had the means to intervene in the equity market, but they consistently resisted strong

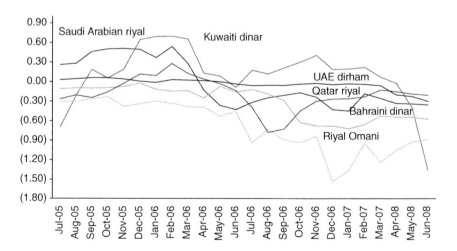

Figure 1.13   Interest rate margin between US dollar and GCC currencies, 2005–07 (Three-month interbank deposit rates)

Source: Saudi Arabian Monetary Agency.

Box 1.1   Main Preventive Policy Measures

Bahrain

■ Quantitative limits on personal loans were tightened so that the ratio of loan service cost to household income cannot exceed 50 percent (2005).

Kuwait

■ An 80 percent ceiling on the ratio of private sector credit to total bank deposits was applied (2004).

■ Monetary policy was tightened to raise the discount rate and reintroduce market-based instruments to mop up excess liquidity (2004–05).

Oman

■ Comprehensive rules on corporate governance, regulations on investment funds, and the money laundering law were introduced (2004).

Qatar

■ The loans-to-deposits ratio was reduced from 95 to 85 percent (2004).

■ The Cabinet of Ministers approved a law allowing foreigners to own up to 25 percent of a company listed in the DSM (2003).

■ The Ministry of Economy and Commerce issued the implementing regulations for the Mutual Fund Law, which allows expatriates to invest indirectly in the stock market (2004).

Saudi Arabia

■ A new capital market law was approved (2003).

■ The CMA was empowered with unified regulatory and supervisory authority on all market participants (2004).

■ Capital charges for market risk were introduced (Basel Tier III capital requirement) (2004).

■ A ceiling per customer to finance IPO purchases was imposed (2004).

■ Reduction in the maturity of consumer loans from 10 to 5 years and introduction of a cap in the amount of debt service at one-third of the borrower's net monthly salary (2004).

The United Arab Emirates

■ Tightening of margin lending regulations: only against tangible securities; loan cap at 70 percent of purchased shares (for companies that have been in operation for more than five years); in case of IPOs, loans cannot exceed five times the amount contributed by the subscriber (2005).

political pressures to do so. Only the Kuwaiti authorities announced they would directly intervene to support market prices. State entities like the Kuwait Investment Authority and the Saudi Government Organization of Social Insurance may also have been behind some buying. These operations, which might have been responses to genuine independent investment policies triggered by the attractive pricing of stocks, did not seem to have a substantial impact on the overall direction of market indices, but may have helped smooth out extreme fluctuations.

A loosening of monetary policy and indirect measures, mainly aimed at increasing market liquidity, were implemented in most markets. Authorities in general avoided raising interest rates despite the increases in the US Federal Funds Rate, in order to avoid tightening liquidity in an environment of rapid market correction. Some of these measures were already under consideration but delayed because of the continuing bull run. The measures focusing on market opening and strengthening of transparency and oversight will have a positive effect in the medium term. However, other measures may have negative side effects on financial stability or on the potential for future market development. The following are some of the most relevant measures:

a. Saudi Arabia opened its market to resident foreign investors (previously constrained to investment funds), and the United Arab Emirates further increased foreign investors' level of participation in some listed companies. Regardless of their immediate effectiveness, these measures will be positive for the medium-term development of these markets.

b. Strengthening of prudential regulations on investment funds, real estate funds, and corporate governance have been approved or are underway in Saudi Arabia. Also, the UAE central bank issued new rules requiring banks, finance, and investment companies to report their direct and indirect exposure to local shares on a quarterly basis. These measures will also reinforce investors' confidence and promote market development.

c. Bahrain enacted a Trust Law that allows for the establishment of financial trusts such as Real Estate Investment Trusts (REITs) and private pension schemes. The law will enable the deepening of the equity market by supporting the development of institutional investors and by broadening the range of investment instruments offered by financial institutions, retaining domestic liquidity, and attracting foreign investment.

d. The United Arab Emirates eased margin lending regulations (increasing the loan cap from 70 to 80 percent) in an attempt to strengthen market demand with a view to injecting liquidity into the market. This measure may increase the banking sector's indirect exposure to the market and, if continued for long, could jeopardize financial stability in the future.

e. The extensions granted by the Saudi CMA to nonfinancial companies to dispose of their stock portfolios[34] may have a negative impact on equity market development, delaying transparency-enhancing measures.

f. Some tinkering with market operational regulations, such as the splitting of stocks and reversal of the decision to narrow the daily price fluctuation band in Saudi Arabia, may have increased liquidity by facilitating small investors' access to the market and may have allowed a larger volume of intra-day operations. However, these changes risk increasing price volatility, the atomization of the market, and the exposure of small households to poorly understood market risk.

g. The Saudi authorities announced the establishment of a risk-free fund shortly after the beginning of the market correction for low income Saudis who want to trade on the stock market.[35] To avoid the appearance of moral hazard, investors' market risk should be hedged through market-based instruments and financial risk for the state should be avoided. However, no further steps to establish the fund have since been taken.

1.5 STABILIZATION AND RECOVERY IN 2007: ARE CURRENT PRICES IN LINE WITH FUNDAMENTALS?

Assessing whether the correction has brought stock prices in line with fundamentals is critical to evaluating the probability of further sudden market movements. The same set of warning signals used in Section 1.3 is applied to this analysis. Thus, examining these warning signals after the correction would serve as an indicator of whether prices are now in line with fundamentals or, on the contrary, if overvaluation symptoms still exist.

The losses in stock prices have brought market gains broadly in line with the improvement in fundamentals since the beginning of the boom. As of end-June 2007, three of the GCC stock market price indices are at new peaks while the remaining four have lost between 43 percent and 66 percent of their peak values (Table 1.12). As a result, the weighted average accumulated gain since 2002 was reduced by over 40 percent, to about 400 percent. The latter is relatively close to the 356 percent increase in world oil prices

Table 1.12   Performance of GCC equity market indices

Country	Index	Index close 6/30/2007	YTD growth (%)	YoY growth (%)	Peak to date growth (%)
Bahrain	Bahrain Stock Exchange	2,409	8.6	17.7	0.0
Kuwait	Kuwait Stock Exchange	12,132	20.5	19.4	0.0
Oman	Muscat Stock Market	6,339	13.6	30.4	0.0
Qatar	Doha Stock Market	7,349	3.0	−3.7	−43.0
Saudi Arabia	Tadawul All Shares Idx.	6,970	−12.1	−47.0	−66.2
UAE	Dubai Financial Market	1,200	6.8	3.1	−48.0
UAE	Abu Dhabi Stock Market	3,545	18.2	−0.3	−43.2
UAE	Natl Bank of Abu Dhabi (Composite)	4,970	10.9	1.4	−38.6

Sources: Bloomberg and Fund staff estimates.

during the same period,[36] and not that far from the region's nominal GDP growth in the last five years (Figure 1.14).

The corrections and developments through June 2007 have brought valuation indicators closer to their historical levels and to emerging market levels. The PER ratios of all GCC stock markets as of June 2007 ranged from 10 to 15.5, well within normal parameters and below the leading industrial equity markets. The analysis of PBV and DY ratios showed the same results. The Price Earnings Growth (PEG) ratio could be used to factor in the markets' expected long-term profitability growth in the valuation of the stock.[37] The profitability growth rates of all companies listed in the Saudi and Qatari stock markets over the last six years were 52 and 34 percent, respectively. Based on these growth rates, the resulting PEG for the Saudi and Qatari markets as of June 30, 2007 were 0.42 and 0.46, respectively, which are significantly below one and compare favorably with average PEG ratios in the leading stock markets. Despite lower expected profit growth rates in the future, the fall in stock prices has corrected the overvaluation. Average profit growth for Saudi listed companies in 2006 was 17 percent. Thus, Saudi Arabia's average PEG ratio as of end-2006 was about 1, showing no sign of overvaluation. The DSM PEG calculated over the year-on-year rate of corporate profitability growth during the first half of 2007 (36 percent) is 0.42, indicating that the correction in Qatari stock prices may have overshot and the market is undervalued. All other PEG ratios in GCC markets are around or below one, indicating the predominance of fair or undervalued stocks.

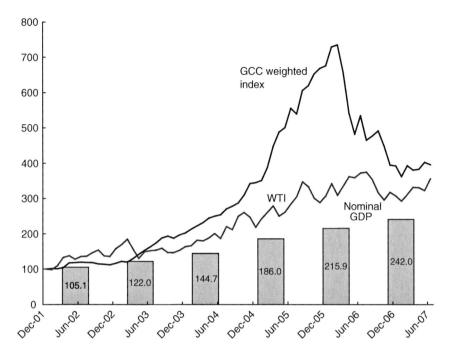

Figure 1.14 Performance of the GCC weighted price index vs. selected variables, 2001–07

Sources: National authorities; Bloomberg; and Fund IMF staff estimates.

Prospects for corporate profits are good, taking into account the projections for continued high oil prices and expansionary fiscal policies including substantial social and infrastructure investment programs. The private sector is benefiting from this favorable economic environment and from the progressive liberalization and structural reforms in the GCC economies. GCC companies will remain attractive to investors, in line with expectations that fundamentals keep improving, corporate profitability remains high, and expansion opportunities continue.

Despite a transitory deceleration in credit to the private sector and (margin lending in particular), immediately after the burst of the bubble, the expansionary fiscal policy, an easing of monetary conditions and the pull of the credit demand from large investment projects have resulted in an acceleration of money growth in the first half of 2007 (Table 1.13). The margin lending and consumer credit components, however, have decelerated markedly reflecting a fall in leveraged speculative positions by retail investors.

Market volatility has declined significantly in 2007, however, it remains high due to structural weaknesses, abundant liquidity, and geopolitical factors (see Figure 1.16). Volatility will continue to be relatively high until

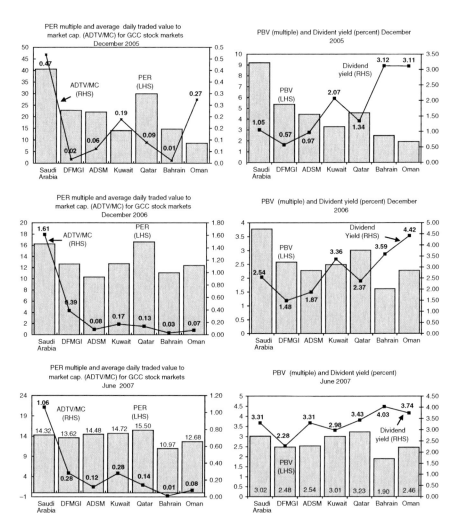

Figure 1.15 The development of valuation indicators for the GCC stock markets,[a] 2005–07

Notes: [a] For 2006 ratios PER is based on trailing 12 months profits up to September 30, 2006 and year-end prices. PBV is based on September 30, 2006 equity figures. Dividends yield is based on 2005 cash dividends and year-end prices. For June 2007, ratios are based on up to March 2006 profits and equity numbers and end-June prices. Yield is based on end-2006 cash dividents and end-June prices.

Source: GCC Equity Markets Monthly Review, December 2006 and June 2007, Kamco Research.

Table 1.13   Money and credit in the GCC (rates of growth in %)

| | Annual cumulative, 2003–06 | | Annualized first half 2007 | |
	M2	Private sector credit	M2	Private sector credit
Bahrain	9.9	17.4	40.1	40.8
Oman	12.0	9.5	38.8	30.5
Kuwait	11.9	16.0	21.6	40.6
UAE	19.4	22.8	41.7	26.9
Qatar	21.0	39.5	61.4	29.1
Saudi Arabia	18.4	20.1	16.2	15.5

Source: National authorities.

some of the key structural weaknesses linked to the lack of transparency, information for small investors, liquidity and depth of the market (free-float), and institutional strengthening are solved. Furthermore, the existence of ample liquidity in the GCC banking systems provides the means for further speculative upheavals, and the region's unstable geopolitical situation further increases the risk for investors.

A substantial level of the equity valuation gains retained after the correction are likely to be consolidated, as long as fundamentals remain strong. New listing, including through IPOs, contained in 2006 and 2007 (Table 1.14). There is room for further price increases following improvements in the structural weaknesses and continuous strengthening of economic fundamentals. However, any increase in stock prices beyond further improvements in economic fundamentals will increase the risk and severity of further corrections, particularly if money and credit growth fuel asset price inflation.

1.5.1   Where do the less-buoyant GCC markets stand?

The recent correction has not affected the Omani and Bahraini markets substantially. The contagion effect suffered by these markets was relatively small, with losses from their respective peaks ranging from 11 to 17 percent, well below the 40 to 70 percent losses registered in the booming markets (with the exception of Kuwait). Stock valuation ratios were always within reasonable limits, with stock price gains broadly in line with the increase in each country's economic fundamentals and corporate profits growth.

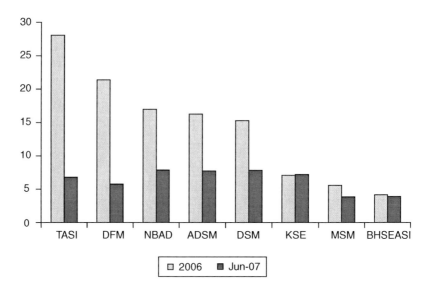

Figure 1.16 Coefficient of variation for GCC markets in 2006 and the first half of 2007 (In percent)

Sources: Bloomberg; and Fund staff estimates.

Table 1.14 Number of listed companies in GCC stock markets

	Bahrain	Kuwait	Oman[a]	Qatar	Saudi Arabia	UAE	GCC
2000	39	86	113	22	76	27	363
2001	43	88	119	23	76	27	376
2002	41	95	127	25	68	37	393
2003	44	108	139	28	70	44	433
2004	45	125	166	30	73	53	492
2005	47	158	176	32	77	89	579
2006	50	180	179	36	86	102	633
Jun-07	52	185	191	36	95	115	674

Note: [a] Includes regular market, parallel market, third market, and other companies.

Source: Global Investment House.

1.6 THE EFFECT OF THE CORRECTION ON FINANCIAL STABILITY AND ECONOMIC GROWTH

The market correction did not undermine the GCC economies' growth potential and the soundness of their financial sectors. GCC banks were financially sound, and have built up reserves to withstand some deterioration in asset quality. The preventive tightening of prudential regulations and strict enforcement of existing prudential regulations have effectively contained equity market risk exposure at manageable levels. The possible negative wealth effect on demand, stemming from the losses in individuals' portfolios, is expected to be offset by the expansionary fiscal stance and strong corporate sector demand resulting from rising confidence in the economy due to high oil prices. However, downside risks remain associated with the overvaluation of the real estate sector, which is particularly important in some GCC markets.

Recent IMF Financial Sector Assessment Program (FSAP) reports confirm that commercial banks, which dominate the financial system in all GCC countries, are well capitalized, have good asset quality, and are very profitable. With capital adequacy ratios well above international standards, high and improving asset quality, and impressive profitability, bank soundness seems to be strong enough to withstand any reasonable correction in stock prices. In fact, despite the substantial market correction, no signs of stress have appeared in any of the GCC banking systems (see Table 1.15).[38]

Although commercial banks' profitability has been affected by the stock market correction, there has been no substantial impact on bank soundness (Table 1.16). Despite the relatively low direct exposure of banks to equity markets throughout the region, their indirect exposure through margin lending (and a part of personal loans) has been growing rapidly, and their current profitability is very dependent on brokerage fees. The loss of income from

Table 1.15 Financial soundness indicators in selected GCC and mature markets (In %; as of end-2006, except when otherwise indicated)

	Capital adequacy ratio	Nonperforming loans	Provisions to total nonperforming loans
Saudi Arabia	21.9	2.0	182.3
Kuwait[a]	22.0	3.9	100.6
UAE	16.6	6.3	98.2
USA	12.4	0.8	147.0
Japan[b]	13.1	1.5	n.a.
Germany[c]	12.2	4.1	n.a.

Notes:
[a] As of end-September, 2006.
[b] Major banks; on a nonconsolidated basis.
[c] As of 2005.

Source: National authorities.

Table 1.16 Financial soundness indicators for GCC countries in 2006
(In percent)

	Bahrain[a]		Kuwait[b]	Oman[a]	Qatar[a]	Saudi Arabia	UAE
	Conventional[c]	Islamic					
Regulatory capital to risk-weighted assets[d,e]	22.0	35.4	22.0	17.2	13.8	21.8	16.6
Capital to assets	8.8	31.9	12.0	12.7	12.4	9.3	12.6
Nonperforming loans to total loans[f]	4.8	2.7	3.9	4.6	2.2	2.0	6.3
Provisions to nonperforming loans	–	–	100.6	102.8	94.3	182.3	98.2
Return on assets[g]	1.4	5.2	2.6	2.7	3.7	4.3	2.3
Return on equity[g]	15.4	17.5	21.6	18.1	27.2	30.5	18.0

Notes:
[a] Commercial banking sector only.
[b] Data as of September 2006.
[c] Onshore sector only (FCBs).
[d] For Oman, capital (own fund) includes common and preferred shares, general bank reserves, revaluation reserves, and undistributed profits. Net of uncovered losses and unallocated specific provisions identified by the CBO.
[e] For Oman, risk-weighted assets net of uncovered and current losses, capital investments and unallocated specific provisions.
[f] For Bahrain, includes nonperforming loans on which payments of interest or repayments of principal are 90 days or more past due and all loans on which specific provisions have been made.
[g] For Bahrain and Qatar, return on average assets and average equity.

Sources: Country authorities and Fund staff estimates.

Table 1.17 Saudi Arabia – Gains from main
IPOs retained after market correction
(end-June 2007, In Saudi riyals)

Company	Listing IPO date	IPO price[a] (per share)	Stock price		Retained gains (in percent)
			2/25/06	30/6/07	
STC	1/23/03	25.50	174.75	58.25	128
Etihad Etisalat	12/19/04	10.00	144.40	48.00	380
NCCI	1/16/05	41.00	207.40	100.00	144
Bank Al-Bilad	4/29/05	10.00	168.40	28.50	185

Note: [a] Adjusted by the split of shares in March 2006.
Sources: CMA; Bakheet Financial Advisor and Fund staff estimates.

brokerage, underwriting, and other equity market-related operations, which were major sources of profits for banks in recent years, was already evident in the second quarter of 2006 across the region, and continued through the first half of 2007 in some GCC countries. Up to 40 percent of banks' net income may be at risk in Saudi Arabia, and this percentage increases to 60 percent in the Emirati and Kuwaiti banks. As a result, banks saw recent investment income gains turn to losses. However, the fall in fees from the security business has been partially compensated by the increase in fees and intermediation margins from the large investment projects that are proliferating in the region. Furthermore, the strong collateral procedures, capital buffers, and relatively limited exposure shielded against a substantial impact on banks' soundness.[39]

The impact of the correction on the non-bank financial intermediaries has also been limited. Since public companies that hold equities (mainly, social security, and pension funds) acquired their portfolios well before the bull market and do not usually mark their portfolios to market, their solvency has not been affected by the stock price correction. Furthermore, since these institutions do not take deposits from the general public, and they carry a state guarantee, they do not pose a threat to systemic stability. A somewhat larger impact could be expected on the net value and profits of insurance companies, although the insurance sector is relatively small in the GCC countries and most of their assets are bank deposits, due to their small size and large liquidity needs. The impact of the correction on non-bank financial intermediaries has been strong, especially in the investment sector. For instance, in Kuwait the correction wiped out the sector's profits for the first half of 2006, which contributed one-third to the total profits of listed companies in 2005. Finally, domestic investment funds are also relatively underdeveloped throughout the region, and a substantial reduction in their holdings will not entail a major reduction in financial wealth nor is it likely to entail a major reputational risk to their parent institutions. However, the correction may slow down the rapid development of this important institutional investment vehicle in the region.

The consequences for the real economy were limited. Some reduction in aggregate demand levels could have stemmed from the wealth effect on a large number of small investors attracted in recent years by the prospects of rapid capital gains. However, the dominant government ownership and large investors' holdings seemed to indicate that the aggregated demand effect was small. Also, a significant reduction in household demand is unlikely since the wealth gain was for a relatively short period and an average household could still retain sizable capital gains in most of the markets if they were active before 2005 (see Table 1.17).[40] Large wage increases announced by various GCC governments in recent years will also support private consumption despite some loss in the stock market.[41]

Highly leveraged households might have delayed bank payments, but the mechanisms put in place (margin calls and preferred creditor status against payroll deposits) were likely to limit the effect on banks' asset quality. Balance sheet effects are likely to be contained for the business sector, despite the relatively large cross holdings in some markets. Furthermore, the increased cost of capital to more realistic levels that might have resulted from a market correction may have also helped eliminate some speculative companies from the market and enhanced efficiency in the allocation of financial resources. Domestic demand was mainly driven by the corporate sector and a continued expansionary fiscal stance. Listed firms remained largely profitable in 2006, and profits were growing again in the first half of 2007 in most markets, as the firms continued with their massive expansion plans. The pipeline of mega projects in the GCC has been growing rapidly, and currently exceeds $1 trillion (Table 1.18). The mega projects include public-private partnerships in most areas of the economy, but construction, oil, and gas seem to be the most dynamic sectors. Despite the loss of income from stock market-related activities, the outlook for bank profits remains strong, supported by growing credit demand from the corporate sector and the need for financial services and lending associated with numerous large projects.

1.7   LESSONS AND RECOMMENDATIONS

The recent events in the region have highlighted the authorities' need to focus on measures that strengthen market resilience to speculative bubble developments. Such measures would not only reduce the propensity of the markets to boom and bust cycles but would also enhance market efficiency. Well-functioning stock markets would help in mobilizing and channeling savings to productive investments and in providing incentives for entrepreneurship and investment. In addition, financing for the ambitious privatization plans and mega projects to diversify the economy and to increase private sector involvement would largely depend on preserving investors' confidence in the markets. A stock price bubble is always costly for investors, listed companies, and the economy as a whole. A preventive policy based on the strengthening of markets is, therefore, the most efficient approach to address this issue.

Strengthening the capital market regulatory framework is a key element in support of market stability.[42] Although a few GCC countries already enforce best international practices on the regulation and supervision of capital markets, others are in the process of strengthening their frameworks. The key areas to be addressed in the short term include (a) creating an adequate incentive and regulatory structure to increase the role of institutional investors and collective investment schemes, which will strengthen

Table 1.18   GCC: investment projects for 2006–12
(In millions of US dollars)

	Amount
Bahrain (Total)	**29,017**
Oil	1,500
Other industries	4,850
Tourism	10,815
Civil and infrastructure	11,852
Kuwait (Total)	**83,000**
Infrastructure	51,000
Hydrocarbons	22,000
Real estate	10,000
Qatar (Total)	**169,868**
Gas	82,500
Oil	7,668
Petrochemicals	32,100
Infrastructure (including electricity and water)	21,100
Other	26,500
Oman (Total)	**38,068**
Oil	8,515
Gas	4,459
Petrochemicals	8,472
Other industries	12,164
Tourism	2,021
Infrastructure	2,437
Saudi Arabia (Total)	**378,948**
Oil	42,800
Gas	37,208
Petrochemicals	47,339
Mining and minerals	13,300
Real estate and housing	111,702
Defense and military	48,800
Infrastructure (railways, power and water)	69,799
Health and Education	8,000
UAE (Total)	**320,000**
Oil and gas	30,000
Infrastructure	100,000
Real estate	190,000
GCC Grand Total	**1,018,901**
of which	Amount
Oil, Gas, and Petrochemicals	324,561
Infrastructure	282,688
Real estate	311,702
Others	99,950

Sources: Fund staff estimates based on various official and unofficial sources.

the market's price discovery process; (b) changing IPO pricing policies to reflect fair market value in order to reduce excessive market volatility and allow firms to receive full value for their shares; and (c) strengthening regulations regarding risk management and the internal control of firms, capital adequacy, and other prudential controls and procedures in case of the failure of an intermediary.

Further integration of capital markets in the GCC region with significant cross-border listings will enhance stability and efficiency. Considerable work will be required to harmonize the region's capital market regulations, structures, and practices. While progress has been made in increasing cross-border listings, further work is needed to fully standardize accounting, auditing, and financial reporting across the region. Full integration will also require the electronic linking of trading systems, harmonization of securities settlement infrastructures, and cross-border supervision of markets and intermediaries.

The authorities should address the remaining structural weaknesses that impede market efficiency and liquidity. In particular, they should encourage the development of institutional investors and open the markets to foreign investors. This would improve the price discovery function since institutional and foreign investors' decisions are driven more by fundamentals.[43] Completing the regulatory framework for non-bank financial institutions and removing the obstacles to their growth could enhance their role as institutional investors. They can provide key capital market activities such as investment advice, fund management, placement, and underwriting. Institutional investors are also more likely to work as market makers due to their relatively bigger size, and thus, can exert downward pressure on stock prices at times of high speculative demand. However, their influence on the market will only be beneficial within a strong financial regulatory environment, with prudential rules and disclosure requirements to ensure they maintain high investment policy standards.

While encouraging IPOs and corporate listings could reduce sector concentration and raise the free-float ratio, care should be given to ensure that the listed companies have audited financial statements and profit records in order to help investors price them based on their fundamentals. Furthermore, the policy of deliberately underpricing IPOs should be reconsidered in light of the impact on market stability. Timely public disclosure of upcoming IPOs may be useful in allowing investors to plan their funding and avoid abrupt changes in market liquidity.

Direct intervention should be avoided, unless systemic stability is at risk. Direct government intervention in the market (for instance, through state-controlled savings vehicles) in order to arrest falling share prices would create a moral hazard and jeopardize the future role of the market to effectively allocate financial resources. In addition, such intervention could reinforce investors' perception that the stocks are overvalued and could carry quasi-fiscal risk. Moreover, moral hazard induced by intervention may substantially increase the size of future speculative bubbles and the costs associated with their correction.[44] In case of a market correction, the authorities should focus on measures aimed at facilitating an orderly return to prices that are in line with the economic value of the companies. Any potential measures to ease hardships resulting from a correction should be channeled through social safety networks that eliminate moral hazard by linking social assistance with the effective income and wealth of households, and not with their losses in the stock exchange.

Strict compliance with prudential requirements and improved risk management practices could enhance financial institutions' resilience to stock market developments. To avoid an increase in banks' direct exposure to equity markets and to contain excessive growth in credit to the private sector, the supervisory authorities should strictly enforce the regulatory limits on lending for stock trading already in place in most GCC countries. Particular attention should be paid to Islamic financing, which is expanding quickly. In case of a new rapid increase in prices, supervisory authorities should intensify their oversight and be ready to further tighten prudential regulations, if necessary, by (a) implementing stricter information requirements on the uses of bank credit; (b) increasing the weight of assets exposed to equity market risk in the capital adequacy ratio; (c) further tightening collateral requirements for margin lending and other loans used directly or indirectly to leverage equity investments; and (d) taking prompt corrective action on any bank with an excessive exposure to equity risk which could be characterized as an unsafe or unsound practice. Authorities should avoid taking any measure to support stock markets that might compromise the soundness of the financial system.[45] In addition, conducting regular stress testing and encouraging financial institutions to do the same would help to identify risks and manage them appropriately. More generally, the supervisory authorities should ensure the implementation of comprehensive risk management strategies, policies, and systems in financial institutions.

Enhancing supervisory coordination and conducting financial crisis simulation exercises at the domestic and regional levels could be very useful. With the increase in the inter-linkages between the financial systems in the GCC region and the exposure to similar risks, enhancing supervisory coordination and conducting financial crisis simulations at the domestic and regional levels could be quite useful. Such measures would reduce regulatory arbitrage possibilities and improve the authorities' readiness to deal with possible future financial crisis by assessing the effectiveness of communication and information-sharing mechanisms, the coordination of decision-making, prevention of conflicts of interest, and, more generally, potential coordination failures during crisis.

Although the scope for monetary policy is limited in the GCC countries, the authorities could help contain speculative demand by keeping liquidity within reasonable parameters. With most GCC currencies pegged to the US dollar and enjoying a high degree of capital mobility, monetary policy independence is limited. However, developing and effectively using market-based instruments would allow for greater flexibility and effectiveness in systemic liquidity management. This will minimize the risk of asset inflation while allowing enough liquidity to support strong private sector-led economic growth. In addition, enhancing the coordination between monetary and fiscal authorities is very important since the latter represent a main source of liquidity expansion in the GCC economies. More generally, the consistency between monetary policy objectives and the fiscal policy stance should be ensured through appropriate coordination. However, the formulation of monetary policy should not be governed by developments in asset markets since this could be perceived as going beyond monetary authorities' mandate and could complicate the future conduct of monetary policy.

APPENDIX I. METHODOLOGIES TO DETERMINE THE EXISTENCE OF STOCK MARKET BUBBLES

Three main methodologies exist in the current literature to analyze the existence of equity market bubbles: (a) rational expectations; (b) behavioral finance; and (c) operational definition.

Rational expectations bubble

Equity prices contain a rational bubble if investors are willing to pay more than what they know is justified by the value of the discounted dividend stream for the equity. They will buy the equity at this high value because they expect that demand from other investors will push prices even higher and they will be able to sell it at a profit, making the current high price an equilibrium price.

A large and growing number of papers propose econometric tests to detect "rational" bubbles (LeRoy and Porter, 1981; Shiller, 1981; West, 1987, 1988; Diba and Grossman, 1988; and Evans, 1991). As noted by Gürkaynak (2005) the existing models' test for the existence of rational expectations bubbles have not yielded conclusive evidence. The problem with these models is that they combine the null hypothesis of no bubbles with an overly simple model of fundamentals. Rejecting the null hypothesis in these models is interpreted as indicating the presence of bubbles. However, in most of these models it is possible to fail to reject the null hypothesis by relaxing some assumptions on the fundamentals. This makes the results depend to a great extent on model specification. In addition to this major shortcoming, these models require long data series, which are not available for the GCC markets.

Measures based on behavioral finance

More recent literature uses behavioral models that allow for irrational pricing and associated "irrational bubbles." These models assume that human patterns of less-than-perfectly rational behavior are central to financial market behavior, even among investment professionals (Shiller, 2001) A lot of the elements that can explain the bubble mechanism in these models have to do with the nature of subjective probability, intuitive and personal judgments, the social environment in which decisions are made, the prominence of the news media, and the nature of human interactions within organizations. The analysis in these models requires collecting data about investors' expectations regarding the performance of stocks and their assessment of the existence of overvaluation. For example, Vissing-Jorgensen (2003) studied investors' expectations and stock holdings for 1998–2002 using the USGallup Investor Optimism Index. Her results showed that (a) investors' expected returns were high at the peak of the market; (b) many investors thought the market was overvalued but would not correct quickly; (c) investors' beliefs depend on their own investment experience; and (d) investors' beliefs do affect their stocks holdings suggesting that understanding beliefs is in fact useful for understanding prices.

Despite recent work on surveying investors' opinions about the future performance of the market, the relatively short length of this index and the lack of other indices render the analysis of such models impossible for the GCC markets. A good example of this work is the HSBC-MEED Middle East Business Confidence Index (MEBCI), which was initiated in the summer of 2004.

Operational definition measure

Recent work by Jeremy J. Siegel (2002) introduced an operational definition and hence, a measure for a bubble. According to this definition, a bubble episode exists when the realized asset return over a given future period is more than two standard deviations from its expected return. According to this definition, the crash of the stock market in 1929 and 1987 – both periods generally characterized as bubbles – proved not to be bubbles but low points in stock prices.

This approach is only operational ex-post, and it cannot be used to predict or to identify a current price increase as a bubble. The model requires information on cash flows realized over a period of time in order to determine whether a specific price increase episode could be identified as a bubble.

NOTES

1. The GCC includes Bahrain, Kuwait, Oman, Qatar, Saudi Arabia, and the United Arab Emirates.
2. These are the Dubai Financial Market (DFM), the Saudi Stock Market (Tadawul), the Doha Securities Market (DSM), and, to a lesser extent, the Kuwait Stock Exchange (KSE) and the Abu Dhabi Securities Market (ADSM). The remaining two markets, the Bahrain Stock Exchange (BSE) and the Muscat Securities Market (MSM), showed little signs of overheating.
3. The index includes the seven regional markets using market capitalization in US dollars at the end-2003 exchange rates as weights. The resulting weights are 51.6 percent for Saudi Arabia; 22.2 percent for Kuwait; 14.4 percent for the United Arab Emirates; 6.5 percent for Qatar; 3.5 percent for Oman; and 1.8 percent for Bahrain.
4. The Egyptian market gained 875 percent in US dollars, while the Jordanian equity market price index increased by over 380 percent in US dollars. The only stock exchange outside the region which has been growing at similar rates (640 percent increase in the last three years in US dollar terms) has been the Colombian market. Colombian equity prices were boosted by the large acquisitions of international firms, and domestic mergers particularly in the financial sector.

5. There are two equity markets in the United Arab Emirates, the Dubai Financial Market (DSM) and the Abu Dhabi Securities Market (ADSM), plus one national market in each of the other five GCC countries.

6. There was no correction in the MSM and BSE, although prices fell slightly in the first half of 2006. The KSE was less affected by the correction, with the general price index falling by 22.5 percent from its peak value to its lowest on August 2, 2006.

7. Including a generalized overhaul of the legal, regulatory and supervisory framework in some equity markets.

8. In addition to weaknesses in the legal and regulatory framework, these include market concentration, limited supply of stocks, lack of alternative domestic financial assets, underdevelopment of institutional investors, and cross holdings of listed companies.

9. The historic earnings growth for the S&P 500 is 10.5 percent, and 9.6 percent for the Dow Industrial index (Stockselector.com, July 31, 2006).

10. Middle East Economic Digest (MEED) March 2005.

11. In addition, many business leaders felt that bubbles were also forming in the real estate market.

12. However, it is worth noting that not all rapid and substantial increases of stock prices are attributable to speculative bubbles. Rapid increases in stock prices are sustainable if they are associated with structural changes in economic fundamentals. This was the case, for instance, in Spain, where the Madrid Stock Exchange Price Index increased by almost 400 percent in the wake of European Union accession (1985–87); in India, where stock prices increased by 500 percent following the implementation of structural measures to liberalize the economy (1990–91); and in several countries of the European Union (Ireland, Portugal, and Spain), where stock price indices increased by about 300 percent in anticipation of the monetary union (1995–98).

13. The favorable valuation indicators in Kuwait are partially explained by the income structure of the listed companies, where profits depend to a large extent on market performance. For example, in 2005, 53 percent of listed companies' income was in the form of investment income.

14. PER and PBV are calculated based on trailing 12-month earnings and prices at the end of 2005.

15. At end-2002, the PER for TASI, KSE, DFM, and ADSM were 21.0, 15.3, 25.1, and 14.0, respectively.

16. Excluding negative earnings (Ned Davis Research, Inc., 2005).

17. Price volatility tends to increase substantially in the period immediately before the bursting of a bubble reflecting considerable uncertainty among investors about being in or out of the market.

18. During the MSM bubble of 1997, the coefficient of variation increased by 121 percent between February and August of 1997.

19. Increases in liquidity and credit extended to the private sector have been associated with the rise in stock prices in most bubble episodes. Eichengreen and Tong (2003), using over a century of data for 12 countries, found a positive association between monetary volatility and stock market volatility in almost every country studied.

20. Bahrain and Oman are excluded since their equity markets are not considered to be overheated.

21. Particularly noteworthy is the link between margin lending (including multi-purpose personal loans) and the opening of subscription periods for large IPOs. Due to the generalized policy of underpricing IPOs, large oversubscriptions resulted in prorated assignments of relatively small amounts of shares, which in turn resulted in heavy leverage on the part of investors to increase their effective final allocation of shares. This phenomenon was readily observed in Qatar, Saudi Arabia, and the United Arab Emirates.

22. For example, in Kuwait the increases in the KSE index and margin loans were 102 and 92 percent in 2003, 43 and 17 percent in 2004, 78 and 47 percent in 2005, and -13 and -6 percent in the first half of 2006.

23. For Saudi Arabia, this includes 15 percent of consumer loans that were used to buy shares according to Standard & Poor's estimates (Volland, 2005).

24. It implied that prices of a few stocks were rising spectacularly, while prices of the majority of stocks were increasing more slowly or decreasing. When money keeps flowing out of a broad group of stocks and into a small list of other stocks, the relative values between them become seriously distorted. This distortion will eventually be corrected, usually with a sudden shock.

25. As identified by Bakheet Financial Advisor (BFA), a local stock market specialist, speculative stocks belong to companies with weak financial indicators that historically do not pay dividends due

to their recurring losses or small profits. According to BFA, the price performance of speculative stocks usually is more dependent on rumors spread by speculators than on the companies' own track record.

26. The BFA Saudi Top 20 Speculative Stocks Index gained 181 percent during the first nine months of 2004 against a 49 percent increase in the TASI. After bursting in September 2004, a new bubble affecting the group of speculative stocks developed from May 2005. During 2005, the BFA Saudi Top 20 Speculative Stock Index gained 236 percent in 2005 vis-à-vis the 104 percent gain in the TASI.

27. In ADSM, six small capitalization companies (9 percent of the market capitalization) accounted for 44 percent of the increase of the ADSM index during 2005. Similarly, four small capitalization companies in DFM (5 percent of the market capitalization) accounted for 18 percent of the increase in the DFM index during the same period. In DSM, five small firms representing 3 percent of market capitalization, contributed 34 percent of the total volume traded in 2005.

28. Average size of listed companies in the NASDAQ at end-2005 was $1.5 billion, similar to the $1.7 billion average size of listed companies in the Japanese Nikkei market.

29. For instance, the banking and investment sectors represent 26 and 24 percent of the KSE market, respectively, compared with 12 percent and 6 percent globally. Similarly, the relative share of the real estate sector is high in the DFM, and the Tadawul and DSM present some concentration in hydrocarbon-related sectors.

30. According to MSCI Barra Equity Research (2006), the domestic free float for the GCC countries ranges from 49 percent in Bahrain and Oman to 70 percent in Qatar. These estimates, however, exclude from free float the holdings of governments and corporations, but not the holdings of large private investors which usually also detract from the stock's liquidity.

31. The volume of domestic debt was dramatically reduced in most GCC countries since 2003 because the authorities used a large part of their growing fiscal surpluses to redeem domestic debt. Notwithstanding some recent progress, bond markets are still very shallow (despite the recent rapid growth of *sukuk* issues), the mortgage market is nonexistent, securitization has not yet been developed at the domestic market level, and there are practically no futures or derivatives trading denominated in local currencies.

32. In emerging markets, the market share for mutual funds is about 15 percent, with the highest share evident in Asia at 22 percent and the lowest in East Europe at 2.4 percent (Global Financial Stability Report, Market Developments and Issues, April 2004).

33. This contagion effect is analyzed by Saadi-Sedik and Petri (2006). They find that Arab stock markets are cointegrated, and that changes in the price indices of the two main regional markets (Saudi Arabia and Kuwait) have a causality effect on other smaller markets (as per the results of Granger causality tests).

34. Nonfinancial listed companies would be able to invest in other listed companies only through mutual funds or portfolios managed by licensed firms.

35. Only individual investors with limited income were to be eligible to participate, up to a maximum investment of SRls 500,000. The proposed fund, which entailed no upfront injection of public money, was aimed at providing a guarantee against a potential portfolio loss for two years.

36. As measured by the West Texas Intermediate (WTI).

37. The PEG is calculated as PER divided by the growth rate of profitability. Therefore, a stock with a PEG greater than one is usually considered overpriced.

38. Although FSAPs in the region were mostly conducted between 2001 and 2005 (with Qatar's FSAP completed in 2007), the speed of the changes in the equity market may have outdated some of the FSAP conclusions. Some of the supervisory authorities, however, reported further strengthening of banks' capacity to withstand shocks based on stress tests conducted by the central banks.

39. In addition, personal loans, which have been the fastest growing component of credit to the private sector in all GCC countries during the period, are guaranteed by (public sector) salaries and seem to have very low (if any) credit risk for the banks.

40. For instance, in Saudi Arabia, retained gains from main IPOs for buy-and-hold investors range from over 100 to almost 400 percent after the market correction (Table 1.17).

41. These include, among others, the 15 percent general salary increase approved in Saudi Arabia in August 2005; the 25 percent increase (15 percent for expatriates) in public sector salaries approved in the United Arab Emirates in March 2005; and the KD200 transferred by the Kuwaiti authorities to every Kuwaiti citizen in January 2005 and July 2006.

42. For an in-depth analysis of the status of the legal and regulatory framework in the GCC equity markets, see the chapter on Institutional and Legal Aspects of Capital Markets in the GCC Countries.
43. For instance, Ofek and Richardson (2003) show that, during the recent NASDAQ bubble, dot.com companies played a larger role in individual portfolios than in institutional portfolios, since institutional investors were reluctant to invest in speculative stocks. As of March 2000, dot.com companies accounted for 4.4 percent of market capitalization, but only for 2.3 percent of total pension fund holdings.
44. Announcements that there will be an intervention, even if they are not carried out, could have similar effects.
45. Including relaxing regulatory limits or supervisory forbearance.

BIBLIOGRAPHY

ABQ Zawya; http://www.zawya.com/

Abu Dhabi Securities Market (ADSM); http://portal.adsm.ae/wps/portal

Arab Monetary Fund (AMF); Quarterly Bulletins; http://www.amf.org.ae/venglish/

Bakheet Financial Advisor (BFA); http://www.bfasaudi.com/bfamain.asp

Bloomberg; www.bloomberg.com

Diba, Behzad and Grossman, Herschel (1988). "The Theory of Rational Bubbles in Stock Prices," The Economic Journal 98 (September), pp. 746–54.

Doha Securities Market (DSM); http://www2.dsm.com.qa/dsm/DSM_Home

Dubai Financial Market (DFM); http://www.dfm.co.ae/dfm/main/main.htm

Eichengreen, Barry and Tong, Hui, 2003. "Stock Market Volatility and Monetary Policy: What the Historical Record Shows," Asset Prices and Monetary Policy conference, Reserve Bank of Australia.

Eichengreen, B. and H. Tong (2003). "Stock Market Volatility and Monetary Policy: What the Historical Record Shows," *Asset Prices and Monetary Policy*: 108–42.

Evans, G.W. (1991). "Pitfalls in Testing for Explosive Bubbles in Asset Prices," American Economic Review 81, 922–930.

Federation of Euro-Asian Stock Exchanges; http://www.feas.org/

Global Investment House; http://www.globalinv.net/

Gulfbase.com; http://www.gulfbase.com/site/interface/index.aspx

Gürkaynak, Refet S., "Econometric Tests of Asset Price Bubbles: Taking Stock," Staff working papers in the Finance and Economics Discussion Series, Federal Reserve Board, 2005.

International Monetary Fund (IMF); International Financial Statistics; www.imf.org

International Monetary Fund (IMF); World Economic Outlook; www.imf.org

KAMCO Asset Management Financial Services; http://www.kamconline.com/

Kuwait Stock Exchange (KSE); http://www.kuwaitse.com/default.aspx

LeRoy, Stephen, and Richard Porter (1981). "The Present-Value Relation: Tests based on Implied Variance Bounds," Econometrica 49 (May), pp. 555–574.

Middle East Economic Digest (MEED), Investment Projects Database.

Middle East Economic Digest (MEED), (2005). "HSBC-MEED Middle East Business Confidence Index (MEBCI)", MEED 25–31 (March).

MSCI Barra Equity Research, (2006). MSCI Gulf Cooperation Council Countries Initial Index Construction Summary (January 2003); www.mscibarra.com

Muscat Securities Market (MSM); http://www.msm.gov.om/

Ned Davis Research, Inc. "NASDAQ Composite Price/Earnings Ratio vs. Margin Debt", Ned Davis Research, Inc., 2005.

Ofek, Eli and Richardson, Matthew, (2003). "DotCom Mania: The Rise and Fall of Internet Stock Prices", Journal of Finance, Vol. 58, pp. 1113–1138, June.

Saadi-Sedik, Tahsin and Petri, Martin, (2006). "The Jordanian Stock Market – Should You Invest in it for Risk Diversification or Performance", IMF Working paper 06/187, August 1.

Saudi Arabian Capital Market Authority; http://www.cma.org.sa/cma_en/default.aspx

Shiller, Robert, "Bubbles, Human Judgment, and Expert Opinion," Cowles foundation discussion paper No. 1303, 2001.

Shuaa Capital; http://www.shuaacapital.com/shuaacapital/

Siegel, Jeremy J., "What is an Asset Price Bubble? An Operational Definition," Working paper, Finance Department of the Wharton School, 2002.

Stockselector.com; http://www.stockselector.com/

Tadawul Saudi Stock Market; http://www.tadawul.com.sa/

Vissing-Jorgensen, Annette, (2003). "Perspectives on Behavioral Finance: Does 'Irrationality' Disappear with Wealth? Evidence from Expectations and Actions," Working paper, Northwestern University.

Volland, Emmanuel, (2005). "Bank Industry Risk Analysis: Kingdom of Saudi Arabia," S&P credit analysis, April.

West K. (1987). "A Specification Test for Speculative Bubbles," *Quarterly Journal of Economics*, 102, 553–80.

West, K.D. (1988). "Bubbles, Fads and Sock Price Volatility Tests: A Partial Evaluation," *Journal of Finance*, 43, 639–56.

World Bank; Emerging Markets Database; www.worldbank.org

World Bank; World Development Indicators; www.worldbank.org

CHAPTER 2

The Bahrain Stock Exchange: Bucking the Regional Trend

Dima Jardaneh and
Mohammed Omran

2.1 INTRODUCTION

During 2002–05, the Bahrain Stock Exchange (BSE) witnessed relatively smaller gains than the boom experienced by other regional stock markets, including Kuwait, Qatar, Saudi Arabia, and the UAE. During the first half of 2006, most regional markets underwent large corrections while Bahrain's stock market posted only modest losses. The aim of this chapter is to survey recent developments in the BSE and to shed some light on the reasons why the BSE has behaved differently than other markets in the region. The BSE's stock price increases were broadly in line with economic fundamentals and the market did not show any evidence of significant overvaluation in the 2003–05 period. This is attributable to Bahrain's underlying economic and financial structure, as well as market-based factors that differentiate Bahraini stocks from the rest of the region. These factors are (a) the country's lesser dependence on oil; (b) the limited impact of privatization and Initial Public Offerings (IPOs); (c) greater opportunities for non-oil private sector investment and funding; and (d) well-established regulatory standards in the capital markets.

This chapter is organized as follows: Section 2.2 analyzes the BSE performance based on selected micro and macro fundamental indicators. Section 2.3 dwells on the factors that explain the different behavior of the Bahrain Stock Exchange (BSE) vis-à-vis the booming Gulf Cooperation Council (GCC) stock markets. Section 2.4 provides concluding observations.

Box 2.1   Bahrain Stock Exchange

Historical background

The Bahrain Stock Exchange (BSE) was established in 1987 and commenced operations in June 1989, with 29 listed companies. As of June 2007, the number of companies stood at 50, including seven non-Bahraini companies. There are three indices that track the BSE: The Bahrain All Share Index, the Dow Jones Bahrain Index, and the Esterad Index. The Bahrain All Share and Esterad indices were introduced in 2004 with the former representing all companies listed on the Exchange, while the latter is comprised of a basket of local publicly listed companies which are selected according to a specific criteria including sector, market representation, and liquidity. Created jointly by the BSE and Dow Jones indexes, the Dow Jones Bahrain Index was introduced in June 2005 to represent all companies domiciled and headquartered in Bahrain whose stocks trade on the BSE. The trading system at the BSE supports the following markets: the regular market, special orders market, IPO market, mutual funds market, and bonds market. Since 1999, GCC citizens are allowed

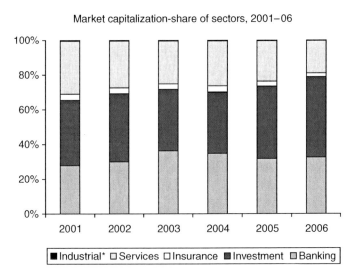

Market capitalization-share of sectors, 2001–06

■ Industrial* □ Services □ Insurance ■ Investment □ Banking

Note: *Share of the industrial sector is less than one percent and therefore does not appear in graph.

▶

to own 100 percent of Bahraini listed companies, while non-GCC nationals are allowed to own up to 49 percent of a domestic joint-stock company's equity, with some exceptions.

Market size

In 1994, BSE market capitalization was estimated at around $5.13 billion. By mid-2007, it reached $22.8 billion (an annualized increase of 54 percent). The steepest increase in market capitalization (40 percent) was in 2004. The ratio of market capitalization to GDP indicates that the BSE has been increasing in importance in terms of size, relative to the overall economy, primarily as a result of the rising share of the financial sector in the stock market. At end-2006, the sector accounted for around 80 percent of overall market capitalization.

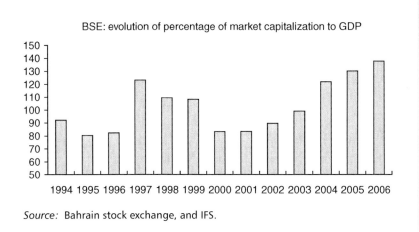

BSE: evolution of percentage of market capitalization to GDP

Source: Bahrain stock exchange, and IFS.

2.2 STOCK PRICE MOVEMENTS AND MICRO AND MACRO FUNDAMENTAL INDICATORS

This section analyzes the performance of the Bahrain stock market based on several selected indicators. These indicators include (a) the recent performance of the stock price index; (b) the correlation between price and economic value of stocks; (c) the volatility of stock prices; (d) the behavior of the money and credit aggregates; and (e) the IPO calendar. Based on these indicators, Bahrain's stock market performance is compared with other developed and emerging markets.

2.2.1   Price index performance

Gains in the BSE have exceeded a number of emerging markets but have fallen well short of the boom witnessed in other GCC markets. The general stock price index (Bahrain All Share Index), which includes all local publicly listed companies, increased by 108 percent from December 2002 to December 2005 – an annualized rate of increase of around 28 percent. During the same period, all other GCC stock markets registered significantly higher increases.[1] While BSE price gains were well below those in other GCC markets, they were in line with the average growth of stock prices in emerging markets, as measured by the Morgan Stanley Capital International (MSCI) emerging markets index. Additionally, BSE gains exceeded other emerging markets during 2002–05, including Chile, Taiwan, and the Czech Republic.

The performance of the BSE All Share Index during 2006 has been flat. In the same tenor as its moderate rise relative to other GCC markets, the change in the BSE All Share Index (0.9 percent during 2006) has left the market undeterred by the sharp correction that occurred in other GCC markets (Figure 1.3). The overall performance of the BSE may have been affected by the increased volatility in the regional stock markets and the underlying risk of contagion arising from cross listings and the unraveling of margin lending positions across the region.[2] Market performance picked up during the first half of 2007 with the BSE All Share Index registering gains of 8.6 percent compared with end-2006.

The movements in the Bahrain All Share Index were accompanied by increased activity in the market. The value of trade, volume of trade, and number of transactions on the BSE hit new records in 2005. Between

Table 2.1   Key market indicators across a sample of emerging markets (%)

	Bahrain	Chile	Czech Republic	Oman	Taiwan	MSCI
Change in local market index (2002–05)	107.6	83.4	75.8	154.1	47.1	141.9
Annualized change in market index	27.6	22.4	20.7	36.5	13.7	34.2
Change in value traded (2002–05)	235.7	504.8	574.7	505.4	−2.2	n.a.
Change in shares traded (2002–05)	29.6	903.0	105.4	142.5	−16.9	n.a.

Sources: Emerging Markets Data Base and MSCI Barra.

December 2002 and December 2005, these indicators grew by 236 percent, 30 percent, and 73 percent, respectively.[3] However, the growth of activity in the BSE seems to have lagged behind other GCC markets, as well as in other emerging markets from the sample, namely Chile and the Czech Republic.

At the same time, market capitalization (reflecting market size) in the BSE increased by 129 percent between December 2002 and December 2005. This increase, although far below that registered in other GCC countries, is sizable considering Bahrain's lesser dependence on oil.

2.2.2 Correlation between price and economic value

During 2003–06, the valuation of stocks as measured by the Price-Earning Ratio (PER), Price-To-Book Value ratio (PBV), and Dividend Yield (DY) compared favorably with the rest of the region, and were also broadly in line with major industrial and emerging markets, indicating that Bahraini stocks were not overpriced. During this period and in contrast with valuations in other GCC markets before the correction, the average PER for the BSE was on a downward trajectory, falling from a peak of 31 in 2003 to 11 in 2006. The low PERs indicate that valuations have lagged behind the growth in company earnings.

Valuations have remained flat over the first half of 2007. As of end-June 2007, the average PER of the BSE was 11, unchanged from its level at end-2006, showing that valuations have continued to lag behind earnings. The largest decline in the PER occurred between January and March 2006, which could indicate that the BSE was affected by the correction taking

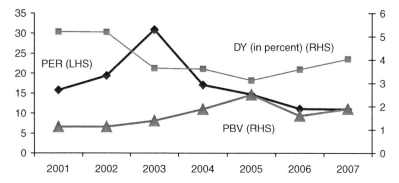

Figure 2.1 BSE – all local-publicly listed companies PER, PBV and dividend yield until May 2007

Sources: Arab Monetary Fund; and KAMCO Research.

Table 2.2 Earnings growth and PERs in a sample of companies

	Net income H1 2006 $ million	Net income H1 2007 $ million	Earnings growth (%)	Market cap. Year-end 06 $ million	PER Year-end 05	PER Year-end 06	PER H1 07
Ahli United Bank	108	151	40	3,221	15.6	15.5	17.3
Bahrain Telecommunications	126	139	10	3,031	12.9	12.8	11.7
Gulf Finance House	117	146	25	1,486	15.0	7.0	6.8
National Bank of Bahrain	49	60	22	1,417	18.0	14.5	12.6
Arab Banking Corporation	111	143	29	1,350	8.9	6.7	7.5
Arithmetic average			25				

Sources: Company annual reports and Fund staff estimates.

hold across the region's stock markets. While the PER appears to have stabilized in later months, the sharp decline from its end-2005 level could indicate that investors were expecting a decline in corporate earnings in 2006, which contributed to a discount in valuations and downward pressure on the PER.

Companies listed on the BSE were selling at a discount relative to their earnings in the first half of 2007. The analysis of the trailing PER for a sample of companies listed on the BSE shows that investors have remained generally pessimistic. Corporate earnings for these companies, which account for nearly 50 percent of overall market capitalization, have risen by an average 25 percent in the first half of 2007 relative to their earnings in the first half of 2006. Nonetheless, changes in the PER for these companies seem to indicate that the change in share prices in 2006 and during the first half of 2007 have not captured the companies' underlying economic value and their earnings potential. This divergence in valuations from earnings potential in 2006 and the first half of 2007 suggests that these shares may have suffered from selling pressures as a result of the stock market corrections in other GCC countries.

2.2.3 Price volatility

The BSE All Share Index enjoyed low volatility, as measured by its monthly standard deviation and coefficient of variation. Comparing the coefficient of variation before and after August 2003, we find insignificant differences. In fact, the coefficient of variation of the Bahrain All Share Index declined in

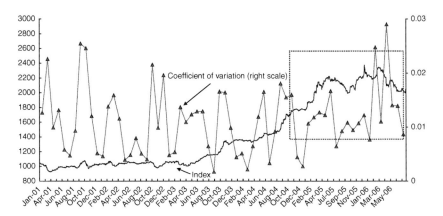

Figure 2.2   Daily Bahrain all share index 2000–06 and monthly standard deviation

Sources: Bahrain Stock Exchange; and Fund staff estimates.

recent years compared with the period of January 2001 until August 2003. It is, however, worth noting that volatility did pick up significantly in the first half of 2006, particularly in the months of January and March, reflecting developments in neighboring countries.

2.2.4 Other factors affecting stock valuations: money, credit, and IPOs

Bahrain experienced one of the lowest growth rates in both the money supply and credit to the private sector among the GCC countries during 2002–05. Bahrain was only preceded by Oman, which had lower growth in both the money supply and credit to the private sector. Nonetheless, private sector credit growth in Bahrain, which reached around 50 percent during 2003–05, is considered high by international standards. The fact that this increase in private sector credit did not fuel an even larger increase in prices could be due to the broader range of financial assets available in Bahrain, the relatively larger proportion of resources absorbed by real private investment, and the perceived higher gains that could be obtained from speculative activities in other GCC markets (see Figure 1.8 and Table 1.14).

There is no indication of an abnormally large number of IPOs in Bahrain. IPOs in Bahrain's market are rare and the size of the offers is very limited. For instance, there were three IPOs, with a total value of just $46 million in 2005, and another three valued at $1.3 billion in 2006. The number of listed companies in Bahrain has not changed markedly over the past five years, while the rest of the GCC countries (except Saudi Arabia) experienced significant increases.

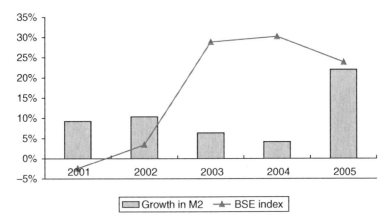

Figure 2.3 Money supply and BSE all share index, 2001–05 (Change in percent)

Sources: Central Bank of Bahrain; and Fund staff estimates.

2.3   WHY IS THE BAHRAINI MARKET BEHAVING DIFFERENTLY?

The divergence in the trend observed in the BSE compared with the rest of the GCC stock markets raises the question as to why the Bahraini market has behaved differently. Not only has stock market growth in Bahrain been slower compared with the rest of the region, but the market continues to suffer from limited diversification and private sector participation. This raises important questions, particularly taking into account Bahrain's non-oil GDP growth rate, which has averaged 8 percent a year during 2002–05. In fact, it may be argued that the BSE has been unjustifiably overlooked by regional and international investors. The reasons for the relatively slower development of the BSE could be attributed to several market-specific factors, ranging from Bahrain's lower dependency on oil production, the structure of its financial sector, and market-related structural factors and regulations. This section looks at the main determinants of the different behavior exhibited by the BSE, including the structure of Bahrain's economy and the market-specific factors mentioned above.

2.3.1   Factors specific to the BSE

Despite its earlier establishment compared with other markets in the region, the BSE remains shallow. Trading on the BSE commenced in 1989, some 11 years before the launching of other equity markets, such as the Abu Dhabi Securities Market (ADSM) and the Dubai Financial Market (DFM), which were established in 2000. However, the Bahraini stock market has not gathered much momentum compared with other regional markets, notwithstanding Bahrain's diversified economy and its strong financial center. To illustrate this point, it is useful to compare the BSE with the Muscat Stock Market (MSM), which was established in 1988. At end-1994, 68 companies were listed on the MSM with market capitalization amounting to $1.86 billion and a turnover ratio of 13 percent, compared with 24 companies listed

Table 2.3   BSE and MSM: selected stock market indicators

	BSE		MSM	
	1994	2005	1994	2005
Listed companies	24	47	68	176
Turnover ratio	3.12	4.08	12.98	25.20
Market capitalization (US$ billion)	5.13	17.7	1.86	11.8

Sources: Arab Monetary Fund and Fund staff estimates.

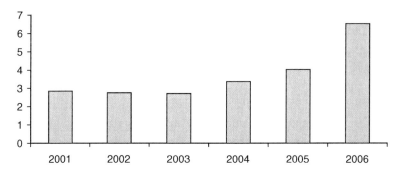

Figure 2.4   BSE: Turnover ratio, 2001–06 (In percent)

Source: Bahrain Stock Exchange.

on the BSE with market capitalization of $5.13 billion and a turnover ratio of 3 percent. By end-2005, these numbers stood at 176 companies listed on the MSM and a turnover ratio of 25 percent compared with 47 companies listed on the BSE and a turnover ratio of 4 percent. These figures illustrate that the MSM has had a more profound deepening than the BSE. As a result, the MSM was better positioned to attract some of the liquidity that has contributed to the buoyancy of stock markets across the region.

The level of activity in the BSE continues to be the lowest among the GCC markets. Turnover data for the BSE reveals a low level of activity, with an almost unchanged turnover ratio, in the range of 3–4 percent during 2003–05, albeit with some acceleration in 2006. This level of activity is markedly lower than in the other GCC stock markets. The lower activity in the BSE may be partially attributed to the smaller number of IPOs, in sharp contrast to the IPO boom observed in many other regional markets. It seems that the BSE index compared unfavorably with the performance of other major GCC indices since the latter experienced a large number of IPOs that registered sharp price increases during initial trading. Also, investor enthusiasm for quick gains through IPO subscriptions may have prompted some Bahraini investors to redirect funds toward other regional markets that offered better opportunities.[4]

Sluggish IPO activity is partially related to the modalities of private sector development in Bahrain. Although guidelines for privatizing a number of sectors (including telecommunications, electricity and water, oil and gas, and transport) have been put in place, thus far the overall strategy has been largely geared toward the extension of management contracts and the liberalization of market entry and exit. Other obstacles to privatization have included parliamentary resistance to the government's plans to divest its equity holdings in certain companies, including the Bahrain Telecommunications Company (BATELCO). The recent sale of the Al Hidd Power and Water Station to a consortium of private sector investors may signal renewed momentum in this area.

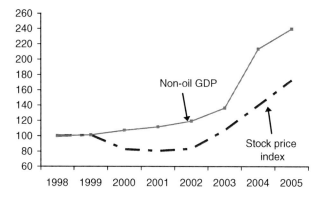

Figure 2.5   Bahrain: Stock price index and non-oil GDP (Normalized at 100)

Source: Fund staff estimates.

2.3.2   Factors related to the structure of the economy

Stock market performance may partially reflect the economy's lesser dependence on oil relative to the rest of the region. At 27 percent of GDP, the contribution of the hydrocarbon sector to GDP is significantly smaller than in other GCC countries, where it ranges between 40 percent and 68 percent of GDP. As a result, Bahrain gained the least from the recent boom in oil prices, with the contribution of the hydrocarbon sector to total GDP rising by a modest 8 percent between 2003 and 2005, compared with increases of around 40 percent and 30 percent of GDP in the cases of the UAE and Saudi Arabia, respectively. In the same vein, Figure 2.6 illustrates that the ratio of non-oil to oil GDP in Bahrain is the highest in the region and it has been less affected by the current hike in oil prices, which attests to the strong growth of non-oil activities and the diversification of the country's economic base.

The more stable behavior of Bahraini stock prices relative to other GCC countries reflects in part a stronger association between market prices and real output. In terms of overall and non-oil sector growth, Bahrain's output exhibits less dispersion and volatility compared with other GCC countries.[5] Given that output is relatively more stable in Bahrain, it can be expected that stock price changes and stock valuations in Bahrain will be stable, as they are more firmly anchored in non-oil fundamentals. Furthermore, the Bahraini stock market can be viewed as better cushioned against the boom and bust cycles that may arise from volatility in the oil sector.

A relatively larger proportion of resources in Bahrain has been channeled to real private investment, rather than the stock market. The implementation of a government-led investment program, with a focus on industrial

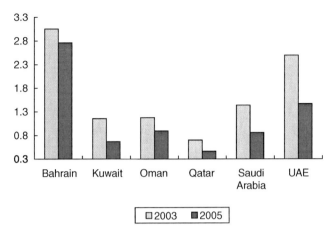

Figure 2.6   GCC: Ratio of non-oil to oil GDP

Source: Fund staff estimates.

Table 2.4   Ratio of private
investment to increase in market
capitalization (2002–05)

Bahrain	56%
Kuwait	19%
Oman	58%
Qatar	44%
Saudi Arabia	15%
UAE	16%

Sources: Country sources and Fund staff
estimates.

and infrastructure development, has crowded in a considerable amount of private sector investment, which has grown, on a compounded basis, by 34 percent a year between 2001 and 2005, compared with compound averages ranging from 5 to 24 percent in other GCC countries. The funding for private investment appears to be a combination of bank lending and retained profits, in addition to foreign participation in joint ventures. In the context of the GCC region, it is useful to consider the scale of real investment by the private sector in comparison with investment in the stock market, measured by the increase in stock market capitalization. The outcome of this exercise shows that GCC countries can be divided into two groups. In the first group, consisting of Kuwait, Saudi Arabia, and the UAE, the proportion of private investment to growth in market capitalization for the 2002–05 period was below 20 percent. In the second group, consisting of Bahrain, Oman, and Qatar, the proportion increased to the 40–60 percent range.

2.3.3 Market-based factors

The earnings growth of companies listed in the BSE has been slower than in other GCC countries. The Bahrain All Share Index increased by 28 percent in 2003, 30 percent in 2004, and 24 percent in 2005. On the other hand, during the same period, the PER was 13.2, 13.6, and 16, respectively, which means that profitability, measured as earnings per share, was increasing at a slower pace than stock valuation. The average earnings growth of the four largest listed companies, which account for about 50 percent of total market capitalization, was around 15 percent a year in 2000–05, well below the levels in other GCC countries. For example, the average earnings growth of companies in Qatar (DSM) and Saudi Arabia (Tadawul) in 2000–05 was 43 percent and 52 percent, respectively. A look at the sectoral breakdown of the stock market can help explain the reasons behind this difference. The BSE does not include any oil and gas companies, the industrial sector accounts for a negligible portion of the stocks listed, and the real estate sector is not present.

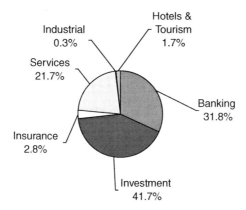

Figure 2.7   Distribution of BSE market capitalization across sectors in 2005
Source: Bahrain Stock Exchange Monthly Statistical Bulletin.

Table 2.5   Earnings growth in the four largest
BSE listed companies (2000–05)

	Average growth (%)	Market share (%)
Bahrain Telecom	11.1	16.8
Ahli United Bank	32.7	14.1
Gulf Finance House	9.5	10.9
National Bank of Bahrain	12.7	8.4
Annualized compound average	15.0	50.2

Sources: Company financial statements and Fund staff estimates.

Moreover, because some important and profitable sectors of the economy such as petrochemicals and aluminum are not listed in the stock market, profitability growth of the BSE was lower compared to other regional markets.

The dominant role played by the financial sector in Bahrain's economy may have directed interest away from the equity market. Bahrain is recognized as a regional financial center, and has developed a comparative advantage in specialized financial services, including off-shore banking and Islamic finance. At 25 percent of GDP, the financial sector is on its way to becoming the leading contributor to GDP. Total banking system assets, including those of Off-Shore Banking Units (OBUs) and investment banks, stood at $140 billion at end-2005, with year-on-year growth of around 18 percent, primarily driven by the increase in foreign assets of OBUs. Contrary to other GCC countries, the growth in Bahrain's banking system assets has surpassed that of market capitalization. The ratio of market capitalization to total banking

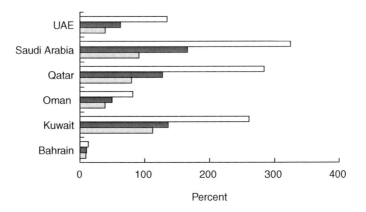

Figure 2.8   Ratio of market capitalization to total banking assets

Sources: Global Investment House; and Fund staff estimates.

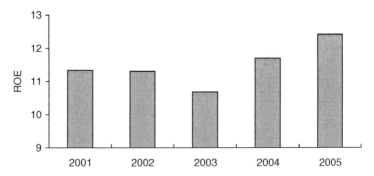

Figure 2.9   ROE of commercial banks listed on the BSE, 2001–05

(In percent)

Source: Company annual reports.

assets was 12 percent at end-2005, well below levels elsewhere in the region. Furthermore, the dominant role of the financial services industry in the stock market, with the sector accounting for around 70 percent of market capitalization, could infer that expectations riding on this sector's performance can largely shape the trends observed in the BSE.

The profitability of Bahraini financial institutions has been healthy and largely stable, with the average Return On Equity (ROE) of commercial banks listed on the BSE reaching about 12.5 percent in 2005. This return, while below the levels witnessed among banks in other GCC countries during the stock boom, indicates that Bahraini banks have not been unduly exposed to stock market-related risk. Given that these banks operate in a mature and highly competitive environment, it can be expected that this trend will continue in the future.

Apart from the equity market, developments in Bahrain's financial market are gaining momentum. With the advent of further innovation and specialization in Bahrain's financial services sector and the deepening of financial markets, there is likely to be a gradual shift in investors' focus away from the equity market toward alternative financial assets. In this regard, it is important to note the important role already played by Islamic instruments, including Islamic treasury bonds (*sukuk*) and shorter-term instruments (*salam*), in providing investors with opportunities to diversify their portfolios. Total outstanding Islamic government and non-government securities increased by $575 million since June 2004, to a total of $1.4 billion as of October 2005.

Tight regulatory standards in Bahrain may have limited speculative demand in the stock market. According to staff findings, Bahrain ranks at the top in terms of the level of implementation of regulatory standards among GCC countries, as measured by the principles of the International Organization of Securities Commissions (IOSCO).[6] In particular, it is important to highlight Bahrain's full compliance with all the principles in the area of prudential regulations, including transparency and disclosure requirements. Moreover, the Bahrain Monetary Agency (BMA) had tightened prudential regulations by placing quantitative limits on personal loans in a bid to curb growth in this type of credit.[7] In sum, the supervisory and regulatory environment in Bahrain aimed at fostering a degree of investor awareness, also helped reduce speculative trading in the stock market.

2.4 CONCLUDING REMARKS

Stock market performance in Bahrain appears to be better aligned with the fundamentals of its non-oil economy. This has contributed to more realistic stock valuations relative to other GCC countries. At this juncture, the

BSE appears to be well poised to receive additional inflows of capital, particularly given the potential for cross regional capital flows as investors may be seeking attractive valuations in the regional markets.

Bahrain needs to promote IPOs and embark on an aggressive privatization program. The BSE was largely ignored by regional investors in the absence of any high profile IPO. Divestiture of state-owned enterprises through Share Issue Privatizations (SIPs) is recommended to improve the operating and financial performance of state-owned companies and to further develop the stock market.[8] This would help increase the market size and activity, and will have spillover effects on private companies by encouraging them to go public. In addition to enhancing liquidity, SIPs can increase investment opportunities for investors to better diversify their portfolios, which in turn will have a positive impact on the risk-sharing function of the market and lead to further market deepening. The success of the innovatively structured IPO of Seef's Properties (a state-owned commercial center) in 2007 and new prospects for further IPOs in the telecomunications and banking sector in 2008, are steps in the right direction. However, further effort is needed to shift the momentum in favor of the BSE.

In order to help small firms go public and increase new issues in the BSE, the authorities should encourage venture capital activities and develop advanced financial instruments. Venture capital can provide crucial financing to enable the development of Small and Medium-Sized Enterprises (SMEs). The characteristic which sets venture capital apart from other sources of financing is its readiness to assume greater risks, thus filling a critical gap in the financing available to SMEs and newly established firms. In addition, venture capitalists frequently offer strategic management support for the firms in which they invest. The introduction of advanced financial instruments, including derivatives and other more-sophisticated instruments, would provide attractive alternatives for investors to manage risk.

NOTES

1. The Dubai financial market (DFM) index increased by 820 percent, followed by Saudi Arabia (563 percent), and Kuwait (380 percent). Stock price indices increased by 376 percent in Qatar, 281 percent in Abu Dhabi, and 154 percent in Oman.
2. Bley and Chen (2006) analyze the impact of the increase in market activity on the return behavior and the dynamic relationships among the GCC stock markets. Their analysis shows that while the return behavior is clearly not homogeneous across regional markets, there is evidence of increasing market integration.
3. By December 2005, the value of trade reached $771 million, the volume of trade recorded 22.5 million shares, and the number of transactions was around 23,000. The level of activity in the first half of 2006, measured as average daily value and volume of traded shares, registered an increase of 85 percent and 93 percent, respectively, relative to the first half of 2005. The boom in trading activity witnessed in the month of May 2006 is attributed to the sale of a number of stakes in the Bank of Bahrain and Kuwait.

4. Another reason behind the low trading volumes in the BSE was that the investor base in the market was dominated by institutional investors such as pension funds, which follow buy-and-hold investment strategies.

5. The issue of links between financial and real indicators, particularly between economic growth and stock market performance has been explored and analyzed, and a strong empirical association has been established in many advanced markets. For example, Fama (1990) found a strong correlation between lagged stock returns and output growth in the US market. In addition, Mauro (2000) showed a significant positive correlation between real stock returns and economic growth in emerging markets.

6. See the chapter titled The Institutional and Legal Aspects of Capital Markets in the GCC Countries.

7. According to the new standards, for a customer to qualify for a personal loan, the maximum permitted ratio of loan service costs to household income cannot exceed 50 percent.

8. See also Summary of Key Recommendations in "Kingdom of Bahrain – Financial System Stability Assessment", International Monetary Fund, 2006.

BIBLIOGRAPHY

Bahrain Stock Exchange (BSE); http://www.bahrainstock.com.

Bley, J. and Chen K. (2006). "Gulf Cooperation Council (GCC) Stock Markets: The Dawn of a New Era," *Global Finance Journal*, Vol. 17: 75–91.

El Nabarawy, M. and Munir, S. (2006). "Ahli United Bank," *Equity Research*, Shuaa Capital.

Fama, E. (1990). "Stock Returns, Expected Returns, and Real Activity," *Journal of Finance*, Vol. 45 (4): 1089–1108.

Garner, J. et al. (2006). "Gulf Equity Markets, Powered by Oil," Credit Suisse.

Global Investment House Economic Research; http://www.globalinv.net

International Monetary Fund (2006). "Kingdom of Bahrain – Financial System Stability Assessment," Country Report No. 06/91, http://www.imf.org/external/pubs/cat/longres.cfm?sk=18991.0

Mauro, P. (2000). "Stock Returns and Output Growth in Emerging and Advanced Economies," IMF Working Paper, IMF/00/89.

MSCI Barra, "MSCI Emerging Markets (EM) Index," http://www.mscibarra.com

Zawya (2006). MSM companies profiles, http://www.zawya.com

CHAPTER 3

Kuwait Stock Exchange Correction: Why Was It Moderate?

Maher Hasan

3.1 INTRODUCTION

This chapter examines the factors that have affected stock market developments in Kuwait during the recent boom and correction periods and why the Kuwait Stock Exchange (KSE) behaved differently from other Gulf Cooperation Council (GCC) markets. While all GCC stock markets, except Bahrain and Oman, witnessed substantial increases in their indices, in excess of 500 percent during 2002–05, followed by large corrections in 2006, the KSE witnessed a relatively moderate correction. In addition, Kuwait recovered strongly in 2007. This chapter also examines the factors that may explain this difference in behavior including the improvement in fundamentals; exuberant demand; the authorities' policy response; and the structural characteristics of the market.

The analysis concludes that the difference in the KSE's behavior is partly attributed to the strengthening of Kuwait's economic fundamentals following the restoration of economic relations with Iraq after 2002. In addition, the authorities' responses to market developments and several structural characteristics of the KSE also made it less prone to the development of exuberant demand and the resulting boom and bust cycles. However, sources for downside risk in the KSE still exist including sectoral concentration, large cross holdings, and the absence of a single supervisory authority.

Section 3.2 provides a regional perspective to KSE developments; Section 3.3 analyzes the key factors explaining these developments; and Section 3.4 provides some concluding remarks.

3.2   KSE DEVELOPMENTS IN A REGIONAL PERSPECTIVE

The KSE led the surge in GCC stock market performance during 2002–05 with the stock price index increasing by 568 percent. Prior to 2002, the KSE experienced three consecutive years (1998–2000) of losses, but it recovered gradually thereafter, and by March 2003, rebounded to its 1997 level. In 2002 and 2003 the KSE outperformed all other markets with the index increasing by 40 percent and 102 percent, respectively (compared with increases of 13 percent and 76 percent, respectively, for the GCC Weighted Index, GCCW[1]). However, the market was less active in 2004, partly due to some tightening of liquidity by the Central Bank of Kuwait (CBK). The index increase was limited to 33.8 percent and the volume of traded shares also declined. In 2005 the KSE index regained its momentum and increased further by 78.2 percent,[2] the value and volume of trade were at record levels, and market capitalization reached $141.5 billion, representing 170 percent of GDP compared with 90 percent of GDP at the end of 2002.

Box 3.1   Kuwait Stock Exchange

Historical background

The Kuwait Stock Exchange (KSE) is the national stock market of Kuwait. Although several share holding companies (such as the National Bank of Kuwait (NBK) in 1952) existed in Kuwait prior to the creation of the KSE, it was not until October 1962 that a law was passed to organize the issue of shares and subscriptions. In April 1977, the first formal over-the-counter stock exchange was opened and it was officially named the KSE in 1983.

The KSE experienced a major crash in 1977 caused by increases in liquidity after the oil price hike in the mid-1970s, and strong speculative demand. As a result, tight government controls, including severely restricting the use of postdated checks on the KSE, were established.

In the late 1970s, an unofficial stock market called Al-Manakh was established by investors to carry out the speculative trading that had been barred on the KSE after the 1977 crash. Traders created numerous companies in neighboring Arab states to avoid domestic regulations governing new companies. Untrained and uncertified brokers were trading worthless securities with very high Price Earnings Ratios (PER) using postdated checks. The bubble burst in August 1982, and in a month securities traded in the market lost about 60 to 98 percent of their value.

▶

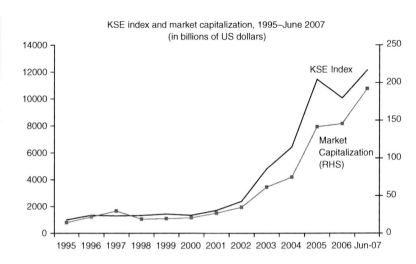

Sources: Central Bank of Kuwait; Gulf Investment Corporation; and MEED.

After the Iraqi invasion of Kuwait in August 1990, the KSE was closed. It resumed operations on September 28, 1992.

Recent developments

During the automation process in November 1995, the KSE Index was introduced. It is based on an arithmetic mean calculation that automatically adjusts for dividends and distributions. The base for the market and sector indices is 1,000 points and December 31, 1993 stock prices. In 2001, the KSE introduced a new weighted Index.

In 1998 the forward trading market was opened and on September 10, 2000, the Foreign Investment Law was issued allowing foreigners to invest in the KSE for the first time.

After several years of weak performance, the market started to recover in 2002. Currently, the KSE is the second largest stock market in the GCC region after the Saudi market. In June 2007, market capitalization was equivalent to $185.4 billion representing about 25 percent of total GCC equity markets.

The KSE index performed better than most other GCC markets, and substantially exceeded the average performance of the emerging markets and the performance of several stock markets during their bubble episodes. The 568 percent increase in the KSE index during the three-year period through 2005 was close to the increase (588 percent) in the Tadawul All Share Index (TASI)[3] and the GCCW index (574 percent) and higher than all other GCC market indices (See Figure 1.2). Similarly, this increase was

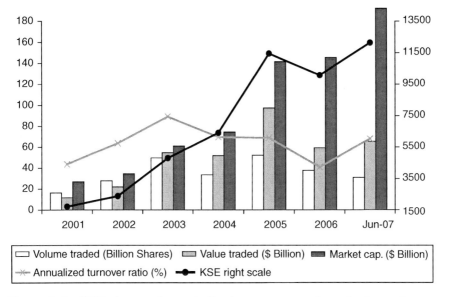

Figure 3.1 KSE index, market capitalization, turnover ratio and value and volume of traded shares (2001–June 2007)

Sources: Kuwait Stock Exchange; Central Bank of Kuwait; and KAMCO Investment Research Dept. Analysis and Fund staff estimates.

significantly higher than the 160 percent increase in emerging markets measured by the Morgan Stanley Emerging Markets Index (MSCI) and it was larger than the price hike observed during the Nikkei bubble of the late 1980s, the Omani (Muscat Securities Market [MSM]) bubble of 1997, and the NASDAQ dot.com bubble of 2000.

By early 2006, investor confidence began to flag. The perception that markets had become overpriced and doubts about the quality and sustainability of corporate profitability increased significantly and triggered widespread sharp corrections in all booming GCC markets except for the KSE, which witnessed a moderate 12 percent correction. For the other expanding markets, the corrections in 2006 ranged from 35 percent in the Doha Securities Market (DSM) to 53 percent in the Saudi stock market, with a 46 percent loss in the GCCW index. The corrections were even sharper when compared with the peaks reached in the expanding markets, (see Table 1.8). While other markets witnessed additional losses or moderate recovery in the first half of 2007, the KSE recovered strongly – the KSE index increased by 20.5 percent outperforming all the other GCC markets.

Although the KSE shares many of the factors that led to the 2002–05 expansion with the other booming GCC markets, its moderate correction

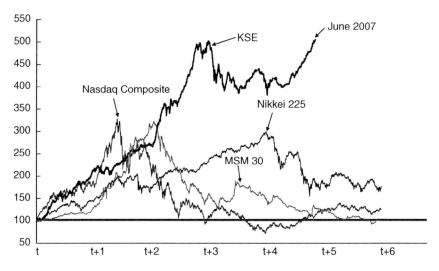

Figure 3.2   Stock price indices during bubble episodes and KSE index
(Nasdaq, Nikkei 225, MSM 30 and KSE are normalized to 100 at start of rapid
price increase periods)

Source: Bloomberg.

and strong recovery is puzzling. Examining the reasons for the KSE's
behavior will help to better understand what can be done to make the equity
markets more resilient to boom and bust cycles. Such an assessment will
also help to determine if downside risks still exist.

3.3 KEY FACTORS EXPLAINING KUWAIT STOCK MARKET DEVELOPMENTS

In addition to higher oil prices, KSE developments can be explained by four
key factors. These are (a) the economic optimism created by the removal
of the previous Iraqi regime and improved fundamentals through strengthened economic relations with Iraq; (b) relatively less exuberant demand in
Kuwait as evident from investors' perception and several market indicators;
(c) the authorities' responses to market conditions; and (d) the structural
characteristics of the KSE compared to other markets.

3.3.1 Economic optimism and improved fundamentals

Like other booming GCC markets, the KSE benefited from improving
economic fundamentals supported by the strength of the oil market. Although

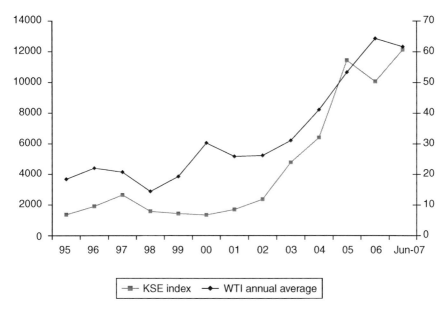

Figure 3.3   WTI oil prices in US dollars and KSE index, 1995–June 2007

Sources: World Economic Outlook; and KSE.

only four small companies related to the oil sector are listed in the KSE, oil price plays an important role in the economy. Corporate profits and stock prices increase with oil prices. This reflects the fact that (a) business opportunities to service public sector consumption and investment demand increased; (b) the spillover effects of higher public expenditure[4] affected private sector income and consumption; and (c) higher fiscal revenues provided assurances of exchange rate stability and easy monetary conditions. Furthermore, abundant liquidity due to high oil prices and a shift in investors' preferences toward regional assets also played an important role in supporting strong demand.

In addition to the above common factors, the removal of the previous Iraqi regime and the prospects for positive repercussions on the local economy played an important role in improving fundamentals in Kuwait. The favorable impact started with prospects for change in Iraq in 2002 and acted as a catalyst to the strong growth of the non-oil sector by boosting business and consumer confidence. After the regime change in 2003, confidence was spurred further and trade and investment opportunities for Kuwaiti companies opened,[5] with Kuwait being a gateway to Iraq. For example, Kuwaiti re-export activities increased by 95 percent in 2003 and averaged 21 percent during 2004–05.

This specific factor partially helps to explain the good performance of the KSE compared to most other GCC markets during 2002–03 and accounts

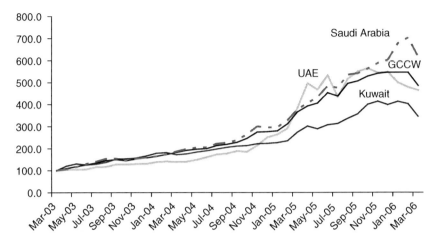

Figure 3.4   Selected GCC stock market indices and weighted average GCC index (March 2003–March 2006)

Sources: Bloomberg; Stock market authorities; Fund Staff estimates; and Global Financial House.

for a large part of the cumulative gains in the KSE index. In fact, comparing the KSE's performance to other expanding GCC stock markets starting in March 2003 when the boom began primarily due to the positive oil price shock, reveals that the KSE performed significantly below other markets, despite the fact that Kuwait is more dependent on oil. This was much more evident in 2004 when the KSE increased by only 34 percent while the GCCW increased by 75 percent.

3.3.2   Relatively less exuberant demand

In addition to the economic optimism created by the removal of the previous Iraqi regime, demand in the KSE reveals a lower level of exuberance compared with other GCC booming markets rendering large correction unwarranted. Assessing the existence and size of exuberant demand is a difficult task because of the absence of complete information about economic fundamentals and their impact on prices. However, examining investors' perceptions about overvaluation and the behavior of specific market and economic indicators (warning signals) could help to assess the level of exuberant demand in Kuwait. These market and economic indicators are (a) a rapid increase in the price index; (b) a weak correlation between the price and economic value of stocks as measured by valuation indicators; (c) a high price volatility; (d) a sizable acceleration in money and credit expansion and heavy use of margin lending; (e) an increasingly narrow market leadership (price hikes are concentrated in a few stocks); and (f) a large initial public offering (IPO) calendar.

As described below, as assessment of the KSE based on these indicators points to a lower degree of exuberance in the KSE compared with other booming GCC markets. Only indicators (a), (c) and (d) pointed to the existence of strong exuberant demand. On the other hand, the KSE's valuation indicators compared favorably with other markets and the narrow market leadership and large IPO calendars that were observed in other booming markets were absent in the KSE.

3.3.2.1 Rapid increase in the price index

The rapid increase in the price index is the market indicator most commonly observed in previous bubbles. As outlined in Section 3.2, the KSE surpassed its average historical performance during the period under review. In addition, it outperformed most other GCC markets and substantially exceeded the emerging markets' average and the performance of several stock markets during bubble episodes. However, not all rapid and substantial increases of stock prices are attributable to speculative bubbles, particularly when economic fundamentals are strong.

3.3.2.2 Correlation between price and economic value

The standard valuation indicators did not point to the existence of exuberant demand in the KSE. By the end of 2005, the markets' returns in most GCC countries outpaced significantly corporate earnings growth, resulting in Price Earnings Ratios (PER) and Price to Book Value Ratios (PBV) being significantly higher than their historical levels and the levels generally seen in emerging and developed markets (Table 1.9). However, KSE valuation indicators compared favorably with most GCC markets and with developed and emerging markets.

Despite the favorable valuation indicators, the market was vulnerable to downside risks. An in-depth analysis of the components of the valuation indicators for the KSE shows that the favorable valuation could be attributable to the profitability structure of listed companies (Box 3.2), which partly depended on market performance due to relatively large cross holdings. This is especially true for the investment companies' sector, which contributed 37 percent of the profits in the first half of 2007, but accounted for only 17 percent of market capitalization. These firms' investments in local shares and the local shares of their fiduciary accounts represented 33 percent of KSE market capitalization as of June 2007.

Table 3.1 Growth in the profitability of the investment
sector and the change in the KSE index (%)

	2000	2001	2002	2003	2004	2005	2006	H1 2007
Profitability growth in investment sector	−19	20	53	295	25	146	−48.2	370
Change in KSE index	−7	27	39	102	34	79	−12	19.4

Sources: Kuwait Stock Exchange; Global investment House; KAMCO and Fund staff estimates.

**Box 3.2   The Profitability Structure of
Listed Companies in the KSE**

Much of the profitability growth of Kuwaiti listed companies was attributable to growth in investment income. The rapid increase in the share of investment income to total corporate income was largely due to the performance of the stock market itself. Furthermore, it is estimated that about 11 percent of listed companies' profits in 2003 were due to the income generated from the implementation of International Accounting Standards (IAS) 39 and 40, relating to the accounting treatment of securities and real estate investment profits. The share of profits from this source increased to 27 percent in 2005. Thus, the actual Price Earnings Ratio (PER) reflecting expected earnings from listed companies' core business is higher than the accounting PER.

Investment, investment income and market performance
of listed companies (2002–05) (in percent)

	2002	2003	2004	2005
Investment income/total income	32	52	36	53
Growth in KSE index	39	102	33.8	79
Listed companies trading and available for sale securities/total assets	10.5	16.5	18.5	20.5

Source: KAMCO research May 2006.

▶

The first half earnings for 2006 (H1 06) show the vulnerability of listed companies' earnings to market performance. The most affected sectors were the real estate, food, and investment sectors. This is not surprising given that investment and insurance companies' earnings largely depend on stock market performance. The least affected sector was the banking sector where earnings increased by 32 percent compared with the first half of 2005, reflecting the sector's resilience to equity market developments. Because of the banking sector's continued strong performance, the decline in overall profitability was limited to less than 17 percent in the first half of 2006, broadly in line with the decline in the overall stock price index during the corresponding period.

Listed companies' results in the first half (H1) of 2006 (in millions of KD)[a]

Sector	H1-05 Profits	H1-06 Profits	Changes in profits (Percent)	EPS 2005[b]	EPS 2006[b]	Changes in EPS (Percent)
Banking	299.4	394.2	31.7	30.0	38.0	26.9
Investment	421.9	212.8	−49.6	27.3	11.8	−56.8
Insurance	36.8	29.1	−21.0	38.3	32.3	−15.8
Real estate	147.2	34.7	−76.4	17.0	2.8	−83.4
Industrial	127.3	123.4	−3.1	29.8	24.2	−18.9
Services	277.8	313.8	12.9	30.2	24.3	−19.7
Food	42.0	17.0	−59.6	49.2	22.0	−55.3
Total/average	1,352.5	1,125.0	−16.8	31.7	22.2	−30.0
Non-Kuwaiti	149.9	150.0	0.0	30.0	33.8	12.5

Notes:
[a] Excluding companies that were listed in 2005 with no available financial results in H1-05.
[b] Simple average for EPS for the companies in the sector.
Source: KSE.

3.3.2.3 High price volatility

Starting in January 2005, the KSE witnessed a substantial increase in volatility as measured by the monthly standard deviation and the coefficient of variation of the KSE index. Since price volatility tends to increase substantially in the period immediately before the bursting of a price bubble, this is an important warning signal. The coefficient of variation increased between January 2005 and December 2005 by 230 percent.[6] This may be compared with the 224 percent increase in the coefficient of variation of the

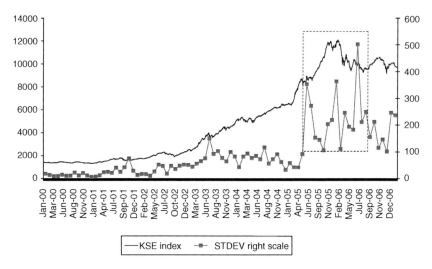

Figure 3.5   Daily KSE index and monthly standard deviation (2000–06)

Sources: Bloomberg; and Fund staff estimates.

NASDAQ price index during the dot.com bubble between October 1999 and April 2000, and the 121 percent increase in the coefficient of variation of the MSM price index during the Omani bubble between February and August 1997.[7] However, the increase in volatility was lower than that observed in the Dubai Financial Market (DFM) and the Doha Securities Market (DSM) (See Figure 1.6) and volatility declined substantially after the mild correction in 2006.

3.3.2.4   *Money and credit expansion and use of margin lending*

Money supply and bank credit expanded rapidly, moving in tandem with the increase in the KSE, albeit at a slower pace than in the other booming GCC markets (Figure 1.8). Money supply, measured by M2, increased by 8 percent and 12 percent in 2003 and 2004, respectively compared with 4.7 percent in 2002.[8] It accelerated further to 18 percent in the first 11 months of 2005. In response, the monetary authorities tightened liquidity conditions significantly, slowing down the growth of M2 to 12.2 percent by December 2005. The increase in the KSE could be partly attributed to the strong increase in credit to the private sector and especially to personal loans (representing 42 percent of total loans). Credit to the private sector and personal loans grew at annual average rates of 18 percent and 23 percent, respectively, between 2003 and 2005 driven mainly by increases in margin and installment loans.[9]

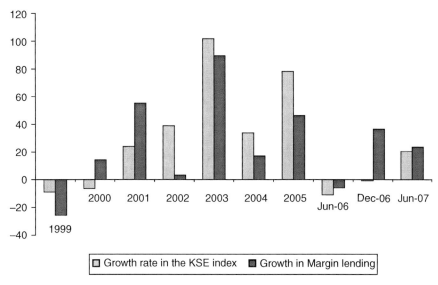

Figure 3.6   Growth in KSE index and margin loans, 1999–June 2007
(In percent)
Source: CBK.

Margin lending increased substantially from an already high level of 6 percent of total private sector loans during 2001–02 to 9 percent during 2003–05.[10] Margin lending represented 25 percent of personal loans at end-2005 compared with an average of 15 percent between 2000 and 2002.[11] It also represented 3 percent of market capitalization as of end-2005[12] and ten times the daily average trading value during 2005. Furthermore, during 2003–05, the increases in the KSE index were in tandem with the increase in margin lending.

3.3.2.5   Narrow market leadership

KSE market development did not show narrow market leadership,[13] contrary to the stock markets in Qatar, Saudi Arabia, and the United Arab Emirates that witnessed this phenomenon during 2003–05. In Saudi Arabia, narrow market leadership was characterized by a group of speculative stocks[14] that showed (since January 2004) recurrent rises, well above the increase in the TASI, and sudden sharp falls. Similarly, groups of relatively small stocks, accounting for 1 to 5 percent of market capitalization, have attracted disproportionate volumes of trade and valuation gains (above 30 percent in some cases) in other GCC markets (DFM, Abu Dhabi Securities Market [ADSM], and DSM) pointing to the existence of an increasingly narrow market leadership associated with exuberant demand.[15]

A careful review of the KSE performance between 2003–06 reveals no evidence of narrow market leadership. The review process includes selecting a group of companies based on the analysis of their financial ratios (including turnover ratio, PER, PBV and dividend yield) and their volatility (measured by beta and the difference between the highest and lowest price in the 52 weeks to the closing price). A high turnover ratio could be due to speculative demand that increases the value and volume of traded stocks, and a high PER or PBV could reflect overvaluation due to speculation, especially if the dividend yield is low. Volatility measures were used because speculative demand increases volatility. The performance of different weighted indices of groups of stocks was compared to the performance of the KSE index and showed no evidence of narrow market leadership.

3.3.2.6   Initial public offerings calendar

The primary market in Kuwait has been less active compared with other GCC markets in terms of the number, size, and oversubscription of IPOs. An abnormally large number of IPOs could be associated with riskier investments (exuberant demand).[16] The number of IPOs in the KSE increased from two in 2003 to six in 2004 and decreased to three in 2005. The oversubscription of IPOs ranged from 2.4 times (Al Qurain Petrochemicals Industries) to 12 times (Jazeera Airways). Although the oversubscription reflects strong demand from investors, it was not high from a regional perspective.[17] However, the number of listed companies increased significantly from 95 at the end of 2002 to 158 at the end of 2005 and further to 185 by June 2007. This increase was the highest among the GCC markets, reflecting the KSE's attractiveness.

Regional investors perceived that the KSE had the lowest degree of overvaluation or market exuberance, given the limited evidence of speculative demand compared to other GCC markets (as discussed above). A March 2005 survey of 740 business leaders in the GCC region revealed that 45 percent of them believed that a price bubble had formed in the Kuwaiti stock market. However, a higher proportion of the same business leaders were of the view that bubbles had formed in other booming GCC markets (Table 1.7).

3.3.3   Authorities' policy response

The authorities' policy response aimed to contain market volatility by limiting credit during the upswing and injecting liquidity during the correction phase through interest rate adjustments and other policies. These may have helped smooth the boom-bust cycle.

During the boom period, the CBK implemented steps to keep liquidity within reasonable limits. It started raising its discount rate in July 2004 and reintroduced market-based instruments to mop up liquidity. By March 2005, the CBK had increased its discount rate by 200 basis points, bringing it to 5.25 percent. This was in line with interest rate developments on the Federal Funds Rate (FFR) since the Kuwaiti Dinar (KD) was pegged to the US dollar. Furthermore, the CBK started auctioning deposits and issued 3-month CBK bonds to mop up liquidity, which helped in keeping the KD deposit rate in line with the CBK's benchmark rate.

In addition, the CBK imposed an 80 percent ceiling on the loan-to-deposit ratio in August 2004 to slow credit growth. The ceiling helped to dampen credit demand in general and credit for purchasing securities in particular. Credits to purchase securities fell by 1 percent between August and December 2004 after rising by 12 percent in the preceding eight months of 2004. This could explain the comparatively slower growth in the KSE index in 2004.

During the correction period, in order to avoid a tightening of liquidity in an environment of rapid market correction, the CBK avoided raising its discount rate, despite the several increases in the FFR. While the Federal Reserve raised the FFR five times between December 2005 and June 2006, the CBK kept the discount rate unchanged.[18] Moreover, between May 2005 and June 2006, the CBK followed the actions of the Federal Reserve only three times out of the total ten FFR increases. This reduced the margin between the CBK discount rate and the FFR from 2.5 percent in March 2005 to 0.75 percent in June 2006.

In the midst of a severe correction in March 2006, the Kuwaiti authorities announced that they would directly intervene in the market by increasing the Kuwait Investment Authority's (KIA) holdings in investment funds. The size and the timing of the intervention were not declared and market news and trading data do not point to any significant market intervention by the KIA. Thus, it is difficult to assess the direct impact of this decision, if any, on prices. Nevertheless, these types of interventions or announcements could increase moral hazard as speculators will discount other possible future interventions from the authorities in their future speculative demand, thereby increasing the probability of the development of new bubbles. In addition, by reducing the already low free-float ratio, such interventions could increase the probability of new bubbles. (See the discussion below.)

The strong recovery in 2007 might have been supported, in part, by the CBK policy of driving short-term interest rates down to dampen speculation on the KD and capital inflows. The speculation was motivated by discussions about the appropriateness of the peg to the US dollar and expectations that the CBK might revalue the KD to lower imported inflation. Speculation intensified further in May when the CBK abandoned the peg to the US dollar in favor of a peg to an undisclosed currency basket. The CBK responded to that by suspending the sales of short-term central bank Certificates of Deposit (CD) used by Kuwaiti banks to park short-term funds. The CBK decision drove short-term interest rates down further and the abundant liquidity and low interest rates might have supported the recovery of the KSE in 2007 (Figure 1.13).

3.3.4   Structural characteristics of the KSE

Several structural characteristics of the KSE have affected market developments. Some of these characteristics have improved the resilience of the market to bubble developments and could explain, in part, the moderate level of exuberant demand including (a) liquidity and openness of the market; (b) the growing role of institutional investors; and (c) the regional and international expansion of many blue-chip companies. Other structural characteristics, however, have been sources of downside risk that could negatively affect future market developments including (a) high degree of sectoral concentration and cross holding; and (b) the absence of a single and independent market regulatory body.

3.3.4.1   *Liquidity and openness of the KSE*

The KSE has the highest free-float ratio[19] among the GCC markets (see Table 1.10). With a free-float ratio of 66 percent, the KSE is the most liquid market in the GCC region.[20] Market liquidity reflects the ability of the market to absorb temporary supply and demand imbalances. It measures how much the price will change for a given amount of incoming transactions. The larger the free-float of stocks, the smaller the impact on prices for a given transaction size.

Furthermore, the KSE is the most open market for non-nationals in the GCC. About 45 percent of KSE stocks could be held by other GCC and non-GCC nationals, almost double the level of other major GCC markets. This market openness helps the price discovery function through the participation of foreign investors whose investment decisions are largely driven by fundamentals rather than exuberant demand.

3.3.4.2   *The role of institutional investors*

Although institutional investors are relatively underdeveloped in most GCC markets, they are relatively well developed in the KSE.[21] In addition to several insurance companies, there are over 75 investment companies in Kuwait, of which more than 40 are listed in the KSE and represent about 17 percent of market capitalization. The assets of these companies are about 50 percent of the banking sector's assets. Their investment in local shares

Table 3.2 Investment companies' assets and contra accounts, 2001–07

(In million KD)

	2001	2002	2003	2004	2005	2006	Jul-07
Total assets	**4,012**	**4,345**	**5,527**	**6,360**	**9,429**	**12,970**	**14,637**
Conventional	3,357	3,465	4,236	4,872	6,679	8,233	9,048
Islamic	655	880	1,291	1,488	2,751	4,737	5,589
Domestic financial investment	540	654	1,048	1,455	2,890	3,732	4,651
Conventional	484	588	909	1,165	2,003	2,240	2,720
Islamic	56	66	139	290	887	1,492	1,931
Credit facilities to residents	737	850	996	1,092	1,290	1,613	1,771
Conventional	445	475	576	686	841	1,012	1,048
Islamic	292	375	420	406	449	601	722
Other assets	2,734	2,842	3,483	3,812	5,249	7,625	8,216
Conventional	2,428	2,403	2,751	3,020	3,834	4,981	5,280
Islamic	307	439	732	792	1,415	2,644	2,936
Contra accounts assets	–	–	–	–	**15,549**	**17,538**	**23,048**
Contra accounts assets in local share	–	–	–	–	9,517	10,462	14,715
Total assets and contra accounts	–	–	–	–	**24,978**	**30,508**	**37,685**
Number of companies	**37**	**38**	**41**	**42**	**56**	**69**	**79**
Conventional	26	27	28	28	33	39	40
Islamic	11	11	13	14	23	30	39

Source: Central Bank of Kuwait.

and the local shares of their fiduciary account represent 33 percent of market capitalization. The rapid growth in the assets of domestic investment companies and the financing of investment companies to residents, as reflected in their balance sheets, point to the stabilizing role played by these companies. In particular, it is noteworthy that investments by residents through the investment companies and portfolio investment in local shares continued to increase throughout 2006 despite the correction and uncertainties in the regional stock markets.

3.3.4.3 The regional and international expansion of many blue-chip companies

The regional expansion of many Kuwaiti blue-chip companies enhanced the stability of corporate profitability. For example, an important part of the National Bank of Kuwait's (NBK) profits comes from NBK's cross-border establishments. Similarly, 40 percent of Mobile Telecommunications Company profits originate from operations outside Kuwait. These two firms account for 20 percent of market share and Kuwait has a number of other such companies. The regional and global expansion of non-Kuwaiti GCC companies is relatively low, although it has increased in recent years.

3.3.4.4 Sectoral concentration

The degree of sectoral concentration in the KSE is high in comparison with global levels and it is a source of downside risk. The banking and investment[22] sectors represent 30 and 17 percent of the market respectively, compared with 12 and 6 percent globally.[23] Combined with the services sector, these three sectors represent about 73 percent of the Kuwaiti market. Furthermore, about 30 percent of traded securities in the first half of 2007 were in the investment sector, which witnessed the largest correction in 2006. This concentration increases market risk because a shock to any of these sectors could result in a large shock to the market.

The risk implied by the concentration could be amplified by the financial sector's dependence on the stock market for its profitability. The large contribution of the trading, investment, and commission incomes to the profitability of the investment, insurance, and other financial sectors, due to high cross holding,[24] (Box 3.2) implies that any major correction could significantly impact the profitability of these sectors and trigger an amplified effect on the market. While this risk did not materialize during the correction in 2006, it still represents a source of downside risk especially with the growing investment in local shares by investment companies.

Table 3.3 Sectors' size and performance, June 2007

	PER	PBV	DY	MKT cap. (KD millions)	Market share (%)	Volume of shares traded (million share)	Volume of traded shares (millions KD)	Volume of traded shares to total traded (%)
Banking	19.59	4.99	2.9	16,632.3	29.8	596.7	627.7	15.1
Investment	9.01	2.21	3.8	9,506.5	17.1	2,818.5	1,257.9	30.2
Insurance	6.3	1.27	7.5	429.8	0.8	8.2	4.6	0.1
Real estate	15.86	1.60	2.9	3,499.8	6.3	2,185.1	490.7	11.8
Industrial	11.97	2.09	3.9	4,423.4	7.9	541.1	435.1	10.4
Services	19.13	4.12	2.2	14,646.2	26.3	983.2	1,086.3	26.1
Food	21.0	3.08	1.8	1,130.8	2.0	74.8	50.6	1.2
Non Kuwaiti	13.57	2.39	3.2	5,458.1	9.8	542.6	214.2	5.1
Total market	14.72	3.01	3.0	55,726.9	100.0	7,750.3	4,167.1	100.0

Source: KAMCO.

3.3.4.5 The absence of a single regulatory authority

The absence of a single regulatory authority in Kuwait could hinder operational independence and accountability, and could potentially create conflicts of interest. A KSE Market Committee oversees the securities in the secondary market; the CBK regulates investment companies; and the Ministry of Commerce and Industry regulates the primary market. This fragmentation may also complicate cross-border supervision and information-sharing with other regional and international supervisory authorities which becomes very important with the increase in the inter-linkages among the regional markets. The complication could arise because of the difficulty in specifying the rights and responsibilities of different parties, ensuring the confidentiality of supervisory information, and possible legal constraints.[25]

The absence of a single regulatory authority could also negatively affect the scope and effectiveness of supervision and hence the investors' confidence and the market's resilience to shocks. The market lacks comprehensive rules regarding inspection of brokerage firms, which is an important tool to discourage and prevent insider trading, price manipulation, and other unsafe and unsound practices. Furthermore, there are no specific regulations on insider trading and the current regulations do not fully promote trading transparency. The systems for clearing and settlement of transactions are not formally subject to oversight, which may increase systemic risk.[26]

3.4 CONCLUSIONS AND RECOMMENDATIONS[27]

The markedly different behavior of the KSE during 2003–07 could be partly attributed to policy measures, some specific political developments in the region, and a number of market-specific factors. In particular, the ceiling on the loan-to-deposits ratio introduced in July 2004, the removal of uncertainties associated with the regime change in Iraq and the resulting strengthened economic and trade relations with Iraq after 2002, and the structural characteristics of the KSE that led to lower demand pressure on share prices are the major factors explaining this difference. The positive economic outlook provides strong support for fundamentals and, given the favorable valuation indicators, there are sound reasons to believe that a substantial part of the current equity valuation gains are likely to be retained. Downside risks to this outlook are adverse geopolitical developments and a strong correction in the real estate market.

The call for direct intervention could have been avoided. Instead of calling for direct intervention through state-controlled savings institutions in order to arrest falling share prices, the authorities should have only focused on measures aimed at facilitating an orderly return to more realistic valuations. Such direct interventions[28] could reinforce investors' perception that the stocks are overvalued and could carry a quasi-fiscal cost. Moreover, moral hazards induced by interventions may substantially increase the size of future speculative bubbles and the costs associated with their correction.

Expediting the drafting and passage of the capital market law would create an independent and accountable regulatory authority that would enhance transparency, increase investors' confidence, and reduce the possibilities of insider and other unfair trading. An effective capital market law will help strengthen the relation between fundamentals and stock prices and reduce speculative demand. It would also help in addressing sectoral concentration by encouraging more companies to be listed in the market. Until the law is in place, it is very important to avoid any gaps or overlaps in the supervisory roles of the different supervisory bodies. This could be achieved through clearly defining roles and responsibilities and implementing functional supervision.

Given the risk that could arise from the sensitivity of listed companies' performance to KSE performance, due in part to relatively large cross holding, the authorities should examine further the level of cross holding and the appropriateness of current regulation in this regard. They also should regularly perform stress testing to assess the resilience of the market and financial institutions to adverse market developments.

NOTES

1. Weighted index for the GCC stock markets using market capitalization weights.
2. The weighted (by market capitalization) average index increased by 69.3, 15.3, and 67.4 percent in 2003, 2004, and 2005, respectively.
3. Saudi Arabia.
4. Annual growth in government expenditure during 2002–06 was 20 percent.
5. Especially in the services sector, which represents 21.5 percent of the stock market.
6. Volatility in the KSE increased significantly in March 2006 with the sharp decrease in the index.
7. The increases in the coefficient of variation for the UAE markets were 318 and 380 percent for the ADSM and the DFM, respectively (between March 2003 and December 2005). The increase in the coefficient of variation for the Saudi stock index (TASI) between September 2004 and January 2006 was 182 percent.
8. The growth in M2 was 4 percent on average during 1996–2002.
9. An "Installment Loan" is a loan utilized by the customer for noncommercial purposes, particularly for renovating or purchasing a private residence.
10. However, this increase was lower than the one observed in the Saudi market where margin lending increased from 3 percent of banks' total lending in 2001 to 9 percent in 2005.
11. It is also possible that some of the personal loans, not specifically declared as margin loans, are used to leverage equity investment positions. It is also believed that part of the non-bank financial institution loans (8 percent of total loans) have been used to leverage equity investment positions.
12. Total margin lending was estimated at about 2.3 percent of the value of common stocks listed on the NYSE and NASDAQ during the dot.com bubble (Peter Fortune, 2001).
13. A narrow market leadership indicates a phenomenon where the prices of a few minor stocks rise spectacularly, while the prices of most major stocks increase more slowly or even decrease. This

phenomenon is also an indicator of excessive exuberant demand in the market. This phenomenon was observed in the dot.com bubble when prices of technology stocks (dominating the NASDAQ index) were increasing astronomically while prices of most other groups of stocks (represented under the S&P 500) had lagged or fallen.

14. As identified by Bakheet Financial Advisor (BFA), a local stock market specialist, speculative stocks belong to companies with weak financial indicators which historically do not pay dividends due to their recurring losses or small profits. (See the chapter on Saudi Arabia for a detailed discussion of these stocks.)

15. In the ADSM, six small companies (9 percent of market capitalization) accounted for 44 percent of the increase in the ADSM index during 2005. Similarly, four small companies in the DFM (5 percent of market capitalization) accounted for 18 percent of the increase in the DFM index during the same period. In the DSM, five small firms (3 percent of market capitalization) contributed 34 percent of the total volume traded in 2005.

16. This was the case, for instance, during the dot.com bubble, the Al-Manakh bubble, and the Omani bubble.

17. For example, the Saudi Sahara petrochemicals IPO was 124 times oversubscribed, and the Ettihad Ettisalat IPO in 2004 was 50 times oversubscribed.

18. The CBK raised the discount rate in July 2006 by 25 basis points.

19. The free float is the amount of shares which are available to ordinary investors for trade (i.e., not held by insiders or in the investment portfolio of institutional investors as strategic holdings), and is expressed as a percentage of the total number of shares.

20. However, the KSE compares less favorably with developed (86 percent) and emerging markets (78 percent) in terms of the free-float ratio, according to Sheldon Gao (September 2002).

21. Institutional investors, such as investment companies, pension funds, and life insurance companies, provide a stabilizing factor in financial markets (see footnote 43). Small investors are usually poorly informed, have less financial culture, lack the ability to analyze fundamentals, and act on the basis of rumors. On the other hand, institutional investors enhance the price discovery function by taking investment decisions based mainly on fundamentals. This stems from the fact that they are long-term investors, and hence, are more oriented towards underlying economic fundamentals as opposed to short-term and transient factors that are frequently associated with speculative price movements.

22. The activities of companies in this sector include providing financial advisory services, trading in local and international securities, underwriting, borrowing, lending, issuing guarantees, managing investment funds, and portfolio management.

23. "Gulf Equity Markets Powered by Oil," Credit Suisse, February 2006.

24. With the exception of the banking sector where regulations limit investment in the stock market.

25. For example, it is difficult to negotiate and sign a memorandum of understanding (the most common mechanism to arrange for cross-border supervision and information-sharing) with a number of regulatory bodies at the same time.

26. As noted in the 2004 FSAP report. http://www.imf.org/external/pubs/ft/scr/2004/cr04151.pdf

27. Many of the recommendations concluded in the overview chapter apply to Kuwait. Hence, here we focus only on a few additional Kuwait-specific recommendations.

28. Announcing that there will be an intervention could have a similar impact.

REFERENCES

Credit Suisse, (2006). "Gulf Equity Markets Powered by Oil" (February).

Financial System Stability Assessment, IMF Country Report No. 04/151.

Fortune, Peter, (2001). "Perspective: Is Margin Lending Marginal?" Regional Review, Federal Reserve Bank of Boston (October).

Gao, Sheldon, (2002). "China Stock Market in Global Perspective" Dow Jones Indexes.

CHAPTER 4

Oman Stock Market: On a Steady Course

Mitra Farahbaksh

4.1 INTRODUCTION

During 2002–05, Oman's Muscat Stock Market (MSM) witnessed relatively smaller gains compared with the boom experienced by the markets in Kuwait, Qatar, Saudi Arabia, and the United Arab Emirates. Similarly, the correction experienced by the MSM in the latter part of 2005 was also modest. In 2006, the MSM was the only market in the region where the price index rose. This chapter examines the factors that have affected stock market developments in Oman and the specific characteristics that have set this market apart from those of the rest of the region. The chapter concludes that the MSM price increases were broadly in line with Oman's underlying economic and financial structure and that the market did not show evidence of overvaluation or a bubble during 2002–06. Market-specific factors, macroeconomic developments, and well-established regulatory standards and structural reforms differentiate the Omani stock market from the rest of the region.

The chapter is organized as follows: Section 4.2 reviews the main market indicators; Section 4.3 analyzes the factors that explain the differences in the developments of the MSM relative to other Gulf Cooperation Council (GCC) markets; and Section 4.4 provides some final remarks.

Box 4.1   Muscat Securities Market

The MSM was established in 1988, and experienced a steady and substantial increase in activity since then – market turnover rose from RO 47 million in 1990 to RO 1.6 billion in the boom year of 1997. The principal stock index, the MSM-30, was established in 1992. It is composed of three different sectors – banks and investment firms, industrial firms, and services and insurance – with ten companies in each sector. There are three markets within the MSM: a regular market for securities of public companies that meet specified profitability, capital, and shareholding criteria; a parallel market for securities of new public companies and those companies that fail to meet one or more of the specified requirements; and a market for share dealings in closed companies and special transactions. The MSM operates through licensed brokers, and has a fully integrated electronic trading system. There are no taxes on dividends or capital gains and foreigners can hold up to 100 percent of the shares in Omani companies.

A combination of significant speculation and a general lack of market transparency led to a severe downturn in 1998. After having increased by about 140 percent in 1997, the market declined sharply in both trading volumes and the share price index. The MSM-30 lost nearly 70 percent of its value from 1998 to 2001. A significant number of new investors that participated in the MSM during the bubble were affected by the correction. Reportedly, thousands of investors who were financially overleveraged went into bankruptcy or serious financial distress. A number of factors were responsible for the build up of the stock market bubble: (a) a surge in money supply and bank credits; (b) an unregulated credit extension for securities investment, which leveraged booming equity investment without a reliable risk control mechanism (regulated margin trading); (c) a flurry of new issues without prudent scrutiny; and (d) a market microstructure without a correction mechanism for overheated prices (regulated short selling).

Following the correction, the government acted to mitigate the social impact of the resulting widespread financial problems through various programs, including (a) a $104 million government fund established in 1999 to invest in MSM-listed securities; (b) a $130 million investment package in MSM-listed securities committed in 2001, entailing government buyouts of MSM-listed shares in "trust accounts" (de facto margin accounts) with negative balances; and (c) a government financial assistance program for brokers that were well-capitalized on a post-merger basis. The government also sought to make the MSM one of the best regulated and transparent markets in the region by establishing the Capital Market Authority (CMA) and passing a number of regulations based on best international practices.

▶

Since 2002, total market capitalization has almost tripled to $12.9 billion, or to about 37 percent of GDP, in 2006. The value and volume of trade, and the number of transactions also hit new records. As of June 2007, the shares of 63 companies were listed in the regular market, 43 companies in the parallel market, and 46 companies in the third market. The MSM also included 10 bonds and 6 mutual funds.

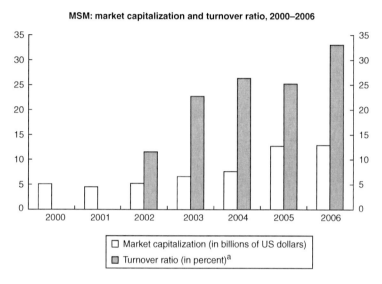

MSM: market capitalization and turnover ratio, 2000–2006

☐ Market capitalization (in billions of US dollars)
▨ Turnover ratio (in percent)[a]

Note: [a] Defined as value of trading as a percentage of market capitalization.
Sources: MSM; and Global Investment House.

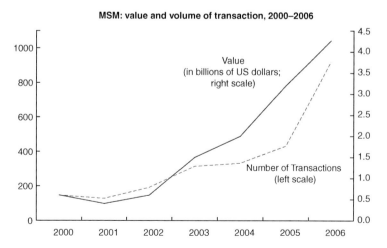

MSM: value and volume of transaction, 2000–2006

Value (in billions of US dollars; right scale)

Number of Transactions (left scale)

Sources: MSM; and Global Investment House.

4.2　KEY MARKET DEVELOPMENTS

Following bearish market sentiments that lasted for several years (Box 4.1), Oman's stock market began recovering in 2002, and by mid-2005 it had increased by over 150 percent. This gain, however, was relatively modest, compared with the boom experienced in some other GCC markets, which in some cases, were three to four times that of Oman.

In contrast to the developments in the regional markets, the MSM-30 continued to register gains in 2005 and 2006. Despite a modest and short-lived period of correction in the second half of 2005, Oman's market ended the year with a gain of over 44 percent. Positive market sentiment carried over into 2006 and the MSM-30 increased by another 14.5 percent. In contrast, most markets in the region experienced retrenchments in 2006, ranging from about 2 percent in Bahrain to 52.5 percent in the Saudi stock market (Tadawul).

The stock valuations in MSM-30, as measured by the Price Earnings Ratio (PER), Price to Book Value Ratio (PBV), and Dividend Yield (DY), compared favorably with the rest of the region, and were also broadly in line with major industrial and emerging markets during 2002–06. These valuation indicators did not point to the existence of exuberant demand.

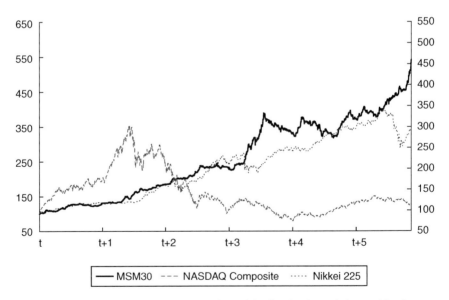

Figure 4.1　Normalized stock price indices (The beginning of the rapid price increase periods = 100)[a]

Note: [a]t = 12/5/2001 for MSM30, 10/8/1998 for NASDAQ composite, 7/23/1984 for Nikkei 225.

Source: Bloomberg.

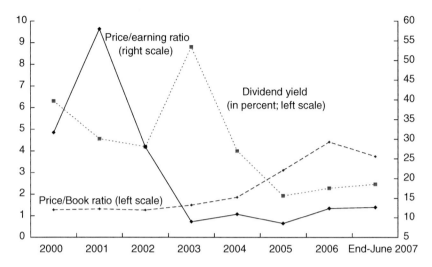

Figure 4.2 MSM: Valuations, 2000–June 2007

Sources: Arab Monetary Fund; and KAMCO Research.

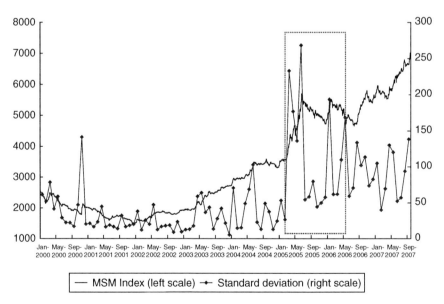

MSM Index (left scale) — Standard deviation (right scale)

Figure 4.3 Daily MSM price index and monthly standard deviation (January 2000–September 2007)

Source: Bloomberg; and Fund staff estimates.

In contrast, the markets' returns in most other GCC countries outpaced significantly corporate earnings growth by the end of 2005, resulting in PERs and PBVs that were significantly higher than their historical levels and the levels generally seen in emerging and developed markets.

The MSM-30 enjoyed relatively low volatility between 2002 and early 2005, as measured by the monthly standard deviation and coefficient of variation.[1] However, volatility increased significantly in 2005, and was considerably higher than the increase in the coefficient of variation of the MSM-30 during the bubble period prior to the 1998 crash. Volatility declined substantially subsequent to the MSM's mild correction.

4.3 FACTORS AFFECTING MSM BEHAVIOR

The divergence in the behavior of the MSM-30 and the rest of the markets in the region can be explained by a number of factors, including market-based factors, macroeconomic developments, and regulatory standards in the capital market.

4.3.1 Market-based factors

The behavior of the MSM-30 relative to the other GCC countries reflects in part a strong link between market prices and growth in the non-oil sector. In contrast to other GCC countries, there were no hydrocarbon-related companies listed in the MSM-30. As a result, stock price changes and valuations tended to remain stable in Oman, despite the significant rise in oil prices, while share prices of listed hydrocarbon-related companies in the other GCC markets, with the exception of Bahrain, skyrocketed along with their profits, leading to significant increases in the region's overall indices. At the same time, companies listed in the MSM-30 registered relatively lower rates of profitability growth (about 22 percent in 2004–05), compared with those in other countries in the region, which ranged from 40 to over 70 percent per year. Overall, the MSM may be viewed as better cushioned against the boom and bust cycles that were related to oil price volatility.

The Oman stock market was relatively broad and had the highest number of listed stocks in the GCC. There were 176 companies listed in the MSM as of end-2005, compared with 158 in Kuwait, 77 in Saudi Arabia, and 89 in the United Arab Emirates. Most listed stocks had relatively small capitalization amounts. At end-2005, the average market value of the listed companies was about $230 million, well below emerging and industrial equity market standards.[2] The broadness of the Omani market helped reduce its vulnerability to speculative operations.

Table 4.1 Key market indicators for the ten largest companies in MSM (End-June 2007)

Company	Closing price	Market cap. (In millions of RO)	PER	PBV	DY (%)	Net profit (In millions of RO)	Return on equity (%)	Market share (%)
Bank Muscat	1.4	1254.3	17.3	3.8	2.3	21.1	23.4	24.0
Oman Telecommunications Company	1.2	888.8	10.3	3.2	5.9	24.4	33.1	18.0
National Bank of Oman	5.9	538.2	13.9	2.8	2.6	9.6	21.6	11.1
Raysut Cement	1.4	286.0	12.3	3.9	3.5	5.2	34.7	6.8
Bank Dhofar	0.5	250.0	11.5	2.6	2.8	3.6	24.1	5.9
Oman International Bank	2.7	224.2	8.7	1.8	7.1	7.9	22.0	4.8
Oman Cement	6.1	200.8	10.2	1.9	5.8	4.1	19.8	4.8
Renaissance Services Holding Company	0.6	140.5	9.5	1.5	21.6	4.1	16.6	3.3
Shell Oman Marketing	1.4	140.6	15.1	7.3	6.4	2.4	48.1	3.2
Oman Cables industry	1.4	125.6	10.8	5.1	5.5	3.2	56.0	3.0

Source: Bloomberg.

Notwithstanding the large number of listed companies, the MSM had a relatively low free float ratio relative to other GCC markets (38.3 percent). The fact that some of the largest listed companies in the Omani market were majority state-owned, de facto, tended to reduce the amount of stocks effectively available for trade. In any case, the breadth of the market probably limited the negative impact of a lower free float ratio in Oman.

The MSM did not show signs of narrow market leadership contrary to the other stock markets in the region where groups of relatively small stocks, accounting for 1 to 5 percent of market capitalization, attracted disproportionate volumes of trade and valuation gains.[3] Nonetheless, the market exhibited some concentration. As of end-September 2005, the five largest companies accounted for about 55 percent of total market capitalization, while the top ten companies accounted for 70 percent.

Margin lending was limited during the study period.[4] Banks' known direct exposure to equity markets was small (2.7 percent of total lending at end-2004) and their profitability depended mainly on interest income. Indirect lending through personal loans may have been higher since the share of personal loans in total loans increased from 34 percent in 2001 to about 41 percent in 2004.[5] However, it is not possible to determine what portion of this increase may have been channeled to financing purchases on the stock market. While some consumer loans have been used to finance investments in the stock exchange, the risk from indirect equity market exposure resulting from these loans is deemed to have been small.[6]

There is no evidence that Initial Public Offers (IPOs) contributed significantly to stock price developments in the MSM, given that the number of IPOs was small during the period under study. A large number of IPOs could signify an increase in risky investments if companies that are launching IPOs are relatively young and lack an established track record. During a bubble period, demand for IPOs would be based on rapid capital gain expectations, rather than on economic fundamentals (profitability, management, assets). In 2004–05, there were eight IPOs with a total offering size of over $1.6 billion. Most IPOs were associated with the privatization of utilities and petrochemical companies (Omantel, AES Barka, and Al Maha Petroleum Products Marketing) and the restructuring of the power and water sector (Al-Kamil Power Company).[7] Moreover, most companies participating in the IPOs were established firms and had solid performance records. Also, price changes reflected mainly the market's proper assessment of the companies' market values. While the largest IPO, Omantel, experienced a significant jump on the very first day of trading, other IPO share prices witnessed declines. This development was in sharp contrast to what was observed in other major GCC stock markets, where a large number of IPOs registered sharp price increases during initial trading.

Table 4.2 Oman: selected IPOs, 2004–07

Company name	Sector	Date	Size of offering (In millions of US dollars)	Over subscription (Times)	IPO price US dollar per share	Closing price (1st day of listings) in US dollar	Percentage equity offered	Number of shares offered
Al Maha Petroleum Products Marketing	Petrol station chain	Apr-04	24.0	9.0	6.6	10.3	60%	3,600.000
Al Kamil Power Company (AKPC)	Utility	Aug-04	15.0	1.0	2.6	4.5	35%	9,625.000
Al Kamil Power Company (AKPC)	Services	Jul-04	15.0	–	4.4	4.5	–	3,368.750
AES Barka	Utility	Dec-04	28.8	17.0	2.6	4.8	35%	11,076.923
Dhofar Power-PRE	Utility	Apr-05	25.4	9.0	3.7	4.9	35%	6,895.700
Oman Telecommunications Company (Omantel)	Services	Jun-05	750.0	3.0	3.3	3.3	30%	225,000.000
Taageer Finance Company	Financial services	Sep-05	10.9	4.3	3.7	4.0	–	3,000.000
Bank Sofar	Banks	Nov-06	156.6	–	1.6	0.6	40%	100,000.000
Oman's Galfar Engineering	Services	Aug-07	52.0	–	1.4	1.0	40%	40,000.000

Source: Bloomberg.

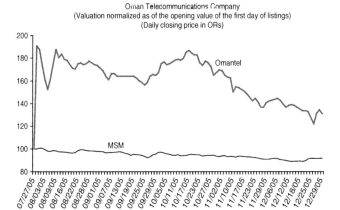

Oman Telecommunications Company
(Valuation normalized as of the opening value of the first day of listings)
(Daily closing price in ORs)

AES Barka
(Valuation normalized as of the opening value of the first day of listing)
(Daily closing price in ORs)

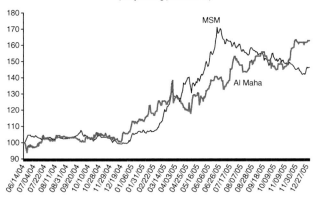

Al Maha Petroleum Products Marketing
(Valuation normalized as of the opening of the first day of listings)
(Daily closing price in ORs)

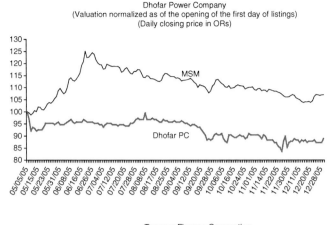

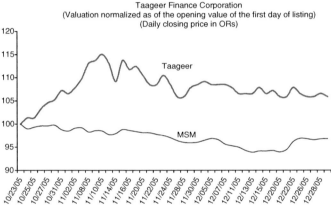

Figure 4.4 Evolution of IPO stock prices relative to the MSM index, 2003–05: while IPOs generally performed better than the MSM index, the gains were relatively modest

4.3.2 Macroeconomic factors

Given the absence of shares of hydrocarbon companies in the MSM, the correlation between market performance and oil prices was present only to the extent that the government increased its expenditures in infrastructure and social projects.[8] Capital outlays increased substantially in 2004 compared to 2002 (about 11 percent of GDP in 2004 relative to about 8 percent in 2002), but was brought down to about 9 percent in 2006. Nonetheless, high oil and gas revenues allowed for a substantial build up of the budget surplus (about 14 percent of GDP in 2006 relative to 5 percent of GDP in 2002). This surplus was used to add to the State General Reserve Fund (SGRF) and to reduce Oman's debt to 9 percent of GDP.[9]

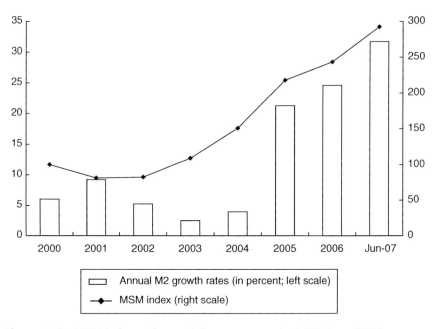

Figure 4.5   MSM index and growth in money supply, 2000–June 2007

Sources: Bloomberg; International Financial Statistics; and Fund staff estimates.

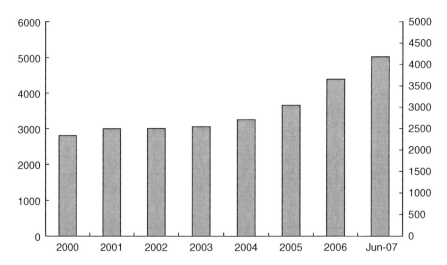

Figure 4.6   Banking sector claims on private sector, 2000–June 2007
(In millions of Rial Omani)

Source: International Financial Statistics.

Oman experienced one of the lowest growth rates in broad money and credit to the private sector among the GCC countries.[10] During 2002–04, money growth and credit to the private sector averaged about 4 percent and 3 percent, respectively. Broad money accelerated in 2005, in part due to an inflow of capital in preparation for the Omantel IPO.[11] Credit to the private sector in the region was considerably higher and ranged from a compound annual rate of 21.0 percent in Kuwait to 36.5 percent in Qatar during 2002–05.

4.3.3 Regulatory framework

Oman has one of the best regulated and most transparent stock markets in the region. In the aftermath of the Omani stock market crash of 1998, the legal and supervisory institutions underpinning the capital market were strengthened considerably. The Capital Market Law issued in 1988 restructured the capital market into three independent entities: (a) the Capital Market Authority (CMA), which is responsible for capital market supervision and regulation; (b) the MSM, which undertakes the registration and trading of securities and acts as an exchange; and (c) the Muscat Depository and Securities Registration Company, which is responsible for safekeeping the shareholders' register and for recording title transfers. The government has put in place clear disclosure and transparency rules and Oman was the only country in the region to have issued a corporate governance code well before the recent surge in stock market activity.

The Capital Market Law, the implementing regulations issued by the CMA, and the strict enforcement of these regulations have created a transparent environment, which has succeeded in boosting investor confidence. The resolve shown by the CMA in addressing quoted companies' noncompliance with the new regulations has also contributed to cementing its reputation and improving the stock market's resilience to shocks.[12] The CMA has also increased efforts to improve investors' access to information and training, including through CMA-sponsored conferences and workshops. Finally, in February 2006, the MSM successfully moved to the Euronext exchange and trading platform, which links 14 exchanges, including Euronet. This move increased both the efficiency and transparency of the trading environment, meeting international trading standards.

4.4 FINAL REMARKS

Oman's stock market performance appears to have been in line with the country's fundamentals, resulting in a more realistic stock valuations relative to other GCC countries. The cumulative effect of structural reforms implemented in recent years has transformed the economic structure of Oman. The private sector has acquired new dynamism due to the substantial progress made in implementing a wide range of structural reforms. Among the reforms which have likely had a permanent impact on the value of Omani companies were (a) the diversification of the economy away from oil;[13] (b) privatization, liberalization, and outsourcing to the private sector of key companies and sectors, including the utilities firms; and (c) trade liberalization, including Oman's membership in the WTO, and economic integration in the context of the planned GCC monetary union by 2010.

These reforms together with market based factors and macro economic developments helped align market valuation with economic fundamentals and reduce price volatility that was seen in other GCC countries.

NOTES

1. Price volatility tends to increase substantially in the period immediately before the bursting of a price bubble.
2. The average size of listed companies in the NASDAQ at end-2004 was $1.14 billion, while the average size of listed companies in the main Japanese stock markets as of September 12, 2005 was $1.09 billion.
3. Narrow market leadership could imply that the price of a few stocks rise well above the price of the majority of stocks, possibly due to speculative demand.
4. Margin lending refers to loans specifically provided to buy stocks where the borrowed money is collateralized by the stocks purchased. If the value of the collateral stock drops, the borrower will be asked to increase collateral, repay part of the loan, or sell some of the stock. Margin lending in Oman is limited to 50 percent of the market value of the shares.
5. The Central Bank of Oman (CBO) maintains a ceiling on the share of bank lending for personal loans equivalent to 40 percent of total credit outstanding.
6. This is due to the special nature of consumer lending in Oman. Consumer loans are secured by direct deposits of public sector payroll (banks can deduct the installments directly from the borrower's payroll).
7. The IPO for Al Kamir Power Company was part of an agreement by its parent company and the government of Oman, under which 35 percent of the company's share capital would be sold to the public.
8. Current outlays declined from 31 percent of GDP to 28 percent of GDP during 2002–06.
9. The SGRF was created in 1980 for saving oil revenues and privatization receipts.
10. Markets in countries with higher rates of money growth tend to outperform those with lower money growth rates.
11. The government sold 30 percent of Omantel for RO 288 million ($750 million), making it the largest public offering in Oman's history; 21 percent was offered to the Omani public and the remaining 9 percent was reserved for pension funds and charities. The IPO was oversubscribed by 240 percent.
12. Measures include (a) preventing and penalizing unfair trading practices by imposing monetary penalties; and (b) warning companies and suspending stocks from trading due to failure to meet disclosure requirements.
13. Diversification entails the development of gas-based industries; the expansion of manufacturing, tourism, mining, and fisheries; and the establishment of free trade zones, water and power projects, steel and iron plants, and industrial and container ports.

REFERENCES

Global Investment House Economic Research; http://www.globalinv.net

Middle East Economic Digest (MEED) (2005). "HSBC-MEED Middle East Business Confidence Index (MEBCI)," MEED 25–31, March.

Muscat Securities Market; http://www.msm.gov.om

Ned Davis Research, Inc. "NASDAQ Composite Price/Earnings Ratio vs. Margin Debt," Ned Davis Research, Inc., 2005.

SHUAA Capital (2006). MSM companies profiles; http://www.shuaacapital.com

Zawya (2006). MSM companies profiles; http://www.zawya.com

CHAPTER 5

The Qatari Stock Exchange: Rising with the Tide?

Fernando Delgado

and Lema Zekrya

5.1 INTRODUCTION

The Qatar equity market has been one of the most exuberant among the Gulf Cooperation Council (GCC) countries, accumulating gains of over 450 percent from January 2003 to its peak in September 2005. Some of this increase reflected improved economic fundamentals that supported the high valuation of Qatari companies. However, as in other booming GCC equity markets, speculative demand also played a part. When the bubble burst in September 2005, the price index lost 40 percent of its value until stabilizing in June 2006. The correction reduced prices to levels broadly in line with the evolution of economic fundamentals. A sizable part of the valuation gains accumulated from January 2003 (over 200 percent as of end-June 2007) is likely to be retained since such gains can be largely explained by the economy's specific characteristics and high expected corporate profitability. The Qatari economy endured the correction well, and economic growth and financial stability were not affected.

Box 5.1   Doha Securities Market

Historical background

The Doha Securities Market (DSM) was established in 1995 and started its activities in May 1997. The market began operations with 17 listed companies and by end-2006 had a total of 36 companies. The DSM price index started in 1998 at a value of 100. With the implementation of electronic trading in February 2002, the index was multiplied by 10 to be more indicative and accurate. Trading value during the first full year of operation (1998) reached QRs 970 million. In 2006, it reached QRs 75 billion, which represents a cumulative annual growth rate of 70 percent. In 2000, GCC citizens were allowed to own up to 25 percent of the shares of 10 companies in the industrial and service sectors. In 2004, the rest of the companies in these two sectors were added to this list. Non-Qataris in general have been allowed to invest in up to 25 percent of newly established or privatized companies.

Market size and sectoral composition

At the inauguration of the DSM, market capitalization was estimated at around QRs 6 billion. By the end of 2006, it reached QRs 222 billion (corresponding to an annual compounded growth rate of about 60 percent).

Market capitalization – sectors' shares

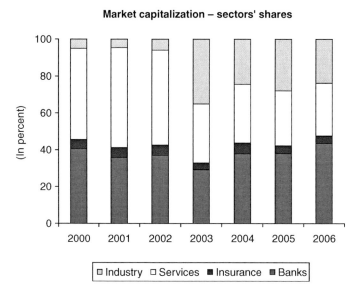

Sources: DSM; and Gulfbase.com.

Market capitalization

Sources: Global Research; and IFS.

Companies included in the DSM General Price Index (December 2007)	
Name of the company	Number of traded shares (Free Float Shares)
Qatar National Bank	91,048,736
Commercial Bank	127,543,722
Qatar International Islamic Bank	69,938,125
Qatar Islamic Bank	119,115,000
Doha Bank	116,080,290
Qatar Islamic Insurance	14,930,000
United Development Company	97,597,500
Industries Qatar	150,000,000
Salam International	66,151,200
Medicare Group	28,135,100
Qatar Real Estate Investment Co	52,638,720
Qatar Navigation	46,360,000
Qatar Shipping	69,700,000
Qatar Fuel	17,980,000
Q Tel	44,975,000
National Leasing	29,288,000
Gulf Warehousing	24,860,000
Qatar Meat & Livestock (Mawashee)	27,950,000
Qatar Gas Transport (Nakilat)	553,100,000
Dlala Brokerage & Investment	19,550,000

Source: DSM.

Within the GCC, Qatar ranks fourth in terms of market size, but first in terms of market capitalization as a percentage of GDP. According to market capitalization, the main sectors are banks, industries, and services. However, in terms of share of profits, the banking and insurance sectors are gaining in importance. The steepest increases in the size of market capitalization to GDP happened during 2003 and 2005 when large Initial Public Offers (IPOs) occurred. In 2003, with the Industries Qatar (IQ) mega IPO, the industrial sector's share of market capitalization jumped from 6 percent to 35 percent.

The composition of the DSM general price index

The DSM general price index comprises 20 companies. The criteria used to select these companies are: market capitalization; number of traded shares; value of traded shares; number of transactions; turnover ratio; and number of traded days.[a]

Note: [a] The methodology for calculating the DSM general price index may be found at http://www2.dsm.com.qa/dsm/DSM_ DsmIndex.

5.2 THE ROAD TO THE BUBBLE: VALUATION INDICATORS, DRIVERS, AND STRUCTURAL WEAKNESSES IN THE QATARI MARKET

The main valuation indicators, including the price index and the Price Earnings Ratio (PER), and the volatility in prices indicate the formation of a speculative bubble in the Qatari market beginning in the final quarter of 2004. The main drivers behind the increase in speculative demand were high liquidity, strong credit expansion, and the increasingly narrow market leadership of speculative stocks. Also, some structural characteristics of the Qatari equity market made it prone to the development of speculative bubbles (the relative underdevelopment of traditional institutional investors, the small supply of stocks, and the relatively weak regulatory environment).

5.2.1 Rapid increase in the price index

The DSM general price index increased 455 percent from January 2003 to its peak in September 2005. This increase is larger than the price hike observed during the Nikkei bubble of the late 1980s and the NASDAQ dot.com bubble of 2000. The value of trade reached $28.26 billion in 2005, representing 2.5 times the cumulative sum of the value traded from 2000 to 2004.

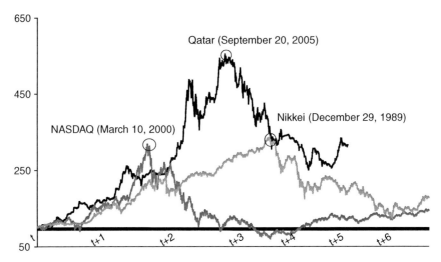

Years since the start of the acceleration in price increases

Figure 5.1   DSM stock price index compared with the Dot.Com and Nikkei Bubbles (Normalized to 100 at the start of the acceleration of price increases "t")
Source: Bloomberg.

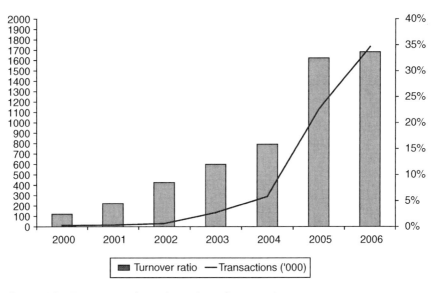

Figure 5.2   Turnover ratio and number of transactions
Sources: Global Investment House; and Fund staff estimates.

5.2.2 Weak correlation between price and economic value

The main indicators showed a growing overvaluation of Qatari stocks. The average PER and Price to Book Value Ratio (PBV) began increasing in 2002. At their peaks in September 2005, the average PER and PBV stood at 40.7 and 6.4, respectively, about three times their 2000–02 average. By end-2005, the PER had decreased to 30.2 and by June 2007, the stock index correction had further reduced the average PER and PBV to 15.5 and 3.2, respectively. These indicators remain slightly above the average of the other GCC equity markets, but are in line with historical values. The Dividend Yield (DY) ratio decreased substantially between 2000 and 2003 to reach 1.3 but later increased to above 3.4 by June 2007.

5.2.3 High price volatility

The DSM experienced substantial increases in volatility as measured by the monthly standard deviation starting in April 2003. Between March 2003 and August 2005, the monthly standard deviation increased by over 16 times, peaking at over 800 percent. This increase was consistent with the market correction that started in September 2005, and seems to have adequately identified the emergence of a speculative bubble in the market. Price volatility declined after the correction, but remained above historical levels (see the discussion on price volatility in the following section).

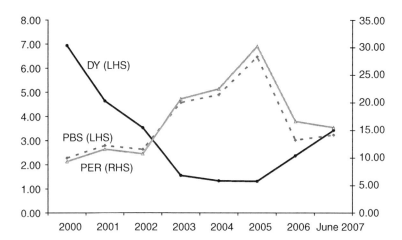

Figure 5.3 PER, PBV, and DY 2000–07

Sources: DSM; Bloomberg; and Fund staff estimates.

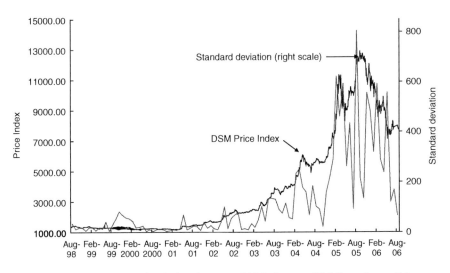

Figure 5.4 Daily DSM price index (August 1998–August 2006) and monthly standard deviation

Sources: Doha Stock Market; and Fund staff estimates.

5.2.4 Sizable increases in money supply and credit

The increase in broad money growth may have contributed substantially to rising DSM stock prices in recent years. Broad money increased by 15.8 percent in 2003, 20.5 percent in 2004, and 43.3 percent in 2005. This acceleration can be explained largely by the strong rate of increase in credit to the private sector. Claims on the private sector increased at an annual compounded rate of 36.3 percent during 2003–05. Although there are no detailed statistical data, it is widely believed that a large proportion of the increase in private sector credit was channeled to leverage investors' stock purchases. Despite the Qatari Central Bank (QCB) prohibition on margin lending, commercial bankers reported that their customers have been borrowing heavily to finance stock market operations, in addition to consumer spending and construction projects.[1] This hypothesis seems to be validated by the correlation observed between the sudden jumps in the claims on the private sector and the opening of subscription periods for large Initial Public Offers (IPOs).[2] Total consumer loans grew from only 3 percent of total Qatari bank loans as of end-2003 to 34 percent of total loans as of end-September 2005. These developments are in line with developments in other GCC countries.

5.2.5 Increasingly narrow market leadership

During the formation of the price bubble, a small group of stocks showed a pattern of behavior consistent with the narrow market leadership warning

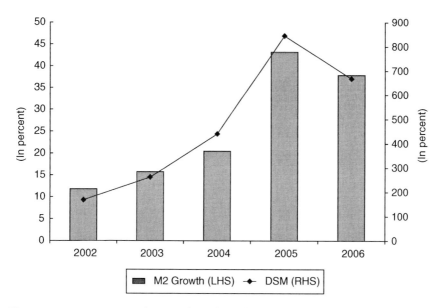

Figure 5.5   Money supply growth and yearly average DSM price index growth
(2000 = 100), 2001–06

Sources: EDSS; Qatar Central Bank; Bloomberg; and Fund staff estimates.

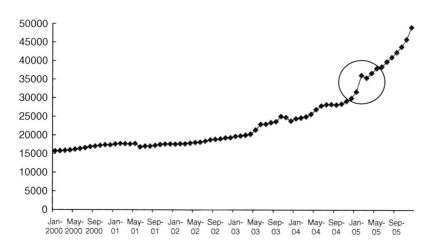

Figure 5.6   Claims on the private sector (In millions of Qatari riyals)

Source: Central Bank of Qatar.

signal.[3] In 2005, five small companies, representing 3.3 percent of the total
market capitalization, contributed 33.6 percent of the total volume of trade,
and 19.6 percent of the total value traded. In addition to the vulnerability derived from their relatively small size, these companies are among
the less profitable ones in the market (their contribution to the market's

Table 5.1   Qatar: developments in small-cap company behavior

DSM – 2005	Percentage of total market capitalization	Percentage of total volume traded	Percentage of total value traded	Percentage of total profits
Five small-cap companies	3.3	33.6	19.6	1.4
Qatar Gas Transport Co.	9.0	28.6	14.4	3.8
Total	12.3	62.2	34.1	5.3

Sources: Doha Stock Market; Gulfbase.com; and Fund staff estimates.

total profits was only 1.4 percent during the same period), thus pointing to the speculative nature of the heavy volume of trade among these stocks. Qatar Gas Transport (QGT), the third-largest listed company, shows similar characteristics, since its trade volume and value shares are 3 and 1.8 times higher than its share in market capitalization. However, contrary to the five highly speculative small companies, interest in QGT seems to be justified by recent developments aimed at greater reliance and use of gas resources as an engine for growth in Qatar.

5.2.6   The relative underdevelopment of traditional institutional investors

Traditional institutional investors, such as pension funds, life insurance companies, and market makers that provide a stabilizing factor in financial markets,[4] are practically nonexistent in Qatar. Although the number of insurance companies has grown, their role and participation in stock market activities is very limited: as of end-2005, the insurance sector accounted for 1.13 percent of total trading value. Furthermore, there are no mutual funds in Qatar. The prioprietary portfolio of banks in the DSM market is very thin, representing only about 1 percent of total market capitalization. The absence of large institutional investors makes the Qatari market particularly vulnerable to speculation.

The largest institutional investor in Qatar is the government, with over 30 percent of ownership in terms of market capitalization. In addition, there are some public funds such as the Retirement and Pension Fund, the Education and Health Care Fund, and the Qatar Foundation that trade on the stock market. However, they are not sizeable investors. Since government institutions typically buy and hold stocks, their investment criteria do not follow market rules, they do not contribute to the price discovery function of the equity market.

Most of the speculative demand in the Qatari market comes from individual investors. The number of investors has grown substantially in the

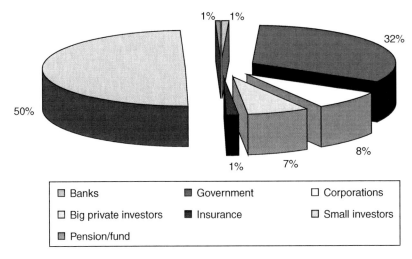

Figure 5.7 Ownership structure of listed companies in DSM (2005)

Sources: Zawya; and Gulfbase.

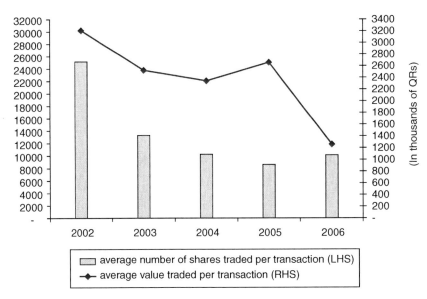

Figure 5.8 Average number of shares and value traded per transaction

Sources: Global Investment House; and Fund staff estimates.

DSM and this has been accompanied by a large increase in the number of transactions and a decreasing size of transactions (number of shares traded per transaction and value of transactions) which points to the growing role of smaller investors in the market.

5.2.7   Limited supply of stocks

The relatively large size of the DSM equity market contrasts with the small number of listed stocks. With only 36 companies listed in the market, the average market value of the Qatari listed companies is $1.69 billion – well above most emerging and industrial equity market standards.[5] This underscores the high concentration of the Qatari market in a few very large firms, which increases its vulnerability to speculative pressures.

Not only are there few Qatari companies listed, but the shares available for trade in the Qatari market are also limited. The fact that three out of the four largest companies in the Qatari market in terms of market capitalization – Industries Qatar (IQ) Company, Qatar National Bank, and Qatar Telecom – are majority state-owned de facto reduces the amount of stocks effectively available for trade.

5.3   THE DSM AFTER THE CORRECTION: ARE STOCK VALUATIONS IN LINE WITH FUNDAMENTALS?

Despite the severe price correction, stock valuation ratios in the DSM are still relatively high compared with regional and international standards. Notwithstanding the loss of 40 percent of its peak value, the DSM price index still retained a 216 percent gain as of mid-2006 when compared with January 2003. Furthermore, as of end-June 2007, the price index has recovered 26 percent over the minimum after the market correction in December 2006. As mentioned in the previous section, due to the fall in prices and the overall good level of profitability of listed companies, valuation ratios have decreased subtantially to levels broadly in line with historical values but remain at the higher end of GCC countries and other emerging markets as analyzed below. Also, some of the structural factors that contributed to the formation of a price bubble still remain. However, to analyze whether Qatari stocks are still overvalued it is necessary to take into account market-specific factors which are not necessarily reflected in valuation ratios and could distort the standard warning signals that usually point to the formation of a speculative bubble. These factors range from economic fundamentals[6] to market-specific structural factors and regulations,[7] and could potentially alleviate some of the concerns arising from the valuation indicators and structural weaknesses mentioned above. The following are some of the main factors relevant for analyzing whether Qatari stock valuations are in line with economic fundamentals.

5.3.1   Global oil market developments and listed companies' performance

There is a strong correlation between the performance of the DSM price index and oil prices. Oil and gas production[8] is most important in overall economic activity in Qatar, accounting for around 60 percent of GDP. This correlation is rooted at the macroeconomic level on the impact of global oil market developments on Qatari economic growth. The change in oil prices[9] explains about 70 percent of the changes in the DSM index during 1998–2005. Not surprisingly, the two leading companies in terms of trading values in 2005 are IQ (petrochemicals and steel) and QGT (Liquefied Natural Gas (LNG)-shipping), which accounted respectively for 18.8 percent and 14.4 percent of total value traded (Box 5.2).

Box 5.2   Major Players in the DSM: Industries Qatar (IQ) and Qatar Gas Transport (QGT)

Industries Qatar is the largest listed company in the Qatari market, accounting for 19 percent of total market capitalization as of end-2006. At the same time, IQ had total assets worth QRs 14.9 billion and total sales of QRs 7.8 billion, equivalent to 7.8 percent and 4.1 percent of Qatar's GDP, respectively. Due to its large size relative to the country's economy, IQ's IPO in April 2003 represented a major change in the sectoral composition and size of the DSM. Also, the DSM is heavily dependent on the company's performance outlook.

IQ was formed with government-owned Qatar Petroleum (QP) as its sole founding shareholder. QP subsequently divested 30 percent of its interest to Qatari individual investors through an IPO in 2003. IQ is a holding company for the following subsidiaries and joint venture companies: (a) Qatar Steel Company (Qasco); (b) Qatar Petrochemical Company Limited; (c) Qatar Fertilizer Company; and (d) Qatar Fuel Additives Company.

IQ profits remain healthy, although the rate of growth slowed significantly from 121 percent in 2004 to 13 percent in 2006. However, year-on-year profits for the third quarter of 2007 reflected a significant rebound with 32 percent growth. Although the price growth of steel, petrochemicals, and fertilizers is expected to moderate, profit growth is expected to strengthen driven by the massive expansion projects undertaken by IQ's subsidiaries, amounting to QRs 28.8 billion as of mid-2007. IQ has a strong client base in growing markets such as Asia, with potential for sustained growth in the future. Part of IQ's competitive advantage comes from lower input costs than those of competitors outside the region, thanks to the

▶

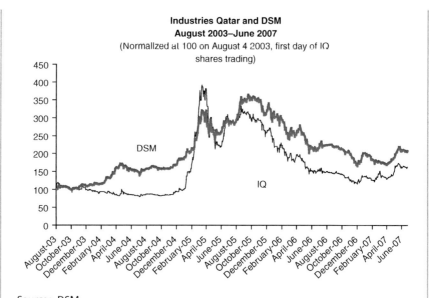

Industries Qatar and DSM
August 2003–June 2007
(Normalized at 100 on August 4 2003, first day of IQ shares trading)

Source: DSM.

2006	Market share		
(In percent)	Volume of trade	Value of trade	Profit growth
Industries Qatar	3.0	7.8	12.6

2006	Market share		
(In percent)	Volume of trade	Value of trade	Profit growth
Nakilat	13.3	9.5	−9.2

long-term low cost agreement with QP to supply natural gas, a main feedstock component for the production of petrochemicals and fertilizers, and IQ's exemption from corporate taxes. In addition, one very significant factor in the sustainability of IQ's profits in the future stems from the fact that Qasco is the only steel producer in Qatar, and it also enjoys the protection of a 20 percent steel tariff imposed on certain imported steel, enabling the company to supply the bulk of the local construction market's booming demand. The ongoing massive infrastructure and real estate developments in Qatar should allow IQ to sustain relatively high profitability growth rates over the medium term.

▶

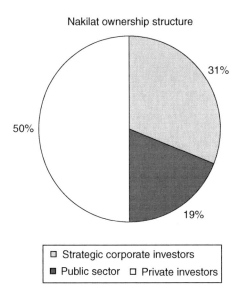

Nakilat ownership structure

31%

50%

19%

☐ Strategic corporate investors
■ Public sector   ☐ Private investors

QGT (Nakilat) is another important driver of the DSM. Nakilat had a market share of 3 percent as of end-2006, with total assets worth QRs 10.8 billion, equivalent to 5.6 percent of Qatar's GDP. The company launched an IPO in January 2005 for 50 percent of its 560 million shares. Nakilat was established to provide transportation services for the Qatar Gas and Ras Gas projects, which have contracts to supply LNG to Asia, Europe, and the US for 25 years and will lease the LNG tankers from Nakilat. The company is expected to become the largest LNG shipping company in the world. By 2012, Nakilat is expected to acquire 77 LNG vessels to transport Liquefied Natural Gas (LNG) to Europe, Asia and the US Profits in 2006, coming mainly from the investment of the company's liquid assets, do not correspond to the regular operations of the firm. The company will be fully operational by the end of 2010, and income is expected to increase rapidly after the vessels already ordered are put into operation in the coming years. Nakilat's relatively large share of the market's volume and value of trade are deemed to be a reflection of the company's growth potential.

The Qatari economy has been traditionally highly dependent on public sector spending which is in turn directly linked to government hydrocarbon revenues. Company profits and stock prices increase with oil prices, since (a) business opportunities to service public sector consumption and investment demand increase; (b) the spillover effects of higher public expenditure affect private sector income and consumption; and (c) higher fiscal

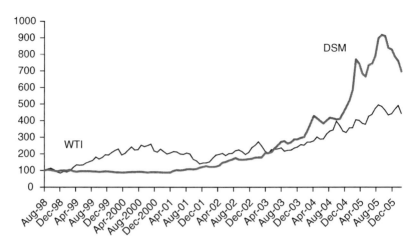

Figure 5.9   Changes in DSM and WTI prices (August 1998 = 100)

Source: Bloomberg.

Table 5.2   Regression analysis

Variable	Coefficient	Standard error	P-value
Intercept	−3494.773583	773.556676	0.0014
WTI	230.847314	41.2159337	0
Adjusted R²	0.7002561		
Durbin-Watson Stat.	1.9427861		
Number of observations	14		

Note: Semi-annual data. To remove the autocorrelation that was detected by Durbin-Watson test, the transformation method was used. The results were transformed back to the original variables and presented in this summary table.

revenues provide assurances of exchange rate stability and easier monetary conditions. Public expenditure has been increasing substantially following the rise in oil prices since 2003,[10] in line with other GCC countries. In addition, a large number of mega-projects involving public and private investments, amounting to about $170 billion, are expected to be implemented in the coming years.

5.3.2   Corporate profitability

The average valuation of Qatari stocks has returned to more sustainable levels after the recent market correction, but remains moderately high by international standards. As of June 2007, the average PER has fallen to 15.5,

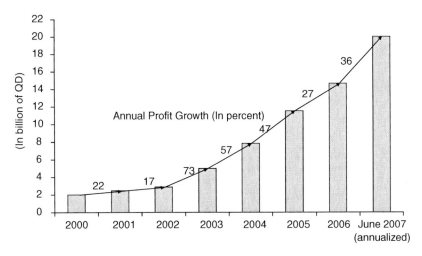

Figure 5.10   Total annual profits for all listed companies (2000–07)

Sources: DSM; and Gulfbase.

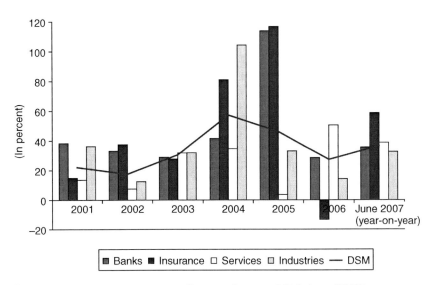

Figure 5.11   DSM corporate profit growth rates, 2001–June 2007[a]

Note: [a] Adjusted by new entries and exits to and from the market.

Sources: Gulfbase.com; and Fund staff estimates.

Table 5.3 Key market indicators for the eight largest companies in the DSM (as of December 31, 2006)

Company	2006 price change (%)	PER	PBV	DY	Market capitalization (QRs)	Market share (%)	Ranking
Industries Qatar	−43.87	11.65	4.93	5.93	42,150,000,000	19.01	1
Qatar National Bank	−20.09	15.4	3.22	2.52	30,860,724,477	13.92	2
Qatar Telecom	−5.10	13.24	5.10	4.44	22,520,000,000	10.16	3
Qatar Islamic Bank	−42.99	15.24	4.51	5.42	15,418,728,000	6.95	4
Masraf Al-Rayan Bank	86.00	–	3.42	0.00	13,950,000,000	6.29	5
The Commercial Bank	−36.09	15.41	2.94	7.14	13,735,477,434	6.19	6
Doha Bank	−43.02	16.68	4.59	0.50	12,406,860,991	5.60	7
Qatar Gas Transport	−73.01	–	3.02	0.00	7,392,000,000	3.33	8
Average/Subtotal	−31.19	13.99	4.30	4.49	158,433,790,902	71.45	
Total DSM	−34.47	16.61	3.01	2.37	221,729,740,160	100.00	

Sources: DSM; KAMCO and Fund staff estimates.

less than half its value at the peak of the stock price index. The correction in stock valuation ratios since September 2005 has been particularly strong among the seven largest Doha Securities Market (DSM)-listed companies, showing an average Year-To-Date (YTD) stock price decrease of 31.2 percent and a decline to a PER of 14 as of June 2007. However, the average valuation of Qatari stocks remains slightly above other GCC markets.

Most of the decline in profitability in 2006 was linked to the fall in GCC stock prices. The insurance sector, which profited from the revaluation of its portfolio in 2004 and 2005, registered a decrease of 13.4 percent in profits in 2006. Banks also experienced a substantial slowdown in the rate of profit growth during the first half of 2006, but ended the year with a healthy profit growth of about 28.5 percent. The emergence of alternative lines of business associated with the booming economy have largely offset the reduction in stock trade-related profits. In fact, the Price Earnings Growth (PEG) ratio,[11] which takes into account expected long-term profitability (instead of a measure such as the PER), was 0.42 based on mid-2007 forecasts for the year. Since this valuation ratio was significantly below one, it pointed to an undervalued market.

5.3.3 Price volatility

Monthly price volatility has declined since its peak in August 2005, but as of mid-2007, still remained well above its historical pre-correction average.

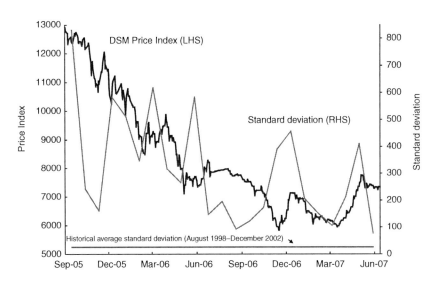

Figure 5.12 Daily DSM price index and monthly standard deviation (September 2005–June 2007)

Sources: Bloomberg; and Fund staff estimates.

The average standard deviation for the period October 2005–June 2007 stood at 265, about ⅔ the peak level of 804. However, the average standard deviation since the beginning of the stabilization of the market in June 2006 declined to 185, but still remained well above the historical average of 26 before the start of the recent boom (August 1998–December 2002).

5.3.4   The impact of privatization, market liberalization, and listing regulations on the DSM index

The increase in the prices of shares offered through IPOs could explain approximately two-thirds of the gain in the DSM price index during 2003–05. The contribution of individual IPOs to the price index gain has varied between 0.2 and 160 percent. This large differential is due to the weight of the company undertaking the IPO relative to the market and the performance of the IPO. In 2003, the IPO for the heavyweight IQ accounted for nearly 160 percent of the DSM index increase, as its market share was nearly 32 percent. The Qatar Meat and Livestock Company, with a very small market share, accounted for only 0.2 percent of the DSM price increase in 2004 following its IPO. In 2005, nearly a third of the DSM increase could be attributed to IPOs, in particular to the large QGT IPO. On average, this impact could be calculated as 65 percent per year, weighting the yearly impact by the yearly increase in the price index.[12]

In all IPOs, the greatest increase in the stock price was achieved on the first day of their trading, thus reinforcing the hypothesis that these increases reflected the market's assessment of their economic values, albeit in an exuberant environment. Most of the stock price increases have since eroded, but have plateaued at prices substantially higher than their offer prices. In the case of IQ, for instance, the stock retained over two-thirds of its initial price gains one year after its IPO. Qatar Gas Transport retained over half of the gains made during the very first few days of trade. The existence of a speculative component in the pricing of IPO shares during the first few days of trade does not invalidate the hypothesis that a large part of the price increase reflected a proper assessment of their market value, to the extent that the underpricing of IPO shares responds to a public policy aimed at increasing the sharing of oil wealth among the population at large.[13] Furthermore, all companies that entered the market through IPOs during 2003–05 had a length of time in business, a solid performance record, large assets, and management depth.[14] These IPOs were all oversubscribed from 1 to 9.5 times. On the other hand, the effect of large IPOs (such as Rayan's) on the market, in a movement of low liquidity, put additional downward pressure in the price index in 2006. A number of retail investors liquidated their positions in other stocks to

Table 5.4 Impact of IPOs on DSM (2003–05)

Issuer	Market capitalization[a] (%)	Date of listing	First day price increase			"Plateau" initial price increase[b]			First year price increase[c]		
			DSM (%)	Stock (%)	Percentage contribution[d]	DSM (%)	Stock (%)	Percentage contribution[d]	DSM (%)	Stock (%)	Percentage contribution[d]
Industries Qatar	31.9	8/4/2003	1.0	521.0	166.2	8.80	567.0	180.9	12.8	499.0	159.2
		Total 2003							69.8		159.2
Qatar Meat and Livestock	0.2	1/21/2004	−0.2	109.0	0.2	2.5	113.0	0.2	61.0	110.0	0.2
		Total 2004							64.5		0.2
Qatar Gas Transport	6.8	10/4/2005	−1.8	609.0	41.2	−5.7	278.0	18.8	11.3	387.0	26.2
Dlala	0.4	5/9/2005	0.3	1,031.0	4.1	1.3	1,150.0	4.6	−16.0	1,111.0	4.4
		Total 2005							70.2		30.6

Notes:
[a] Market capitalization as of end of the first year of listing or closest end-of-year date.
[b] Includes the price increase during the first few days of listing, until a "plateau" price was established.
[c] Price increase from the date of listing to end-December of the IPO year.
[d] Stock price increase weighted by its market capitalization.

Sources: Zawya, Authorities and Fund staff estimates.

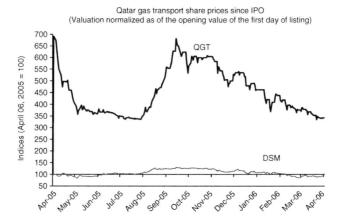

Qatar gas transport share prices since IPO
(Valuation normalized as of the opening value of the first day of listing)

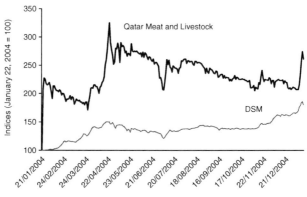

Qatar meat and livestock – first year of listing
(Valuation normalized as of the opening value of the first day of listing)

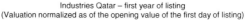

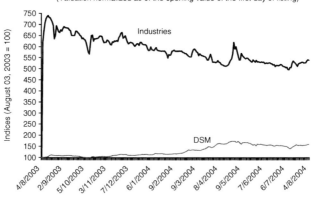

Industries Qatar – first year of listing
(Valuation normalized as of the opening value of the first day of listing)

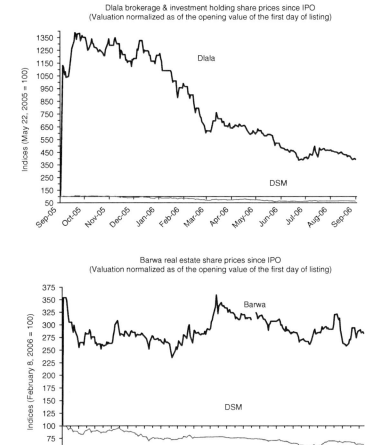

Figure 5.13 Evolution of IPO stock prices (First year of listing) and DSM, 2003–06

leverage their investments in the new IPOs since these were perceived as better short-term investments.

5.3.5   The shift in investors' preferences

To the extent that the increase in regional liquidity responds to the shift in investors' preferences (and thus in the pattern of capital flows) for regional assets, there may be a permanent increase in the demand for stocks. A substantial part of the region's capital remained close to home in the last few years, due to heightened international security concerns and the low rate of return in international markets.[15] The change in the pattern of capital flows has increased the GCC region's narrow and broad money stocks since 2002. The relative scarcity of available domestic assets has been pushing up local stock prices as well as real estate prices. Also, allowing foreigners to invest directly in up to 25 percent of shares in many companies in the Qatari stock market brought more liquidity to the market and this in turn had a positive impact on stock prices. Although foreign stock investments may be volatile, if properly matched with structural reforms aimed at strengthening market transparency and corporate governance they could constitute a substantial source of liquidity, thus moderating the effect of regional cycles.

5.4   SUMMARY OF THE RESULTS

The stock market's sharp correction has reduced substantially the gap opened in 2005 between the stock price index and the main economic fundamentals. As of end-June 2007, the price index stood at about 200 percent above its January 2003 level. This valuation gain was broadly in line with the increase in oil prices, as measured by the West Texas Intermediate (WTI) spot prices (226 percent), and below the expected accumulated increase in corporate profits by the end of 2007 (268 percent). The valuation indices, however, are still somewhat above most other GCC and emerging equity markets. In order for prices to be sustainable, it would be necessary that the rebound in corporate profits of the first half of 2007 is consolidated further, which may be possible as the losses associated with equity market positions have been already taken. Furthermore, continued banking sector profitability, and buoyant profits for petrochemicals and other oil-related companies, supported by strong global demand and higher prices, provide a sound basis for the growth of stock prices in the medium term.

Volatility will continue to be relatively high, associated with structural weaknesses, abundant liquidity, and geopolitical factors. Differences in the transparency of the market, particularly in the information for small investors, and other institutional weaknesses continue to affect volatility. The existence of ample liquidity in the banking system provides the means for further speculative upheavals, as money and credit growth in Qatar have continued expanding rapidly during 2006, as in most GCC economies. Furthermore, the Qatari market will continue to be sensitive to the developments in the larger regional equity markets, particularly Saudi Arabia, given the observed contagion effects.[16] Finally, the region's unstable geopolitical situation further increases the risk for investors.

Stock market developments in the near future will continue to be determined by future IPOs, the level of liquidity, economic fundamentals, and oil prices. As long as oil prices stay high, macroeconomic fundamentals remain favorable, and corporate profitability continues to be strong, it is expected

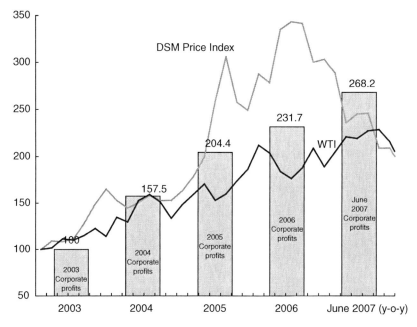

Figure 5.14   DSM price index, WTI and corporate profits, January 2004–August 2006 (December 31, 2003 =100)

Sources: Bloomberg; Gulfbase.com; and Fund staff estimates.

that a substantial part of the DSM stock price gains will be retained and the market will resume its upward trend in a sustainable manner.

5.5   THE STOCK MARKET CORRECTION: IMPLICATIONS FOR FINANCIAL STABILITY

Despite the substantial market correction in stock prices, economic growth remained strong at 10.3 percent in 2006, and there was no sign of financial sector stress, other than a decline in profitability. Several reasons explain why the impact of this correction was relatively moderate and did not affect systemic stability, despite falling profits for financial intermediaries. In particular, the large Qatari banks are well capitalized, profitable and possess a strong asset quality, and their sources of business are being diversified along with Qatar's rapid economic growth.[17] The ratio of shareholders' equity to total assets averaged more than 12 percent as of end-2006, while the average capital adequacy ratio for Qatari banks was 13.8 percent, well above the minimum international standard and over the regulatory minimum of 10 percent. Asset quality has improved steadily since 2000, in the wake of rapid economic and credit expansion. As of end-2006, average Non-Performing Loans (NPL) represented 2.2 percent of total loans, and provisions covered 94.3 percent of NPL. Despite the reduction in trading and brokerage activities in 2006, banks' profitability, as measured by the return on assets, was high at 3.7 percent (up from 2.5 percent in 2003). The return on equity in 2006 was a hefty 27 percent.

Thus, the sharp stock price fall eroded slightly Qatari banks' profitability, but did not affect their soundness or asset quality given the country's high economic growth and financial diversification. Due to the Qatari banks' substantial direct exposure to the stock exchange (averaging 40 percent of total shareholders' equity for the three largest banks, as of end-September 2005), the correction turned past investment profits into losses. In addition, the reduction in the level of stock exchange activity further reduced revenue derived from brokerage commissions, asset management fees, and underwriting fees.[18] The correction did not have an impact on asset quality, despite the fact that part of the consumer loans were diverted to stock market speculation, because consumer loans are guaranteed by (generally public sector) salaries, thus substantially reducing the banks' credit risk. Even though the amount of consumer loans increased substantially in the wake of the stock exchange boom, loans to the public sector still accounted for some 30 percent of total loans as of end-September 2005. Also, credit demand from the main Qatari companies increased following the financing of large public-private partnership based mega-projects and the diversification of the economy, providing a rapidly expanding alternative business base for Qatari banks.[19] Finally, government deposits accounted for 37 percent of total banking system deposits as of end-September 2005, thus providing a substantial base of stable deposits de-linked from fluctuating share prices.

Table 5.5 Qatar: mega projects pipeline (2007–12)

Projects by sectors	Billions of US dollars
Gas	83
Oil	8
Petrochemicals	32
Infrastructure	21
Other	27
Total	170

Sources: Oxford Analytical Report and discussions with the Qatari authorities and business entities during the 2007 Article IV consultation mission.

The impact of the negative wealth effect was limited. Household demand remained mainly stable as the stock market-related wealth gain was for a relatively short period and an average household could still retain sizable capital gains if they were active in the market before the speculative spree that started toward the end of 2004. The expansionary fiscal stance and the large number of mega-projects to be implemented, particularly in the gas sector, also helped boost household spending. Finally, strengthened investor confidence arising from high oil prices and a generally strong corporate sector exerted a countervailing force on the short-term contractionary wealth effect.

NOTES

1. "A large proportion of new lending finds its way to the equity market," according to the 2006 Moody's banking system outlook.
2. For instance, the 14 percent increase in claims on the private sector observed in February 2005 corresponds to the period for the Qatar Gas Transport IPO. The decline in claims on the private sector in the following month is due to investors' repaying loans for the amounts in excess of the IPO's share allocation.
3. This warning signal implies that the prices of a few stocks are rising well above the prices of the majority of stocks, possibly as a consequence of speculative demand. This was the case, for instance, with the dot.com companies during the NASDAQ bubble (see footnote 68).
4. See footnote 43 in chapter 1.
5. The average size of listed companies in NASDAQ as of June 22, 2007 was $1.42 billion, slightly below the $1.09 billion average size of listed companies in the main Japanese stock markets as of May 31, 2007.
6. Such as the profitability growth rate, structural factors affecting corporate profits, and the impact of developments in the oil market on the performance of listed companies.
7. Such as the privatization policy, the role of the government as a major holder of stocks, and the opening of the market to foreign investors.
8. Currently oil receipts represent about 60 percent of total Qatari oil and gas receipts. Gas is expected to increase its share to about 65 percent of total hydrocarbon receipts by 2011.
9. As measured by West Texas Intermediate (WTI) oil spot prices.
10. Total expenditure grew by 38 percent a year during 2004–06, while the rate of growth during the previous three years had been only 8 percent a year.
11. See footnote 37.
12. This is a theoretical calculation since firms are not eligible to integrate with the DSM general price index until after one year of listing. However, it illustrates investors' euphoria associated with these IPOs, which drove the market upward.
13. H.E. Abdullah Bin Hammad Al-Attiyah, Minister of Energy and Industry and Chairman of IQ, formulated this policy in the following terms at an introductory meeting for the IQ IPO on May 4, 2003: "the emergence of IQ comes as a blessing from His Highness which will benefit the largest possible number of Qataris as individual investors" (Al-Attiyah, 2003).
14. In addition to the leading companies, Industries Qatar and Qatar Gas Import, Dlala has a sound position as a brokerage company, strengthened by the regulatory changes introduced by the QCB. Other IPOs listed in 2006 include Barwa, a leading company in the booming real estate sector; Maaraf Al-Rayan Bank, a leading Islamic bank; and Gulf Cement. All of these companies were backed by strong economic fundamentals.
15. See, for instance, Chapter II of the World Economic Outlook, April 2006, on the changing patterns of petrodollar recycling.

16. See footnote 33.
17. Recognizing this trend, Moody's recently upgraded Qatar's ratings for long-term foreign currency bonds and bank deposits to A1 in 2005, and upgraded the country's long-term foreign bank deposits to Aa2.
18. The Qatar Central Bank decision to terminate all banks' brokerage licenses as of 2006 and transfer all related business to Dlala Brokerage Co. and Dlala Islamic Brokerage Co. also affected banks' earnings.
19. The good prospects for Qatari banks have been attracting new competitors to the market. During 2004 two GCC banks (Al-Ahli United Bank of Bahrain and National Bank of Kuwait) acquired minority stakes in two Qatari banks (Al-Ahli and Grindleys Qatar Bank, respectively), and a number of other GCC banks have applied for a license to operate. In addition, two new banks are expected to start operations in 2006, including Al-Rayyan Bank. Furthermore, the start of operations of the Qatar Financial Centre (QFC) in 2006 should also attract new banks, given the low tax rate on profits (10 percent) following a three-year tax holiday and the possibility of 100 percent foreign ownership and profit repatriation.

REFERENCES

Al-Attiyah, Abdullah Bin Hamad. Speech on the introductory meeting for Industries Qatar Company, Sheraton Hotel, Doha, May 4, 2003. http://www.zawya.com/story.cfm?id=ZAWYA20031028100549&query=al%2Dattiyah&searchmethod=keywords
Doha Securities Market (2002, 2003, 2004). Annual Bulletin.
Doha Securities Market (2005). Investor's Guide.
Doha Securities Market (2005 and 2006). Monthly Bulletins and Reports.
Doha Securities Market (2005 and 2006). Financial Ratios.
El Nabarawy, M. and Shahin, M. (2006). Industries Qatar Initial Coverage. SHUAA Capital Equity Research. Dubai, March 22, 2006.
Garner, J. et al. (2006). Gulf Equity Markets: Powered by Oil, Equity Research: Credit Suisse.
Global Investment House KSCC (2003). Qatar Economic and Strategic Outlook I. Global Investment House Economic Research. Kuwait, September 28, 2003.
Global Investment House KSCC (2004). Qatar Economic and Strategic Outlook II. Global Investment House Economic Research. Kuwait, July 10, 2004.
Global Investment House KSCC (2005). Qatar Economic and Strategic Outlook III. Global Investment House Economic Research. Kuwait, December 21, 2005.
Grigorian, David (2004). *Financial Sector Overview*, in Qatar – Selected Issues and Statistical Appendix, IMF, SM/04/350, October 6, 2006, pp. 52–65.
Gulfbase (2006). DSM companies profiles and financial ratios. http://www.gulfbase.com/site/interface/MarketWatch.aspx?m=7
International Monetary Fund (IMF). World Economic Outlook; www.imf.org
Industries Qatar (IQ). http://www.industriesqatar.com.qa/
Moody's Investors Service Global Credit Research. London, May 18, 2005.
Moody's (2006). Banking system Outlook: Qatar. Moody's Investors Service Global Credit Research. Limasol, January 2006.
SHUAA Capital (2006). DSM companies profiles. http://www.shuaacapital.com
Zawya (2006). DSM companies profiles. http://www.zawya.com

CHAPTER 6

The Saudi Stock Market in a Regional Context

Fernando Delgado
and Maher Hasan

6.1 INTRODUCTION

From the second half of 2004 to the first months of 2006, the Saudi stock market (Tadawul) experienced one of the fastest price increases in emerging and mature equity markets alike, followed by an equally fast and deep correction. It is particularly noteworthy in the case of Saudi Arabia that the correction in 2006 has had no major impact on financial stability or economic growth. Furthermore, a mostly bearish market during the first half of 2007 has not diminished the prospects for strong non-oil GDP growth. Equally striking is that in the first half of 2007, Saudi equity prices seem to have been oblivious to the sustained increase in economic activity and the bright medium-term economic outlook, while all the neighboring markets have started to regain part of their losses.

This chapter examines the developments of the Saudi stock market during the boom and correction periods in a regional perspective (Section 6.2). It analyzes the reasons behind the depth, length, and volatility of the Saudi equity market correction compared with other regional markets and its poor performance in the first half of 2007 (Section 6.3). It also assesses the impact of the correction on financial sector stability and economic growth (Section 6.4). Finally, it provides some specific recommendations to enhance market resilience (Section 6.5).

Box 6.1   Saudi Stock Exchange (Tadawul)[a]

Historical background

Saudi joint stock companies had their beginnings in the mid-1930s, when the first company, Arab Automobile, was established. The rapid economic expansion and nationalization of foreign banks in the 1970s led to the establishment of a number of large corporations and joint venture banks. Major share offerings were made to the public during this period. The market, which was created in 1983, remained informal until a Ministerial Committee of the Ministry of Finance and National Economy, Ministry of Commerce, and the Saudi Arabian Monetary Agency (SAMA) was formed in 1984 to regulate and develop the market. SAMA was authorized to monitor market activities. With the aim of improving the regulatory framework, share-trading intermediation was restricted to commercial banks. In 1984, the Saudi Share Registration Company (SSRC) was established by the commercial banks. The company provides central registration facilities for joint stock companies, and settles and clears all equity transactions. Automated clearing and settlement was introduced in 1989. The Electronic Securities Information System (ESIS), developed and operated by SAMA, was introduced in 1990. Tadawul, the new securities trading, clearing, and settlements market was launched in October 2001.

The capital market authority (CMA)

On July 31, 2003, the Capital Market Authority (CMA) was established pursuant to the "Capital Market Law" which was promulgated by Royal Decree Number (M/30). The CMA's main objective is to organize and develop the stock exchange by enacting and enforcing rules and regulations to protect investors and ensure the fairness and integrity of the Tadawul. The CMA reports directly to the chairman of the Council of Ministers. On March 19, 2007 the Council of Ministers approved the formation of the Saudi Stock Exchange (Tadawul) Company converting Tadawul into a joint stock company with capital of SR 1.2 billion and fully owned by the state-owned Public Investment Fund (PIF). The company is envisaged to play a greater and more effective role in the management and development of the stock market by setting necessary rules and regulations and carrying out the requirements for listing on the market. The new company will have 120 million shares of equal value. A part of the company's shares will be floated for public subscription.

▶

General index and market capitalization of the Saudi Market, 1985–2007

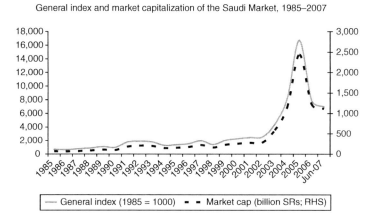

Source: SAMA.

Saudi stock exchange activity (1983–07)

In the first two decades following its inception, the stock exchange index gained very little. After the Gulf War in 1991, this situation changed temporarily as the market attracted a large number of investors seeking shorter-term investments. Share prices and trading volumes grew sharply and by early 1992 had reached unprecedented levels, creating the first Saudi bubble. The market index, which had remained relatively dormant in the late 1980s, roughly doubled by the end of 1991. Confidence in the Saudi economy spurred by high oil prices and greater confidence in the regional geopolitical situation, following the Iraq War in 2003, and low international interest rates prompted domestic investors to repatriate foreign funds and boosted stock prices to unsustainable levels leading to the bursting of the bubble. Market performance remained moderate until the recent boom and bust cycle.

Note: [a] Based mainly on information from the Saudi Stock Exchange.

6.2   SAUDI STOCK MARKET DEVELOPMENTS IN REGIONAL PERSPECTIVE

The Tadawul All Shares Index, (TASI, the general price index) which includes all shares listed in the market, increased by 564 percent in the three years to end-2005, and further to 719 percent at its peak on February 25, 2006. This increase is several orders of magnitude larger than the price hikes observed during the Nikkei bubble of the late 1980s and the NASDAQ dot.com bubble of 1999. Furthermore, the increase in the TASI during this period was

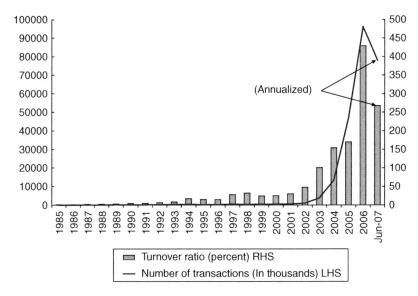

Figure 6.1 Turnover ratio and number of transactions, 1985–June 2007
Sources: SAMA; and CMA.

the second largest in the Gulf Cooperation Council (GCC) region, after the Dubai stock market, and well above the weighted average of the Arab equity markets, as measured by the Shua'a index, which grew by 396 percent. TASI growth accelerated to nearly 104 percent in 2005, and it grew by over 23 percent until February 25, 2006, recording the highest growth since the inception of the Tadawul stock exchange in 1985. As a result, the increase in market capitalization was also phenomenal. Trading value reached SRls 4.1 trillion in 2005, more than double the 2004 level and higher than the cumulative sum of the 19 years since the market's creation. The number of transactions, the trading value, and the turnover ratio (defined as the value of transactions over market capitalization) have also increased substantially in the last three years.

However, this boom was followed by a sharp and deep correction in 2006. The TASI fell to only 40 percent of its peak value in February 2006 (Figure 1.3, 1.12, and Table 1.8). This loss was the highest among all GCC markets[1] and close to the loss recorded in NASDAQ during the dot.com bubble. Except for the Saudi market, which lost 12 additional percentage points, all GCC stock markets recorded gains in the first six months of 2007. In addition, market activity has declined in line with this poor performance, with a 34 percent fall on the average value of daily traded stock in the first six months of 2007 compared with 2006.

The sharp correction in the TASI was associated with the highest level of volatility in the region in 2006. This volatility, as measured by the coefficient of variation of the TASI, reflected investors' concerns about market direction and was proportional to the size of the correction when compared with other GCC markets. However, despite further correction in the first six months of 2007, TASI volatility declined to levels broadly in line with other GCC markets (Figure 1.16).

While all GCC markets recovered in the first half of 2007, the TASI lost an additional 12 percent. GCC stock market gains ranged from 21 percent in Kuwait to 3 percent in Qatar. The continuation of the Saudi market correction in the first half of 2007, despite the positive medium-term outlook for both oil and non-oil sectors, has brought market valuation indicators in line with the regional emerging market level (See Figure 1.15, lower panel).

6.3 WHAT EXPLAINS THE DEPTH, LENGTH, AND VOLATILITY OF THE SAUDI MARKET CORRECTION COMPARED WITH OTHER REGIONAL MARKETS?

The magnitude of the Saudi bubble, the depth of the correction, the high volatility, and the lag to pick up in the recovery during 2007 could be attributed to a number of factors including (a) the high level of exuberant demand during the boom period; (b) structural weaknesses in the Saudi market; and (c) the pre- and post-correction policies, including Initial Public Offering (IPO) pricing policies.

6.3.1 Exuberant demand

Assessing the existence and size of exuberant demand is a difficult task because of the absence of complete information about economic fundamentals and their impact on prices. However, examining investors' perceptions about overvaluation and the behavior of specific market and economic indicators ("warning signals") could help to assess the level of exuberant demand in the Saudi market during the boom period. These market and economic indicators are (a) a rapid increase in the price index; (b) a weak correlation between the price and economic value of stocks as measured by valuation indicators;[2] (c) a high price volatility; (d) a sizable acceleration in money and credit expansion and heavy use of margin lending; (e) an increasingly narrow market leadership (price hikes are concentrated in a few stocks); and (f) a large IPO calendar. The previous discussion shows that the first warning signal pointed to a higher degree of exuberance in the Saudi market.

6.3.1.1 Weak correlation between price and economic value

Standard valuation indicators pointed to the overpricing of Saudi stocks beginning in late 2004 and peaking by end-February 2006. The Price Earnings Ratio (PER) and the Price to Book Value Ratio (PBV) grew rapidly and reached levels significantly higher than their historical levels in the Saudi market. Similarly, the Dividend Yield (DY) decreased substantially during the same period. Furthermore, at the peak of the market, Saudi average PER, PBV, and DY levels showed a generalized overpricing of Saudi stocks vis-à-vis other industrial and emerging markets (Table 1.9). At its peak on February 25, 2006, the average PER of the Saudi market was 47.3, with a maximum PER of 72,302 for the Saudi Cable Co. The average Saudi PER ratio approached the average PER of 61 and 50 for NASDAQ[3] and the S&P 500, respectively, at the peak of the dot.com bubble, and had almost reached 49, the high point of the short-lived first Saudi market bubble between January 1991 and June 1992, when the price index increased by 130 percent before losing all its gains in the following three years.

During the boom, regional investors perceived the Saudi market as the market with the highest degree of overvaluation or market exuberance (Table 1.7). A March 2005 survey[4] of 740 business leaders in the GCC region revealed that 63 percent of them believed that a price bubble had formed in the Saudi stock market. Since then, however, the TASI increased by about 100 percent, enforcing the bubble perceptions, before the correction started in 2006.

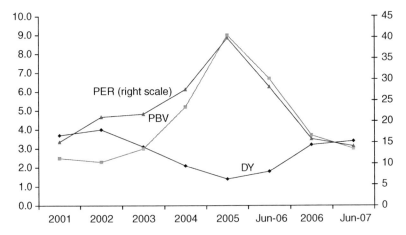

Figure 6.2 All companies PER, PBV, and DY 2001–June 2007

Source: Bakheet Financial Advisors.

6.3.1.2 High price volatility

The Saudi market witnessed a substantial increase in volatility as measured by the monthly standard deviation and coefficient of variation of the TASI starting in October 2004. In particular, the increase in the standard deviation was particularly acute prior to and immediately following the start of the correction on February 25, 2006. In April 2006, the standard deviation of the TASI increased to over 1,900, well beyond the 376 standard deviation registered by the NASDAQ price index at the peak of the dot.com bubble in April 2000. However, the volatility declined significantly in 2007 to levels broadly in line with other GCC markets (see Figure 6.3).

6.3.1.3 Sizable acceleration in money and credit expansion and heavy use of margin lending

Money supply and bank credit in Saudi Arabia expanded rapidly in tandem with market evolution, fueling exuberant demand. The acceleration in money growth is attributed mainly to the strong rate of increase in credit to the private sector, which grew by a 38 percent compound annual rate, during 2003–05[5] in Saudi Arabia. This rate of credit growth is substantially above rates observed in the two years preceding the bursting of the dot.com bubble (10.8 percent) or the five-year boom period preceding the Nikkei bubble

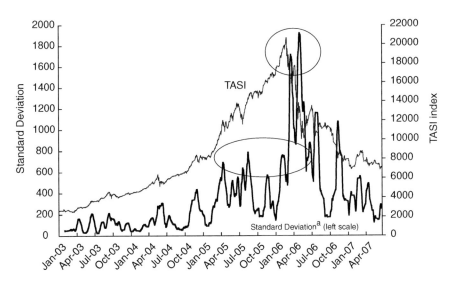

Figure 6.3 TASI and monthly standard deviation, January 2003–June 2007

Note: [a] Moving 25 trading days.

Source: Backheet Financial Advisor.

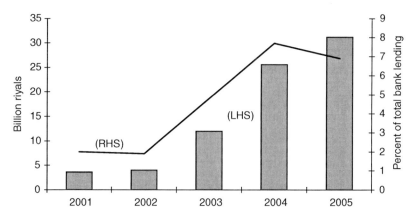

Figure 6.4 Margin lending, 2001–05

Source: SAMA.

burst (15.5 percent). An important part of this credit increase was directed to finance trading in the stock market.

Margin lending increased from 2 percent of banks' total lending in December 2001 to 8 percent in 2005. This compares to a corresponding increase in Kuwait from 6 percent to 9 percent during the same period.[6] Furthermore, consumer credit was the fastest growing component in credit to the private sector since 2003, and a sizable part of the consumer loans not specifically declared as margin loans were used to leverage equity investments. In addition to the high capital gains, several other factors contributed to increased financing of stock trading. The introduction in 1999 of the Murabaha margin trading scheme, in addition to already existing "conventional" margin trading schemes, enabled investors to trade Tadawul-listed stocks at leveraged ratios of 150 percent to 200 percent in a Sharia-compliant manner.[7] This opened the way for many Saudi investors concerned about compliance with Sharia to leverage their positions. Also, the introduction of payroll direct deposits through the RTGS payment system (SARIE), and legislation securing repayment of consumer loans through payroll retention by banks, allowed a substantial expansion of consumer credit from 7.2 percent of total private sector credit in 1998 to 43.9 percent as of end-2005. The banking system's ample liquidity enabled banks to meet the increasing demand on margin and consumer loans at relatively low interest rates.

6.3.1.4 Narrow market leadership and large IPO calendar

The Saudi market showed partial and recurring signs of narrow market leadership. A small group of speculative stocks[8] has shown a pattern of behavior

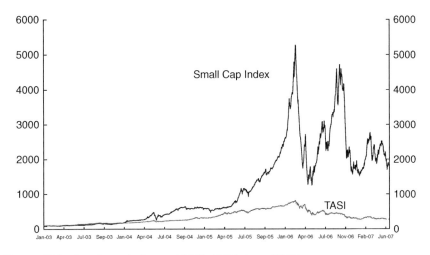

Figure 6.5   Small cap index and TASI, 2003–June 2007

Source: BFA.

consistent with this warning signal. Recurrent rises (well above the increase in the TASI) and falls occurred in the periods between January and May 2004, May and September 2004, and started a new cycle in the second half of 2005 which lasted until the bursting of the speculative bubble at end-February 2006. In each of these cycles, sharp price increases were followed by sudden declines that wiped out most of the earlier gains. During 2005, the Bakheet Financial Advisor (BFA) Small Cap index gained 236 percent vis-à-vis the 104 percent gain in the TASI. Along with this rise, there was heavy trading in the speculative stocks that did not correspond to their small market capitalization.[9] Speculative stocks soared well beyond TASI growth during the first two months of 2006 and by February 21, 2006, the BFA Small Cap Index had accumulated a gain of 100 percent compared to a 17 percent gain in the TASI.

The correction beginning on February 25, 2006 has also been particularly strong with regard to this group of speculative stocks, as their prices fell more sharply than the TASI. Overshooting on both price gains and losses on the group of speculative stocks is one of the reasons explaining the persistence of high volatility in the Saudi market. The accelerated fall of these speculative stocks, accounting for a large part of trading volume, also helped spread the panic to small investors in general. In 2006, the speculative stocks' volatility was 25 percent higher than TASI volatility. During the first half of 2007, it was 133 percent higher. This phenomenon has affected most of the fast-growing GCC equity markets during the 2005 boom period.[10]

Exuberant demand was also evident by the large increase in the number of IPOs[11] and the size of their oversubscription (see below).

6.3.2 Structural weaknesses

Several structural weaknesses increased the Saudi market's propensity to the development of boom and bust cycles and volatility. These structural weaknesses were (a) the underdevelopment of institutional investors; (b) high sector and trading concentration; and (c) a relatively low level of liquidity and openness. These structural weaknesses have affected the size of the boom, the length and the depth of the correction, and the associated volatility.

6.3.2.1 Underdevelopment of institutional investors

Despite their rapid growth in the last two years, institutional investors are still relatively underdeveloped. Traditional institutional investors, such as pension funds and life insurance companies, provide a stabilizing factor in financial markets given that their trading decisions are more informed and based on fundamentals. Their small market share in Saudi Arabia was an important factor that contributed to both the exuberant demand generating the bubble and the overshooting of the correction. In general, institutional investors are relatively underdeveloped in GCC markets, with the possible exception of Kuwait. However, the Saudi market is particularly lacking in this area due to the relative underdevelopment of the insurance industry and mutual funds; more stringent limitations to banks' proprietary portfolios; and low degree of openess to foreign institutional investors.

Until 2007 there was only one licensed insurance company. Although a number of foreign-based insurance companies were allowed to conduct business in Saudi Arabia, none of them managed their assets domestically. Following the 2003 insurance law, 13 licenses have already been issued for new companies in 2007, but these firms have not yet started the asset management side of their operations in Saudi Arabia. Furthermore, the size of the National Company for Cooperative Insurance (NCCI), the only insurance company booking its assets in Saudi Arabia, is relatively small, with total investments

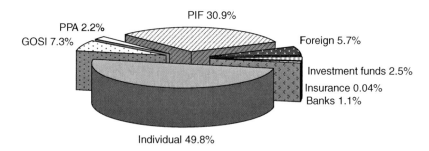

Figure 6.6 Market share of investors in the Saudi Stock Market, 2006

Source: Capital Market Authority.

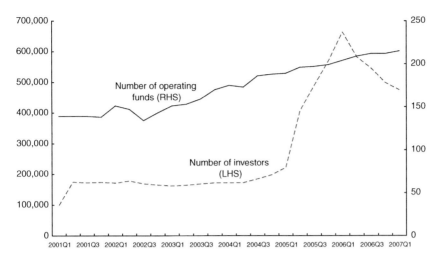

Figure 6.7   Mutual funds: number of funds and investors, 2001–07

Source: SAMA.

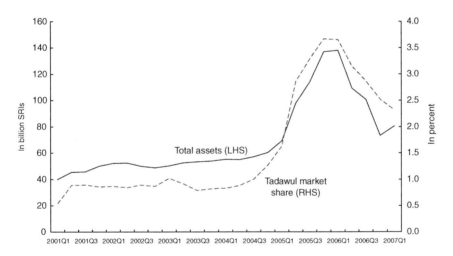

Figure 6.8   Mutual funds: total assets, 2001–07

Source: SAMA.

in listed shares equivalent to about 0.04 percent of market capitalization as of end-2006. The market share of corporate investors as of end-2004 was deemed very small (below 1 percent), but it grew rapidly during 2005, prompting the CMA to issue a regulation in January 2006 (implemented in October 2006) prohibiting direct portfolio investments in listed companies, and limiting them to investments in mutual funds or portfolios managed by licensed firms.

Despite their recent growth, mutual funds have a small market share. Mutual funds grew rapidly during 2005 and decreased markedly after the correction in February 2006,[12] and their relative size remains small, with total assets of SRls 84.2 billion (6.4 percent of GDP) as of December 2006 and a share in the domestic stock market of about 2.5 percent. It is expected that the recent licensing of financial companies by the CMA will foster the development of mutual funds by breaking the previous bank monopoly and introducing competition and independent professional valuation and assessment to the sector. Because of strict prudential regulations, Saudi banks have very limited proprietary portfolios, accounting for between 0.6 percent and 1.1 percent of market capitalization as of end-2005 and end-2006, respectively.[13]

The Autonomous Government Institutions (AGIs) are the only sizable institutional investors in the Saudi market. These include the two large public pension funds and the Public Investment Fund (PIF). Their public institutional nature has so far effectively prevented an active role of AGIs in the Saudi equity market, and their passive investment policies do not qualify them as traditional institutional investors from the point of view of price discovery, but they may play a stabilizing role as core investors in a number of companies.

Most of the speculative demand in the Saudi market comes from individuals rather than companies or institutional investors. This could explain the high volatility and large price movements in the Saudi capital market. More than 8 million Saudis, over half of the Saudi population including children, have trading accounts in Tadawul. Taking into account that most of these small investors have very limited market knowledge, no previous asset management experience, and limited sources of unbiased information, their behavior both during the bull and bear market periods exacerbated

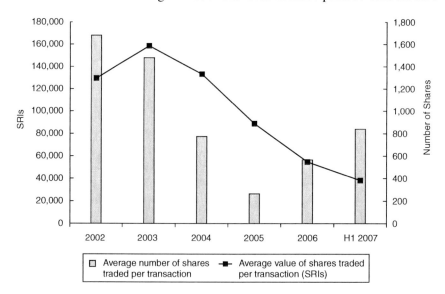

Figure 6.9   Average number and value of traded share per transaction, 2002–June 2007

Sources: SAMA; and Fund staff estimates.

Table 6.1 Equity markets in selected emerging economies, April 2007

Market	Number of companies	Market capitalization (millions of US dollars)	Market capitalization (percent of GDP)[a]	Value traded (millions of US dollars)	Turnover ratio	Average company's market value (millions of US dollars)
Bahrain	44	21,036.5	130.9	73.1	0.4	478.1
Brazil	408	846,002.7	79.2	38,765.5	4.7	2,073.5
Chile	246	202,250.1	139.3	2,767.5	1.4	822.2
China	1,478	3,428,617.6	130.4	707,918.0	22.4	2,319.8
Egypt	558	97,662.6	91.0	2,319.9	2.4	175.0
India	4,826	929,433.6	104.8	60,029.0	6.7	192.6
Israel	626	199,369.7	142.2	9,633.8	4.8	318.5
Jordan	230	32,362.0	226.0	1,069.2	3.3	140.7
Korea	1,703	904,248.4	101.8	152,329.2	17.4	531.0
Morocco	65	64,857.9	113.0	1,519.3	2.4	997.8
Nigeria	202	52,927.0	45.9	1,096.2	2.2	262.0
Oman	127	13,759.1	38.2	337.1	2.2	108.3
Russia	311	1,112,458.9	113.6	54,253.7	4.8	3,577.0
Saudi Arabia	88	308,555.7	88.5	70,253.0	22.4	3,506.3
South Africa	388	812,064.8	318.3	25,585.1	3.1	2,093.0
Taiwan	1,214	648,653.9	n.a.	82,780.4	12.8	534.3
Turkey	314	192,516.7	49.1	22,985.7	12.1	613.1

Note: [a] GDP is end-2006 value.

Sources: World Bank Emerging Markets Database (EMDB); World Economic Outlook (WEO) and Fund staff estimates.

market movements, resulting in the overshooting of prices, and propelling speculative demand.[14] The number of small investors has grown substantially in the Saudi stock market since the beginning of the boom, reducing the average size of transactions substantially.[15] However, data on ownership concentration is not available.

6.3.2.3   Sectoral and trading concentration

The relatively large size of the Saudi equity market contrasts with its small number of listed stocks. Despite the large number of IPOs in 2005 and 2006, only 88 companies were listed in the Saudi market as of end-2006, one of the lowest in the region taking into account the size of the Saudi economy. As a result, the average market value of Saudi listed companies was over $3.5 billion, despite the substantial contraction in 2006,[16] well above emerging and industrial equity market standards (Table 6.1).[17] This points to the high concentration of the Saudi market in a few very large firms, which increases the vulnerability of the market to speculative operations. The sensitivity of the largest listed company in the market Saudi Basic Industries Corporation (SABIC) to oil market developments amplifies the impact of market concentration on volatility (see Box 6.2).

Box 6.2   SABIC Financial and Market Performance

The Saudi Basic Industries Corporation (SABIC) is the largest listed company in the Saudi market, accounting for 26.4 percent of market capitalization as of May 2007. However, trading of SABIC stock has declined from 9.6 percent of total market trade in 2005 to only 2.2 percent in the first five months of 2007. Thus, although the market's valuation indicators and performance are heavily dependent on the company's performance and outlook, they have less impact on investors' capital gains or losses.

While SABIC's financial performance improved significantly over the last three years, its market value grew at a multiple of the company's profits during the boom period, as reflected in the 16-fold increase in the share price in the period from 2003 to February 2006. To some extent, this outstanding market performance could be traced to investors' discounting of future profits associated with SABIC's ambitious medium-term expansion plans,[a] the positive oil price outlook and the steady growth of its profits (in September 2006, S&P raised SABIC's rating to "A+"). However, the correction brought its valuation indicators (as of May 2007, PER equal to 13.8) close to historical levels and international petrochemical companies' average PER of 11.7.

▶

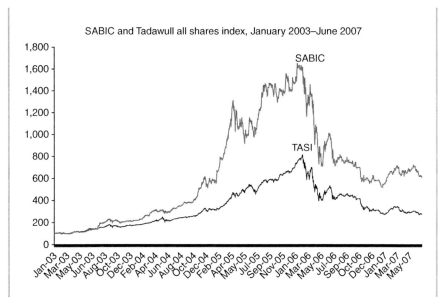

Source: Bakheet Financial Advisor.

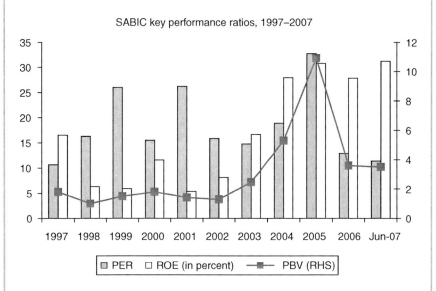

Source: Bakheet Financial Advisor.

▶

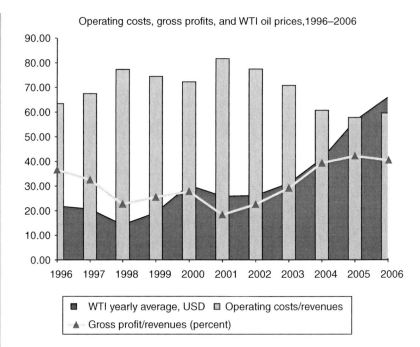

Operating costs, gross profits, and WTI oil prices,1996–2006

Legend:
- ■ WTI yearly average, USD □ Operating costs/revenues
- ▲ Gross profit/revenues (percent)

Sources: Bakheet Financial Advisor; and Fund staff estimates.

SABIC profitability depends largely on international oil prices. Thus, investors' expectations in this regard greatly influence SABIC's share prices. Since the domestic prices of the main feedstock are administratively fixed,[b] an increase in international oil prices (which usually entails a corresponding increase in petrochemical product prices) increases SABIC's competitiveness and reduces the cost of production as a percentage of total revenue.[c] This sensitivity to international oil prices makes SABIC's stock a source of volatility to the market (SABIC's stock volatility measured by the coefficient of variation exceeded TASI's volatility by 26 percent in 2006).

Notes:
[a] SABIC was established as a wholly government-owned joint stock company in 1976. In 1984, 30 percent of its equity capital was sold to the private sector, starting a period of rapid and continuous expansion. In 2002, SABIC acquired the Dutch firm DSM Petrochemicals for around $2.6 billion. The deal gave SABIC technological knowledge, a European marketing network, and production facilities in the Netherlands and Germany. The acquisition made the company the 11th largest petrochemicals producer in the world and the 4th largest polymers producer. SABIC plans to increase its production capacity by 36 percent to 66.8 million tons (mt) by 2010 and to 100 mt by 2015.
[b] SABIC purchases ethane at a fixed price of 75 cents per MTBU. The price of propane is linked to changes in the price of naphtha in Japan.
[c] This does not apply equally to SABIC's subsidiaries outside Saudi Arabia.

6.3.2.4 Relatively low level of liquidity and openness

The Saudi market is characterized not only by a small number of companies, but also by a limited amount of shares available for trade (free float). The fact that some of the largest listed companies in the Saudi market – including SABIC, Saudi Electricity Company, and Saudi Telecom – are majority state-owned de facto reduces the amount of stocks effectively available for trade and hence market liquidity.[18] Three government agencies, PIF, the Public Pension Agency (PPA) and the General Organization for Social Insurance (GOSI), which are not involved in active share trading, held over 40 percent of the total market share. Despite the substantial progress that has been made in the last three years regarding the amount of dematerialized shares[19] (as of end-2006, these accounted for 78 percent of all Tadawul-listed shares), big strategic holdings still keep the free float ratio relatively low.

Furthermore, foreign investors' access to the Saudi market was very limited. As of end-2005, only 24 percent of Saudi stocks could be held by other GCC nationals, and non-GCC nationals were not allowed to invest in the market (Table 1.10). This limited openness barred the price discovery function through the participation of foreign investment funds whose investment decisions are largely driven by fundamentals rather than exuberant demand.

The Saudi listing regulations introduced in 2004 include stringent trading restrictions for the issuer and controlling shareholders, similar to lock-up clauses that are common in IPOs in equity market contracts in industrial countries. In particular, the issuers and controlling shareholders cannot issue or dispose of any securities for six months after the date of the official

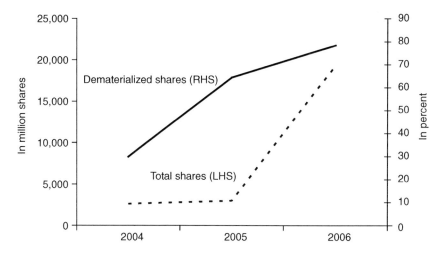

Figure 6.10 Dematerialized shares, 2004–06

Source: Capital Market Authority.

Table 6.2 Impact of IPOs on TASI (2003–06)

Issuer	Market capitalization[a] (%)	Date of listing	First day price increase TASI (%)	First day price increase Stock (%)	First day price increase Percentage contribution[d]	"Plateau" initial price increase[b] TASI (%)	"Plateau" initial price increase[b] Stock (%)	"Plateau" initial price increase[b] Percentage contribution[d]	First year price increase[c] TASI (%)	First year price increase[c] Stock (%)	First year price increase[c] Percentage contribution[d]
Saudi Telecom	21.5	1/25/2003	5.6	39.4	151.6	3.01	30.1	6.5	69.7	148.7	32.0
Total 2003									76.2		32.0
Sahara	0.5	7/7/2004	0.9	200.0	1.0	4.9	250.5	1.2	40.3	277.5	1.4
Ettihad Etisalat	2.9	12/20/2004	−2.1	500.0	14.4	−2.3	650.0	18.7	−1.5	652.0	18.7
Total 2004									84.9		20.1
NCCI	0.3	1/17/2005	0.1	81.2	0.2	2.0	76.6	0.2	110.0	242.4	0.7
Bank Al Bilad	2.1	4/30/2005	−2.6	1,430.0	29.9	−2.5	1,388.0	29.0	44.8	1,596.0	33.4
SADAFCO	0.2	5/23/2005	−1.5	94.4	0.2	0.6	123.2	0.2	31.3	159.3	0.3
Almarai	0.7	8/17/2005	0.4	14.6	0.1	0.4	14.6	0.1	18.0	65.0	0.5
Total 2005									103.7		34.8
Yanbu	1.5	2/20/2006	0.3	1,120.0	16.9	−34.4	307.5	4.6	−33.8	427.5	6.5
Aldrees	0.2	3/14/2006	−4.7	87.6	0.2	−16.6	285.1	0.5	−16.0	369.6	0.7
Research & Marketing	0.3	5/15/2006	0.2	106.5	0.3	−11.2	49.5	0.2	11.0	70.1	0.2
Saudi Paper	0.2	6/14/2006	0.9	130.2	0.3	5.8	146.4	0.3	10.1	160.5	0.3
Total June 2006									−21.3		7.6

Notes:

[a] Market capitalization as of end of the first year of listing or closest end-of-year date.

[b] Includes the price increase during the first few days of listing, until a "plateau" price was established.

[c] Price increase from the date of listing to end-December of the IPO year. For IPOs listed in 2006, price increase until end-June 2006.

[d] Stock price increase weighted by its market capitalization.

Source: Bakheet Financial Advisors and Fund staff estimates.

listing or the first trading date. The percentage of equity capital offered at most IPOs has been kept to the legal minimum of 30 percent,[20] and the ownership of stocks not included in the IPOs remains very concentrated, thus further reducing the free float of shares. Although lock-ups have a preliminary positive impact on share price stability and growth by avoiding an increase of the float and keeping the supply of shares stable, this effect could have been reversed upon expiration of the lock-up period.

6.3.3 The impact of market and supervisory policies

Several market and supervisory policies have affected market developments. These include the authorities' measures to contain asset inflation, prudential measures, and IPO pricing policies during the boom period, and liquidity supporting and enhancing measures during and after the correction.

The authorities emphasized asset inflation containment measures and prudential oversight during the market's boom period. The CMA strengthened capital market regulatory and supervisory frameworks since its establishment and enforced these regulations through corrective actions. These measures helped enhance transparency and discourage insider trading and hence speculation and exuberant demand. To limit banks' direct and indirect exposure to the market and contain liquidity channeled to the market, SAMA introduced capital charges for market risk and a ceiling per customer on bank financing of IPO purchases in 2004. In addition, the tenor of consumer loans was reduced from 10 to 5 years and a cap on the amount of debt service at one-third of the borrower's net monthly salary was introduced. While these measures did not prevent the forming of the bubble, they may have limited the bubble's size and impact on the banking system and household net worth.

The policy of privatization and opening of regulated industries to private capital, that has been carried out through IPOs in which shares were offered at prices below their estimated economic values, may have contributed to the fueling of exuberant demand and volatility. About 30 percent of the increase in the TASI between January 2003 and June 2006 was due to the increase in the prices of shares offered through IPOs. Although this pricing policy has been common in other GCC countries, only the Doha Stock Exchange registered a higher impact on its general price index. While it has been an effective way of transferring part of the state's wealth to the Saudi population and deepening the capital market, it may have fueled investors' positive expectations and exuberant demand. In addition, this policy was extended to newly licensed firms entering sectors previously reserved for the public sector (such as telecommunications) or newly liberalized and regulated sectors (such as insurance).[21] Most IPO share price increases occurred in the first

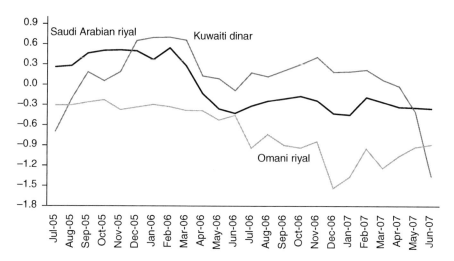

Figure 6.11 Interest rate margin between US dollar and selected GCC currencies, 2005–07 (Three-month interbank deposit rates)

Source: Saudi Arabian Monetary Agency.

few days of trading, thus reinforcing the hypothesis that this increase reflects mainly a proper assessment of their fair economic value by the market.[22]

After the start of the correction, the authorities eased monetary policy and applied indirect measures in an attempt to increase market liquidity. SAMA did not raise interest rates despite the increases in the US Federal Funds Rate during the second half of 2006, in order to avoid tightening liquidity in an environment of rapid market correction. In addition, a number of measures to open the market and increase transparency and oversight were implemented. Some of these were already under consideration, but had been delayed because of the continuing bull run.

Despite the sharp correction, the authorities refrained from direct intervention. The authorities had the means to intervene massively in the equity market, but they consistently resisted strong political pressures to do so. It is possible that state entities like GOSI may have been behind some buying. These operations, which might have been responses to genuine independent investment policies triggered by the attractive pricing of stocks, did not seem to have a substantial impact on the overall direction of market indices, but may have helped smooth out extreme fluctuations.

Some other measures implemented during the bubble episode, noted below, might have an impact on the market's future performance.[23]

■   Saudi Arabia opened its market to resident foreign investors (previously restricted to investment funds) during the correction periods. While the decision did not help to mitigate the correction, it will enhance market liquidity and hence the medium-term development of the market.

■ Prudential regulations governing investment funds, real estate funds, and corporate governance have been strengthened. These measures will also reinforce investors' confidence and promote market development.

■ The authorities allowed the splitting of stocks in early 2006. The decision has increased liquidity by facilitating small investors' access to the market and may have allowed a larger volume of intra-day operations. However, it might increase price volatility, the atomization of the market, and the exposure of small households to poorly understood market risk.

6.4   THE MARKET'S POOR PERFORMANCE DURING THE FIRST HALF OF 2007

The comparatively poor performance of the Saudi market in the first half of 2007 can be traced mainly to the fall in banking sector profitability. The stock market correction affected Saudi banks and financial institutions more deeply than it did its GCC peers. This is due to the stronger magnitude of the Tadawul correction, the lower income diversification of Saudi banks with a larger proportion of income from trading commissions and brokerage fees,[24] and their constrained asset/liability management.

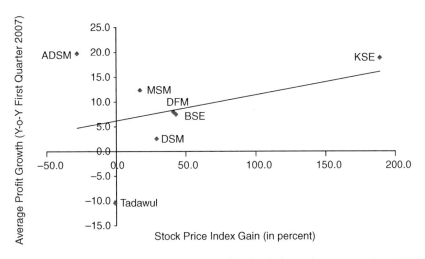

Figure 6.12   Corporate profitability vs. stock price index gain, January–June 2007

Sources: KAMCO; and Bloomberg.

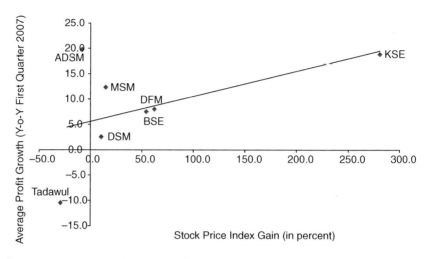

Figure 6.13   Financial sector profitability vs. stock price index gain, January–June 2007

Sources: KAMCO; and Bloomberg.

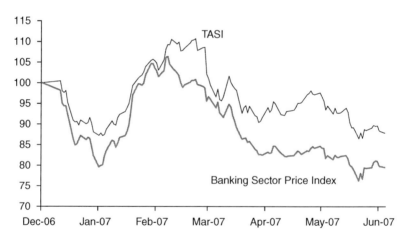

Figure 6.14   Saudi Arabia Stock Exchange: TASI and banking sector price index, December 2006–June 2007 (December 31, 2006=100)

Source: Bakheet Financial Advisors.

Also, financial institutions in other GCC countries, particularly in the United Arab Emirates, already reflected the impact of the correction in their 2006 financial statements,[25] while in Saudi Arabia, in part due to the lag in the correction, this impact started to appear in the results for the first half of 2007. Listed banks' average profit growth in 2006 was a healthy 31 percent, as income from the record-high first quarter compensated for a lower level of activity over the rest of the year. However,

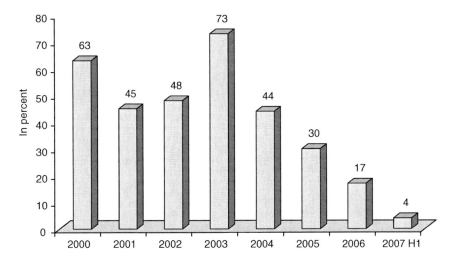

Figure 6.15   Average corporate profit growth, 2000–07 H1

Source: Bakheet Financial Advisors.

profits for the first half of 2007 have declined by an average of 15 percent, as banks have, in general, been unable to find alternative sources
of business to compensate for the missing stock market-related revenues.
This resulted in downward pressure on bank stock prices that, due to the
large capitalization of the sector,[26] pulled down the TASI. However, the
impact of the reduction in stock market-related income in banks' profits
is a short-term phenomenon. Profits will increase once the 2006 slump is
accounted for and banks begin to provide financing for the large number
of mega-projects slated for the near future.

The decreasing profitability trend since the beginning of the market
boom in 2003 has contributed to the low performance in the first half
of 2007. The profitability of Saudi Arabia's listed companies had been
remarkably high during the last decade, with rates of annual profit growth
well above 40 percent during 2000–05. However, profit growth rates
started to decline after the record growth in 2003, to the (still healthy, but
much lower) 17 percent in 2006. Prospects for 2007 are even lower, with
a disappointing 4 percent growth during the first half of the year, vis-à-vis
the first half of 2006.

The relatively less favorable valuation indicators and speculations on the
Saudi riyal in the first half of 2007 might have contributed to this weak
performance. As indicated in the panel chart (Figure 1.15), the correction
in the first half of 2007 has brought the valuation indicators of Saudi stocks
in line with regional levels indicating that the stocks were still overvalued
by regional standards in early 2007. The speculations on the Saudi riyal and

bidding on a stronger riyal, might have shifted some liquidity away from the market. This is especially true in the case of petrochemicals given that the revenues of this sector are indexed to the US dollar.[27]

6.5   WHY WERE FINANCIAL SECTOR STABILITY AND DOMESTIC DEMAND NOT AFFECTED BY THE STOCK MARKET CORRECTION?

Despite the sharp market correction in 2006, banking system soundness was not affected. The capital adequacy ratio increased for the banking system in 2006 to almost three times the minimum international standards (Table 1.17). The quality of assets, as measured by the non-performing loans ratio, is very high, with over 100 percent provision coverage. Banks were able to preserve their financial soundness because of the preemptive tightening of prudential regulations by SAMA, which limited banks' exposure to equity market risk. The banks' policy of using a large part of the profits recorded in 2006 to increase owners' equity also enhanced their financial strength.[28] The decline in profitability in the first half of 2007 is unlikely to have a significant impact on the solvency of the banking system.

The impact of the market correction on domestic demand was very limited. Domestic economic activity remained strong with non-oil GDP growing by 6.3 percent in 2006 from 5.2 percent in 2005. Although investors entering the market at its peak have lost about 60 percent of the value of

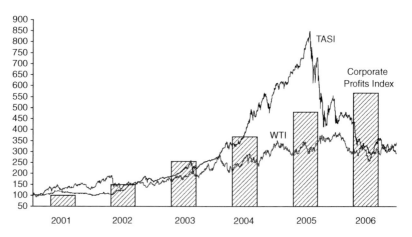

Figure 6.16   Saudi Arabia: Indices on stock prices, oil prices, and corporate profits of listed companies (2001=100)

Sources: Bloomberg; and Bakheet Financial Advisors.

their investments, those who invested at the beginning of 2003 and stayed in the market saw a hefty accumulated profit of about 300 percent. In addition, the authorities' policy of increasing public expenditure and reducing gasoline prices, as well as stronger private sector investment activity, more than offset the negative wealth effect of the correction.

Barring a further decline in the profitability of listed companies, another large correction in the TASI is unlikely. Currently, stock prices are in line with fundamentals, and in some cases below their historical values given their earning potential. High oil prices played an important role in improving the hydrocarbon sector's profits and strengthening investor confidence by providing assurances of exchange rate stability, easy monetary conditions, and better business opportunities due to higher public sector consumption and investment plans. The positive economic outlook provided strong support for fundamentals. However, structural weaknesses and speculative stocks could continue to fuel market volatility. Downside risks to this outlook are adverse geopolitical developments and a sharp decline in oil prices.

6.6 POLICY RECOMMENDATIONS

Authorities should continue focusing on measures that strengthen market resilience to speculative bubble developments and should address the structural weaknesses affecting market efficiency and liquidity. Many of the measures suggested in Chapter 1, Section 1.3, are relevant for the Saudi authorities. In addition, the authorities should enhance investors' financial education and awareness. Efforts to educate retail investors and to create professional and accountable financial advisory firms will go a long way toward eliminating the exuberant demand phenomena that characterized the Saudi market during 2005 and the early months of 2006. While such a program is part of the regulatory authority's ongoing efforts to enhance market stability, a more focused and well-coordinated program will pay for itself in terms of insurance against future potential unstable periods.

The authorities should examine options to reduce the volatility induced by small speculative stocks. While the current listing rules are consistent with international best practices and promote confidence in the market by enhancing transparency and improving the quality of investments available by creating quality hurdles for companies, they might not be effective in dealing with the problems associated with speculative stocks.[29] Despite the authorities' suspensions and corrective measures related to unfair trading on several occasions, such activities still represent an important source of instability in the market. Compliance with existing listing requirements should be strictly enforced, and an exit alternative for non-compliant firms should be designed.

The authorities should also consider the merits of establishing a second market for small capitalization (cap) companies. Creating a second market where such stocks could be listed, should be considered at a future stage, following the development of a stronger institutional investor group. This second tier market should be initially restricted to institutional and professional investors, thus reinforcing the message that retail investors should focus on the main market and see it as an exercise in investment based on the analysis of information disseminated by issuers rather than pure speculation. The small cap market could include companies delisted temporarily or permanently from the first market as well as companies that fail to fulfill the listing requirements for trading on the first market but meet the listing requirements for the second market. This market would also promote trading in stocks of small and medium-sized companies in a reliable and transparent environment and encourage family-owned businesses to go public.

NOTES

1. The average loss for the other booming markets was 35 percent.
2. The economic value of a stock should theoretically reflect the present value of the dividends the investor will receive.
3. Excluding negative earnings (Ned Davis Research, Inc., 2005).
4. Middle East Economic Digest (MEED), March 2005.
5. For other GCC countries, the compound annual rate ranged from 18.6 percent in Kuwait to 36.3 percent in Qatar, during 2003–05.
6. This does not include personal and corporate loans that are then used to purchase shares.
7. "Conventional" terms typically involve an overdraft line at an agreed interest rate based on the bank's base rate or the Saudi Interbank Offer Rate (SIBOR), with a one-year agreement to rollover, subject to review. "Murabaha" is a contract with a "cost plus" financing structure. A purchaser asks a bank to acquire a commodity or asset on its behalf with the understanding that the purchaser will re-purchase the item from the bank, on pre-determined terms (i.e., the profit margin and payment terms are agreed in advance). Usually the bank pays the seller on a spot basis and receives payment from the purchaser during a deferred payment period.
8. As identified by Bakheet Financial Advisor (BFA), one of the first investment firms licensed by the Capital Market Authority (CMA), speculative stocks in the Saudi market belong to companies with weak financial indicators, which historically do not pay dividends due to their recurring losses or small profits. The price performance of speculative stocks usually is more dependent on rumors spread by speculators than on the companies' own track record. Bakheet Small Cap index consists of the 20 smallest listed companies ranked by market capitalization is a good proxy for them.
9. The cumulative market capitalization of the 20 speculative stocks included in the BFA index did not exceed 2 percent of the total, while they accounted for 28 percent of the total market value of shares traded in 2005.
10. In the Abu Dhabi Stock Market (ADSM), six small capitalization companies (9 percent of market capitalization) accounted for 44 percent of the increase in the ADSM index during 2005. Similarly, in the Dubai Financial Market (DFM) four small capitalization companies (5 percent of market capitalization) accounted for 18 percent of the increase in the DFM index during the same period. In the Doha Securities Market (DSM), five small firms representing 3 percent of market capitalization contributed 34 percent of the total volume traded in 2005.

11. An abnormally large number of IPOs could be associated with riskier investments (exuberant demand). This was the case, for instance, during the dot.com bubble, the Al-Manakh bubble in Kuwait (1982), and the Omani bubble (1997).

12. The number of mutual funds has increased from 121 as of end-1998 to 215 as of March 2007. The number of participants grew dramatically in 2005 and the first quarter of 2006 from less than 200,000 to over 600,000, but began to decline after the correction.

13. Banks' total proprietary stock portfolios amounted to SRls 25.2 billion, or 2.9 percent of total assets, as of end-2006, out of which domestic stocks accounted for SRls 13.2 billion (1.5 percent of total assets, down from 1.9 percent at the end of 2005). The magnitude of the banks' proprietary stock portfolios has not changed substantially in the last six years relative to their asset size, but has been declining relative to market capitalization, following the rapid increase of the stock market until 2005.

14. The CMA introduced regulations to improve market information dissemination to individual investors by introducing competition in the brokerage of stocks and explicitly allowing brokers to render investment advisory services if they are licensed as investment advisors. However, investors may continue to rely on market rumors and trends.

15. The increase in the average number of shares traded per transaction in 2006 is due to the 5-to-1 split approved for all shares in April 2006, reducing the nominal value of shares from SRls 50 to SRls 10. Adjusting for the split, the average number of shares per transaction would have continued to fall in 2006.

16. Due to the severe price fall, market capitalization contracted in 2006 and the size of the Saudi market went from oversized to undersized in the regional and emerging markets context in a single year. In fact, Saudi Arabia went from being the biggest emerging equity market in the world, excluding Hong Kong, according to HSBC estimates (The Economist, August 18, 2005, http://www.economist.com/displaystory.cfm?story_id54304230) to falling below countries with lower GDP such as Chile or South Africa, according to the World Bank Emerging Markets Database. As a result, the once oversized Saudi capital market (market capitalization-to-GDP ratio of 210 percent as of end-2005) seems now undersized vis-à-vis the size of the country's economy, with a market capitalization-to-GDP ratio of 88.5 percent, well below most of its emerging market peers, including other Middle East and North African equity markets.

17. The average size of listed companies in the NASDAQ as of June 22, 2007, was $1.42 billion, slightly below the $1.94 billion average size of listed companies in the main Japanese stock markets as of May 31, 2007.

18. Market liquidity reflects the ability of the market to absorb temporary supply and demand imbalances. It measures how much the price will change for a given amount of incoming transactions. The larger the free float of stocks, the smaller the impact on prices for a given transaction size.

19. Since only dematerialized shares are allowed to trade on the stock exchange, this is considered a good proxy for the float of shares.

20. This rule was maintained for all IPOs until mid-2006, except for National Company for Cooperative Insurance's (NCCI) IPO, which reached 70 percent of its shares, and Al-Bilad Bank, with 50 percent. From 2006 onwards the range of shares offered has varied, but most issues are still within the range of 30–40 percent of capital.

21. Although article 98 of the Company Law allows shares of a joint stock company to be issued at a premium, the authorities have generally not allowed a joint stock company or its substantial shareholders to freely price the company's newly issued or resold shares at IPOs. The findings of Al-Hassan, Delgado, and Omran (IMF WP/07/149, July 1, 2007) confirm that the companies undergoing IPOs were a key determinant of abnormal returns. This shows the important impact on market prices of this wealth distribution policy.

22. In fact, despite the bear market in Saudi Arabia, the share prices of all the companies after one year of having launched an IPO have been above their IPO offer price in all cases except one.

23. Other GCC authorities introduced similar measures to cool down the market during the formation of the bubble and to expand demand and liquidity after the beginning of the correction.

24. Until 2007, only banks were allowed to provide these services.

25. All UAE banks, except one (Abu Dhabi Commercial Bank), have registered profit growth from the first half of 2006 to the first half of 2007.

26. Banking sector capitalization remains at about one-third of total market capitalization, despite its decline from 36.2 percent of total capitalization as of end-2006 to 32 percent as of end-June 2007.
27. SABIC PER was 11.4 in June 2007 compared with 14.1 for the market. The size of the hydrocarbon sector is small in other GCC stock markets.
28. In turn, this resulted in low dividends that further affected the market correction during January 2007.
29. The CMA Board was appointed in 2004 and hence many of these companies preceded its establishment and the recent listing regulations that were issued in early 2006.

REFERENCES

ABQ Zawya; http://www.zawya.com/

Backheet Financial Advisor; http://www.bfasaudi.com/bfamain.asp

Capital Market Authority; http://www.cma.org.sa/cma_en/default.aspx

The Economist, August 18, 2005, http://www.economist.com/displaystory.cfm?story_id=4304230

International Monetary Fund (IMF), (2004). Global Financial Stability Report, Market Developments and Issues (April).

International Monetary Fund (IMF); World Economic Outlook; www.imf.org

Middle East Economic Digest (MEED), Investment Projects Database.

Middle East Economic Digest (MEED), (2005). "HSBC-MEED Middle East Business Confidence Index (MEBCI)," MEED 25–31 (March).

NCCI; http://www.ncci.com.sa/

Ned Davis Research, Inc. "NASDAQ Composite Price/Earnings Ratio vs. Margin Debt" Ned Davis Research, Inc., 2005.

SABIC, Financial Statements, (2004–05). http://www.sabic.com/sabic-www/index_Latest_Results.htm

SAMA, Table 12a, Monthly Statistical Bulletin, April 2005. http://www.sama.gov.sa/indexe.htm

Tadawul Stock Market; http://www.tadawul.com.sa/wps/portal/!ut/p/_s.7_0_A/7_0_49I/.cmd/Change Language/.l/en

CHAPTER 7

Myth vs. Reality: Stock Price Bubbles in the UAE

Mohammed Omran[1]

7.1 INTRODUCTION

After an unprecedented increase in stock prices during the period 2003–05, both the Abu Dhabi Security Market (ADSM) and the Dubai Financial Market (DFM) experienced sharp declines in 2006, in line with other stock markets in the region (Box 7.1). During 2003–05, UAE stock prices increased at a rate far beyond the growth in economic activity in nominal terms. This vigorous increase was due largely to the improvements in macro- and microeconomic fundamentals, speculative demand, and market specific factors. As of end-June 2007, the ADSM and the DFM had declined by about 43 percent and 48 percent from their peaks in May and November 2005, respectively. This reflected the fact that stock prices were overpriced and did not match the firms' fundamentals.

The chapter concludes that (a) as of end-December 2005, UAE stocks were significantly overvalued; (b) with the latest waves of corrections in the market, the speculative bubble has virtually disappeared; (c) despite the sharp drop in equity prices, significant capital gains are likely to be retained as long as fundamentals remain strong; (d) the bursting of the bubble has adversely impacted many retail investors, but the real economy has not been significantly affected; and (e) further strengthening of capital market regulations and financial sector supervision will lead to greater market stability and better growth prospects in the future.

The rest of this chapter is organized as follows: Section 7.2 examines the main macroeconomic and market specific factors that pushed stock

Box 7.1   Capital Markets: Key Market Characteristics and Developments Leading up to the Market Correction

The Dubai Financial Market (DFM) and the Abu Dhabi Security Market (ADSM) were established in March and November 2000, respectively. From December 2003 to December 2005, the DFM index increased by about 748 percent, versus 255 percent for the ADSM index. Although both markets showed significant increases in terms of all market activity indicators (value of trade, volume of trade, number of transactions, and the turnover ratio), the DFM surpassed the ADSM in all of the above-mentioned market activity indicators. For example, the value of trade and the turnover ratio in the DFM in 2005 was $107.5 billion and 95.2 percent, respectively, some four times the corresponding indicators for the ADSM.

The firm level and fundamental indicators also showed differences. Although both markets had similar Price Earnings Ratios (PER) in 2003, the sharp increase in the DFM index pushed the PER to a much higher level when compared with the ADSM. As of November 2005, the PER and Price-to-Book Value Ratio (PBV) for the six largest companies that accounted for 60 percent of the ADSM's market capitalization – which stood at 45.2 and 9.2, respectively – were significantly lower than those reported for similar companies in the DFM (66.5 and 13.8). Also, the Dividend Yield ratio (DY) at 0.56 percent for the ADSM sample firms was much higher than that of the DFM at 0.24 percent.

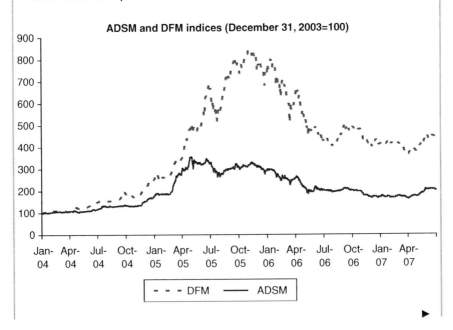

ADSM and DFM indices (December 31, 2003=100)

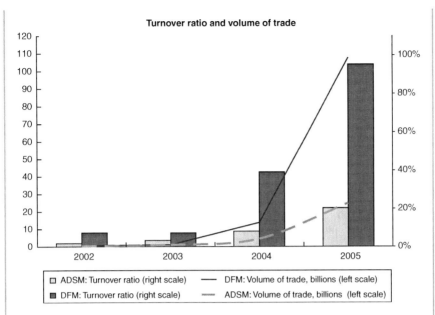

Sources: DFM; ADSM; and Fund staff estimates.

Key market indicators for the biggest 10 companies in the UAE as of November 2005 (6 companies for ADSM and 4 companies for DFM)

Indicators	ADSM	DFM
YTD%	112.40%	274.30%
Market share	60.10%	63.40%
Market cap. (in $ billion)	73.7	71.5
PER	45.2	66.5
PBV	9.2	13.8
DY%	0.56%	0.24%
Beta	1.4	2.9

Sources: Shuaa Capital; and Fund staff estimate.

While the ADSM was dominated by the telecom (Etisalat) and banking sectors in terms of market capitalization, the DFM was dominated by the real estate and banking sectors. The DFM index was heavily driven by Emaar Properties, which accounted for around 50 percent of index movements. Moreover, following the correction, the DFM declined somewhat more precipitously than the ADSM. As of end-June 2007, the

▶

DFM had declined by about 48 percent from its peak, while the ADSM had dropped by around 43 percent from its highest point in May 2005. It should be noted, however, that as of June 2007, both markets remained substantially higher than their pre-bubble valuations. Specifically, the ADSM and the DFM indices were about 102 percent and 341 percent higher than their levels at end-December 2003, respectively.

prices beyond their fundamentals. Section 7.3 discusses the warning signals that pointed to the emergence of a bubble prior to the recent correction. Section 7.4 discusses the implications of the stock price correction on the UAE's financial stability and economic growth. Finally, Section 7.5 discusses a few policy recommendations.

7.2   FACTORS THAT CONTRIBUTED TO THE STOCK PRICE BUBBLE IN THE UAE

Several factors contributed to the stock price bubble in the UAE markets. These factors can be classified into three main categories: economic fundamentals, which laid the foundation for the market to grow in all its dimensions; factors contributing to speculative demand, which pushed the stock prices beyond the fundamentals; and structural weaknesses in the UAE equity markets.

7.2.1   Economic fundamentals underpinning the increase in stock prices

There is a strong relationship between the performance of UAE capital markets and oil prices. The increase in oil prices since 2003 resulted in higher economic growth and improved corporate profitability. A regression analysis of the semi-annual ADSM and DFM indices and the semi-annual price of West Texas Intermediate (WTI) oil for the period June 2000 to December 2005 shows that there was a strong relationship between oil market developments and the performance of the UAE stock market.[2] Although oil comes mostly from Abu Dhabi, the effect of higher hydrocarbon prices spilled over to the neighboring Dubai market. Moreover, other Gulf Cooperation Council (GCC) investors, enticed by high oil prices, targeted Dubai as a preferred destination for their investments. As indicated in Figure 7.1, the relationship was particularly strong until mid-2004. Thereafter, speculative forces pushed stock prices well beyond what could be justified by oil price developments.

Table 7.1 Regression of the relationship between oil prices and UAE stock market indices, June 2000–December 2005

Abu Dhabi Security Market

Dependent variable	ADSM Index
Intercept	−1969
	(−2.86)**
Oil prices (WTI)	122.5
	(6.96)***
No. of observations	9
Adjusted R^2 (%)	85.6
F - Ratio	48.4***

Dubai Financial Market

Dependent variable	DFM Index
Intercept	−717
	(−5.42)***
Oil prices (WTI)	28.9
	(8.1)***
No. of observations	12
Adjusted R^2 (%)	85.4
F - Ratio	65.6***

UAE Stock Markets (Fixed effect model-unbalanced panel)

Dependent variable	UAE Stock Markets
Oil prices (WTI)	61.1
	(4.26)***
No. of observations	21
Adjusted R^2 (%)	63.2
F - Ratio	24.6***

Notes:
** and *** refers to 5 and 1% significance level respectively.
Figures between parentheses are *t* statistics.
All regression results are based on semi-annual data (December 2001–December 2005 for ADSM and June 2000–December 2005 for DFM.

Unrealistic earnings expectations led to the apparent overvaluation of UAE stocks. The profitability growth rate of the biggest companies listed in the UAE stock markets grew substantially over the period leading up to the correction. A closer look at the performance of UAE stocks during 2005 reveals that earnings grew by approximately 80.5 percent for ADSM-listed companies and 116 percent for DFM-listed companies. As an example, Emaar Properties, a DFM-listed company with the largest market capitalization, achieved earnings growth of 180 percent in 2005. However, such high profitability growth rates could not persist for long and there were

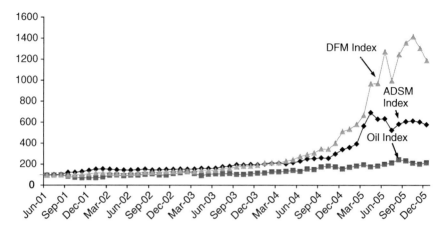

Figure 7.1 ADSM, DFM, and oil prices (Normalized at 100)

Sources: ADSM; and DFM.

Table 7.2 Key market indicators, November 2005

Market	PER	PBV	Dividend yield (%)	Earnings growth% (2002–04)	Last year (2005) earning growth %
Dow 30 averages	24.1	3.9	1.9	9.6	13.4
S&P 500	30.5	2.9	1.5	10.5	21
TASI	35.2	8	1.7	53	n.a.
Kuwait[a]	16.2	3	2.9	30.4	n.a.
UAE-Abu Dhabi[b]	57.7	10.9	0.56	24.3	80.5
UAE-Dubai[b]	74.37	15.4	0.24	58.7	115.9
UAE Total[b]	67.57	13.4	0.45	37.1	96.8

Notes:

[a] May 2005, earnings growth between 1998 and 2004.

[b] Earnings growth based on average 2002–04 growth rate. Data cover the biggest market capitalization firms in both markets (the average is 60% for ADSM, 63% FOR DFM and 62% for the entire UAE market).

Sources: Bloomberg; stockselector.com; Bakheet Financial Advisor; KAMCO (Kuwait Economic Brief & Market Outlook, June, 2005); ADSM; DFM and Fund staff estimates.

already some signs that many of the leading companies listed on the stock market were not able to meet investors' expectations in the first half of 2006 as earnings growth slowed significantly. During that period, and in contrast to 2005, earnings grew at a rate of 23 percent and 19 percent for companies listed on the ADSM and the DFM, respectively.

7.2.2 Speculative demand factors

The increase in equity prices was partly driven by the substantial increase in money and credit expansion.[3] The annual growth of broad money increased from 23.2 percent in 2004 to 33.8 percent in 2005, compared with the 15.5 percent annual average during 2000–03. This acceleration in money growth can be partially attributed to the strong rate of increase in credit to the private sector, which grew by 24.7 percent in 2004 and 44.5 percent in 2005 (compared with an annual average of about 11 percent during 2000–03). In particular, personal loans increased sharply and accounted for 27.6 percent of total bank

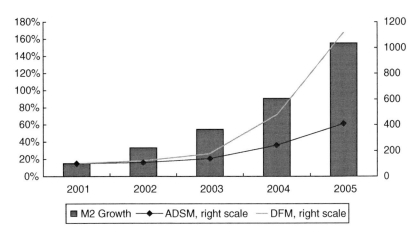

Figure 7.2 Cumulative growth in money supply and ADSM, DFM 2001–05
(Indices are Normalized to 100 in 2001)

Sources: IMF; information notice system; and country authorities.

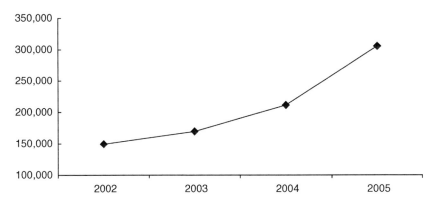

Figure 7.3 Claims on private sector (in millions of UAE dirhams)

Sources: IMF; Information Notice System; and Country authorities.

loans in 2005, as opposed to 24.1 percent in 2004. Taking into account that a substantial portion of personal loans may have been used to leverage investor positions, the maximum absolute value of leveraged positions in the UAE markets might be similar to the ratios observed in the dot.com bubble.[4] Moreover, the banking system's ample liquidity and high profitability enabled financial institutions to continue their lending policies and meet the increasing demand on margin and personal loans at relatively low interest rates.[5]

The large number of Initial Public Offerings (IPOs) in the UAE markets during 2004–05 appears to have fed the bubble phenomenon. This seems to be similar to the greater than average number of IPOs placed during the dot.com episode.[6] Furthermore, the incredible and somewhat irrational euphoria surrounding IPOs raised concerns as many of the issuers were start-ups or greenfield companies that did not have a financial track record. As an example of the market's exuberance, the IPO launched by the start-up Aabar Petroleum Investments in April 2005 was 800 times oversubscribed, drawing applications worth $100 billion – approximately equal to the UAE's GDP at that time.

Increased regional liquidity, reflecting a shift in investors' preferences (and thus in the pattern of capital flows) toward regional assets, helped move

Table 7.3 Summary indicators on the most actively traded companies in the ADSM and DFM (As of November 2005)

Description	Market	Big market cap.[a]	Small market cap.[a]	Total
No. companies	ADSM	4	6	10
	DFM	7	4	11
No. transactions (% of the market)	ADSM	19%	47%	66%
	DFM	61%	29%	90%
Volume of trade (% of the market)	ADSM	14%	42%	56%
	DFM	58%	314%	89%
Value of trade (% of the market)	ADSM	34%	40%	73%
	DFM	76%	17%	93%
Market cap. (% of the market)	ADSM	59%	9%	68%
	DFM	74%	5%	79%
Weighted average return	ADSM	138%	478%	
	DFM	278%	354%	
Contribution to the index	ADSM	82%	44%	125%
	DFM	205%	18%	224%

Notes:
[a] Big market cap. refers to the largest companies in the market capitalization and small market cap. refers to the smallest companies on same term.

Sources: ADSM; DFM and Fund staff estimates.

prices above their fundamentals. Net private capital outflows from the region decreased in the period preceding the correction, partially due to heightened international security concerns. The change in the pattern of capital flows contributed to the increase in the narrow and broad money aggregates in the GCC region. Given the relative scarcity of available domestic assets, this helped shore up local stock and real estate prices.

7.2.3 Market specific characteristics

The UAE markets showed partial and recurring signs of narrow market leadership. Between 2004 and 2005, the four largest companies in the ADSM, represented 59.3 percent of market capitalization, but accounted for only 19.1 percent of the total number of transactions, 4.1 percent of the volume of trade, and 33.7 percent of the value of trade. Their weighted average price index increased broadly in line with the ADSM index and they accounted for about 82 percent of the market's gains.[7] At the other end, six small cap companies (9.1 percent of total market capitalization) accounted for 46.9 percent of the total number of transactions, 41.6 percent of the volume of trade, and 39.5 percent of the value of trade. Also, their weighted average price index increased by 478.4 percent – substantially above the increase in the ADSM index. The activity and performance of these small and volatile companies signaled some sort of bubble. The DFM also experienced a similar trend. Moreover, in the DFM, one company

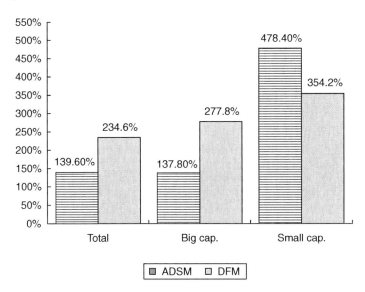

Figure 7.4   YTD for DFM and ADSM and most actively traded big cap. and small cap. companies

Sources: ADSM; DFM and Fund staff estimates.

(Emaar Properties) dominated the market. Because of the market's thinness, changes in one company could potentially affect the whole market. During January to November 2005, Emaar alone contributed 118 percentage points, or 50 percent of the total gain in the DFM index.

The large size of the UAE equity market in terms of market capitalization contrasted with the relatively small number of listed stocks. In December 2005, the UAE market was the second largest market by capitalization in the Arab world. However, only 80 UAE companies were registered on the ADSM and the DFM. As a result, the average market value of the UAE listed companies approached $3 billion – well above emerging and industrial equity market standards.[8] The concentration of market value in a few large firms increased the vulnerability of UAE equity markets to speculative operations. Not only were there relatively few UAE companies, but the volume of shares available for trading in the market was also limited. Empirical studies show a negative relationship between the size of the free float of shares[9] and the propensity for speculative bubbles. The fact that some of the largest listed companies in the UAE market – including Emaar Properties and Emirates Telecommunications – are majority state- and institution-owned, de facto reduces the amount of stocks effectively available for trade.[10] The ADSM ownership structure indicates that more than 50 percent of the market capitalization of listed companies is owned by the state and public corporations.

The privatization policy and listing regulations of IPOs led to sharp increases in share prices, which explained a significant portion of both ADSM and DFM growth. As an effective way of transferring part of the state's wealth to the UAE population at large, while deepening capital markets, privatization was carried out through IPOs in which shares were offered at prices below their estimated economic values. The IPO offering price of both state-owned and private companies was set by the Ministry of Economy at nominal value and often did not reflect the fair market value of the issuing company. The valuation of the issuing companies was also complicated by the fact that a number of them were new firms that had no prior financial track

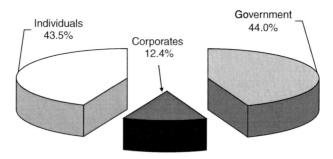

Figure 7.5   Ownership structure of listed companies in ADSM in 2005

Source: Fund staff estimates.

Table 7.4 Summary information on some recent IPOs in the UAE markets, December 2005

Panel A: Abu Dhabi Security Market

Company	Date	$ millions	% Equity offered	Over-subscription (times)	Offer price (Dirham)	First day price	Return since floatation
Al Dar Properties	Nov-4	224.5	55%	448	1.0	7.59	930%
Emirates Food Stuff and Mineral Water Company	Jan-5	80.0	49%	8	1.0	7.41	226%
Sorouh Real Estate Company	Jan-5	378.0	55%	176	1.0	6.72	500%
Aabar Petroleum Investments Company	Apr-5	134.7	55%	796	1.0	5.34	431%
Abu Dhabi National Takaful Co.	Apr-5	9.0	55%	n.a.	1.0	5.00	581%
RAK Properties	Apr-5	299.3	55%	57	1.0	4.25	295%
Finance House	May-4	29.9	55%	75	1.0	14.55	1730%
Abu Dhabi National Energy Co.	Sep-5	163.3	14%	350	1.0	7.92	423%
Dana Gas	Oct-5	567.0	35%	140	1.0	4.12	350%
Emirates Driving Company	Oct-5	14.1	63%	n.a.	10.0	15.00	60%

Panel B: Dubai Financial Market

Company	Date	$ millions	% Equity offered	Over-subscription (times)	Offer price (Dirham)	First day price	Return since floatation
Dubai Islamic Insurance and Reinsurance	Oct-2	3.2	55%	5	3.5	17.21	1622%
Amlak Finance	Feb-4	112.0	55%	33	1.0	2.52	1835%
Arab International Logistics Company	Jul-5	149.7	55%	80	1.0	4.25	440%
Arab Technical Construction Company	Aug-4	60.0	55%	65	1.0	4.88	620%

Source: Shuaa Capital; and Fund staff estimates.

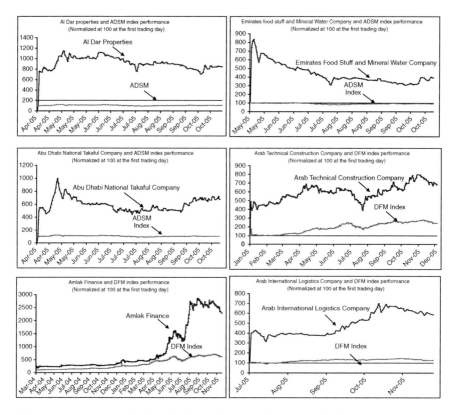

Figure 7.6   UAE: Evolution of selected IPO stock prices in both ADSM and DFM indices, 2004–05

record. Moreover, the initial undervaluation of IPOs may have been compounded by the exuberance of market participants whose over-subscriptions were often financed through excessive borrowing. During 2005, IPOs contributed 77 percent and 10 percent to the increases in the ADSM and DFM price indices, respectively.[11] The fact that the initial returns on IPOs in the United Arab Emirates were far greater than in other developed and emerging markets further reaffirms this evidence.[12] However, a certain degree of investors' over-optimism about the IPOs when the market is booming could be observed in the UAE equity market, as indicated by the extraordinary over-subscription and the relatively short track record of some of the IPO firms.

Traditional institutional investors, such as pension funds, life insurance companies, and market makers that provide a stabilizing factor in financial markets, are relatively underdeveloped in the UAE. Although the number of insurance companies is growing in the UAE, their role and participation in stock market activities tend to be limited. Moreover, given the size of the UAE market, the evolution of mutual funds has lagged behind other emerging markets.

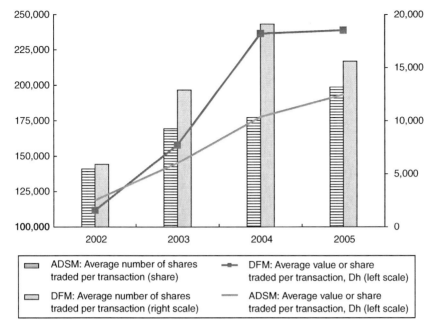

Figure 7.7   Average number and value of shares traded per transaction
Sources: DFM; ADSM; and Fund staff estimates

Most of the activities in the UAE market came from individuals rather than companies or institutional investors. A substantial increase in the number of investors has been associated with a number of stock market bubbles, particularly in emerging markets.[13] Most of these new investors, lacking the ability to analyze fundamentals and acting on the basis of rumors, helped propel speculative demand.[14] Although the number of investors grew substantially along with the huge increase in the number of transactions, the average size of transactions has also increased. This might indicate that the average unit price of shares has increased and the market is driven by more liquidity along with a greater number of wealthy investors.

7.3   WARNING SIGNALS IN THE UAE MARKET

This section analyzes whether there were significant warning signals pointing to the existence of a stock market bubble. Looking back, it seems that there were three major warning signals indicating the development of a speculative bubble in the UAE stock markets: (a) a rapid increase in the price index; (b) a weak correlation between the price and economic value of stocks; and (c) high price volatility.

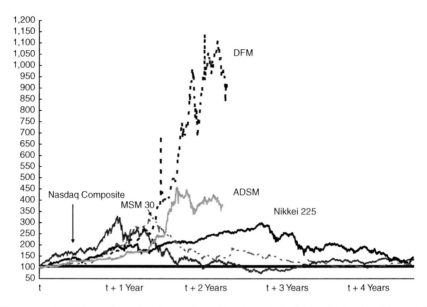

Figure 7.8 Selected stock price indices (Nasdaq, Nikkei 225, MSM 30, DFM and ADSM are normalized to 100 at start of rapid price increase periods)

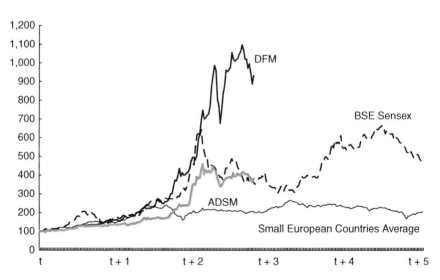

Figure 7.9 Selected stock price indices average of the Spain, Ireland and Portugal stock price indices (from 1995), DFM (from 2003), and Bombay Stock Exchange index (from 1991), Normalized to 100 at the start of rapid rice increase periods

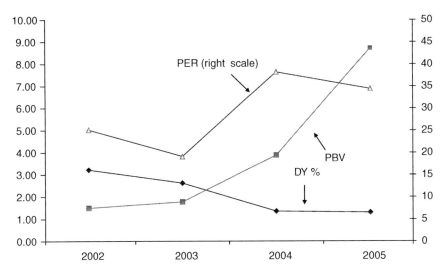

Figure 7.10   DFM: All companies PER, PBV, and DY (2002–05)

Source: DFM.

7.3.1   Rapid increase in the price index

The ADSM and the DFM general price indices increased by 280 and 832 percent, respectively, from March 2003 to December 2005. These increases were larger than the price hikes observed during the Nikkei bubble of the late 1980s, the Omani (Muscat Securities Market [MSM]) bubble of 1998, and the NASDAQ dot.com bubble of 1999. The value of trade in the ADSM reached $24.9 billion in 2005, almost 25 and 5.6 times its 2003 and 2004 levels, respectively. It was also four times the cumulative sum of value traded since the establishment of the formal market in November 2000. The volume of trade, the trading value, and the turnover ratio, all continued to grow in 2005. The DFM experienced even more significant increases in the above-mentioned indicators.

7.3.2   Weak correlation between price and economic value

An assessment based on the Price-Earning Ratio (PER), Price-to-Book Value ratio (PBV), and the Dividend Yield Ratio (DY) would conclude that stocks in both the ADSM and the DFM were highly overpriced by end-2005. In both markets the average PER and PBV grew rapidly and stood at record high levels.[15] Similarly, the DY decreased substantially as prices began to accelerate. When compared with other industrial and emerging markets,[16] it is evident that the average of these indicators point toward a

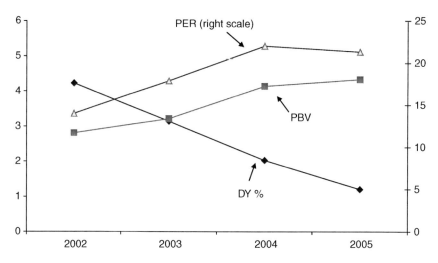

Figure 7.11   ADSM–all companies PER, PBV, and DY (2002–05)

Source: ASDM.

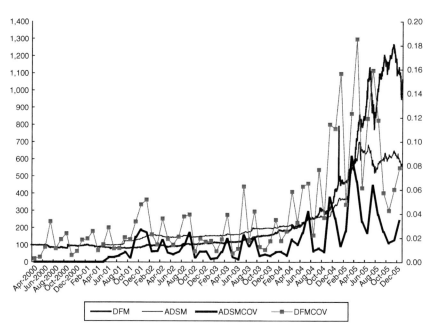

Figure 7.12   Daily ADSM and DFM indices (Normalized at 100 at the beginning of each index and monthly coefficient of variation)

Sources: ADSM; DFM; and Fund staff estimates.

Table 7.5 Key market indicators for the biggest ten companies in the UAE (2004 earnings and November 2005 prices)

Company	Stock exchange	YTD	PER	PBV	DY	Market cap. ($Billion)	Market share	Ranking
Emaar Properties	DFM	369.2%	75.7	17.1	0.2%	40.3	17.2%	1
Emirates Telecommunication Corporation – Etisalat	ADSM	34.3%	25.6	6.5	0.9%	25.2	10.8%	2
National Bank of Abu Dhabi	ADSM	218.8%	38.5	9.1	0.7%	14.6	6.2%	3
Dubai Islamic Bank	DFM	256.5%	96.4	17.2	N.A.	12.7	5.4%	4
Abu Dhabi Commercial Bank	ADSM	205.9%	46.3	8.1	N.A.	11.8	5.1%	5
Emirates Bank International	DFM	47.1%	41.6	7.0	0.7%	11.4	4.9%	6
Dana Gaz	ADSM	N.A.	N.A.	N.A.	N.A.	8.0	3.4%	7
National Bank of Ras Al Kheimeh	ADSM	N.A.	128.4	26.2	0.8%	7.5	3.2%	8
Mashreq Bank	DFM	131.0%	34.3	5.7	1.0%	7.0	3.0%	9
First Gulf Bank	ADSM	273.4%	93.9	13.4	0.3%	6.5	2.8%	10
Weighted average		315.7%	53.1	11.3	0.5%	145. 2	62.0%	

Sources: Shuaa Capital; and Fund staff estimates.

generalized overpricing of both the ADSM and the DFM. Furthermore, the average PER of the ten largest UAE companies (listed on the ADSM and the DFM), which accounted for 62 percent market capitalization, was 53 as of end-2005. This was at least twice the international standard and was closer to the average PER of 61 for the NASDAQ[17] and 50 for the S&P 500, at the peak of the dot.com bubble. Similarly, the PBV of the ten largest companies was 11.3, a level that is hard to observe in other markets. Additionally, the average DY at 0.45 percent was much lower than in other markets. Another striking figure was that the price index of the ten largest companies in the UAE market increased by 315.7 percent over the preceding 12-month period[18] – a rate of return that far exceeded the observed figures for most countries around the globe.

7.3.3   High price volatility

Both the ADSM and the DFM experienced substantial increases in volatility as measured by the monthly standard deviation and coefficient of variation of the price indices. Price volatility tends to increase substantially in the period immediately before a price bubble bursts. The increases in the coefficient of variation of the ADSM (318 percent) and the DFM (380 percent) between March 2003 and December 2005,[19] are higher than those recorded for the NASDAQ price index during the dot.com bubble (224 percent increase in the coefficient of variation between October 1999 and April 2000) and the MSM price index during the Omani bubble (121 percent increase in the coefficient of variation between February and August 1997).

When we split the indices to compare the monthly standard deviation and coefficient of variation in the periods before and during the sharp stock price increases, we find significant differences. The results show that the mean (median) standard deviation and coefficient of variation of the ADSM and DFM stock price indices increased significantly after March 2003. The differences are statistically significant at the 1 percent level.

7.4   IMPACT OF THE STOCK MARKET CORRECTION

In general, the UAE economy has not been significantly affected by the correction in equity markets. Whether in terms of financial sector stability or wealth effects affecting household consumption, the economy proved to be resilient to the sharp drop in asset prices.

The effect of the stock price correction does not seem to have had a significant effect on the household sector. Given that the UAE equity markets were dominated by individual investors, one could have expected that the

Table 7.6 Test for significance differences in monthly standard deviation and coefficient of variation in the pre- and post-March 2003[a]

Variables		Before March 2003		After March 2003		Difference (after-before)		T-statistic for difference in mean		Z-statistic for difference in median	
		ADSM	DFM	ADSM	DFM	ADSM	DFM	ADSM	DFM	ADSM	DFM
Standard deviation	Mean	13.46	1.47	88.14	22.48	74.7	20.98	3.22***	4.24***	3.60***	4.38***
	Median	11.53	1.57	35.61	8.07	24.1	6.91				
Coefficient of variation	Mean	0.011	0.016	0.023	0.038	0.012	0.022	2.36**	3.51***	1.78*	3.49**
	Median	0.009	0.012	0.019	0.027	0.003	0.017				

Notes: [a]The table shows the results of sub-period comparisons of monthly standard deviation and coefficient of variation over two intervals; the pre- and post-stock price bubbles for the ADSM and the DFM. The parametric t-test has been employed to determine the significance in the differences in the mean values and the non-parametric Wilcoxon signed-rank test has been used for the significance to determine differences in median values ***, ** and * indicate statistical significance at 1, 5 and 10 percent significance levels, respectively.

reduction in household wealth resulting from the sharp correction would significantly impact the economy at large.[20] However, this does not seem to have occurred. The UAE's robust and diversified economy was able to weather the sharp blow to the equity markets, with real domestic demand and real non-oil GDP both increasing by about 9 percent in 2006. Moreover, it should be noted that although a number of late entrants were burnt by the bursting of the bubble, others investors who entered the market during 2003–04 have made substantial gains. In fact, as of June 2007, the ADSM and the DFM indices were still considerably higher than their earlier levels in December 2003 (Box 7.1).

7.5 SOME POLICY RECOMMENDATIONS

During the correction phase, the authorities have appropriately not intervened in the stock market. The authorities' conscious policy of non-intervention in the market has sent a clear signal and will help prevent future stock market bubbles. This section spells out some policy recommendations aimed at protecting the financial sector from future shocks and sustaining the economy's growth momentum.

It is difficult to judge the appropriate role of monetary policy within the context of a stock market bubble. Given the difficulty of assessing the size of the bubble and the impact of monetary instruments on stock prices, monetary intervention needs to be applied judiciously. As a rule, monetary authorities should generally react to key macroeconomic challenges and not to specific stock price shocks,[21] unless the stability of the financial and payment systems is threatened. Moreover, the type of exchange rate regime in place has a direct effect on the degrees of freedom available to policy makers. In the future, the UAE monetary authorities could help contain speculative demand by maintaining the amount of liquidity within reasonable parameters. Central Bank-issued Certificates of Deposits (CDs) are the main vehicle by which excess market liquidity is currently mopped up. However, there is no secondary-market for these securities, which are issued on demand. By developing a market for sovereign debt, the authorities would introduce new monetary tools that could allow them, for example, to conduct open market operations in the future. This would also help create a benchmark yield curve for domestic debt that is essential for the proper pricing of risk in the UAE financial markets.

Strict compliance with existing prudential regulations will limit the impact of a possible future correction on the soundness of financial institutions. To avoid an increase in banks' direct exposure to the equity market, the UAE Central Bank had already introduced a number of new measures when the markets were still moving upward.[22] It has also tightened regulations on consumer lending, in an attempt to contain the increase in other sources of credit that are being used to leverage investors' positions in the equity market. Additionally, the adoption of comprehensive risk management strategies, policies and systems, and their implementation in financial institutions would be important for the supervisory authorities. These actions will require close oversight by the UAE Central Bank and it should be ready to further tighten prudential regulations, if necessary, by (a) implementing stricter information requirements on the uses of bank credit; (b) increasing the weight of assets exposed to equity market risk in the capital adequacy ratio; (c) further tightening the collateral requirements for margin lending and other loans used directly or indirectly to leverage equity investments; and (d) taking prompt corrective action on any bank with excessive exposure to equity risk which could be characterized as an unsafe or unsound practice.

The authorities could continue to build on the broad-based structural reforms implemented in recent years that helped transform the economic structure of the United Arab Emirates. While acknowledging that aggressive structural reforms – including efforts to diversify the economy away from oil – have enhanced the private sector's role in the economy, more needs to be done. Among the favorable reforms which are likely to have a permanent impact on the stability and growth of UAE capital markets are (a) the privatization, liberalization, and outsourcing to the private sector of key companies and activities previously dominated by the public sector; (b) the public listing of quasi-public companies – such as Dubai Holding and Dubai World – that are coveted by global investors; (c) further trade liberalization within the context of the WTO, the Greater Arab Free Trade Agreement (GAFTA), and possible free trade agreements with the EU and other countries; and (d) progress toward economic integration through the formation of the planned GCC monetary union by 2010.

Strengthening the capital market regulatory framework and further developing the supervisory capabilities of the Emirates Securities and Commodities Authority (ESCA) will create more stability in the market.[23] Over the last few years, the legal and institutional underpinnings of the capital market have been going through major transformations. The legal and institutional enhancements accompanied the rapid and substantial growth in the stock markets. The regulatory and supervisory functions have been transferred to ESCA, while the operational responsibilities remain with the stock exchanges. However, ESCA should continue to strengthen its supervisory capabilities by (a) strictly enforcing regulations, including disclosure requirements; (b) taking prompt corrective actions against violators; (c) increasing efforts to improve investors' access to information through timely dissemination requirements; (d) expeditiously developing the supervisory skills and mechanisms that are necessary to oversee investment funds;

and (v) updating current regulations governing capital markets, generally, and investment funds, specifically.

Encouraging the participation of institutional investors and the development of the corporate bond market will increase the efficiency of capital markets and mitigate speculative demand. This could be achieved through (a) creating a more active role for the insurance sector in stock market activities; (b) analyzing the causes for the underdevelopment of mutual and private pension funds, and removing the obstacles to their growth; (c) accelerating the development of the corporate bond market; and (d) further liberalizing foreign investors' access to the local market. Although the United Arab Emirates is considered a leader among the GCC countries in allowing foreign investor participation in direct stock trading, further liberalization will also lead to better stock market monitoring and more diversification and entrepreneurship.

The careful introduction of more sophisticated financial instruments would be conducive to a more efficient allocation of risk among market participants, hence greater efficiency. Introducing derivatives and applying more sophisticated approaches to measuring and managing risk could be key to the development of UAE capital markets. Additionally, given that margin trading is widely used in the UAE market, short-selling – which is the other face of the coin and is currently not allowed – should be carefully examined as it could help enhance market stability in the long run.

In conclusion, although the UAE economy has proven its resilience to a sharp swing in equity prices, its ability to maintain a robust growth rate depends on continued financial and structural reforms. To this end, greater efforts are needed to increase the depth and diversification of capital markets, while developing the information base available to domestic market participants and opening the door to foreign investors. The UAE capital markets have certainly come a long way since their establishment in 2000. Their future success will now depend on their ability to successfully adapt to the constantly evolving world of international finance.

NOTES

1. This paper has benefited from useful updates provided by Mr. Mohamed Jaber.
2. The relationship is positive and significant at the 1 percent level.
3. Barry Eichengreen and Hui Tong (2003), using over a century of data for 12 countries, found a positive association between monetary volatility and stock market volatility in almost every country studied.
4. Total margin lending was estimated at about 2.3 percent of the value of common stocks listed on the NYSE and the NASDAQ during the dot.com bubble (Peter Fortune, 2001).
5. Anecdotal evidence shows that the increase in liquidity and credit extended to the private sector have been associated with the rise in stock prices in most bubble episodes.
6. We were able to find only five IPOs for the period 1995 to 2001. In contrast, about 16 IPOs were issued over the period 2002–06 (although most of these IPOs were placed on the ASDM in 2005).

7. January to November 2005. The same time frame was applied to the DFM.

8. The average size of listed companies in the NASDAQ at end-2004 was $1.14 billion, similar to the $1.09 billion average size of listed companies in the main Japanese stock markets as of September 2005.

9. The free float is the amount of shares available to ordinary investors for trade (i.e., not held by insiders or in the investment portfolio of institutional investors) and is expressed as a percentage of the total number of shares. The balance of a company's share capital traditionally will be in the form of strategic holdings, effectively excluded from normal dealing.

10. Hong, Sheinkman, and Xiong (2005) find that the role of lock-up expirations is relevant in explaining the burst of the dot.com bubble in the US stock market in 2000. Also, they find empirical evidence that the impact of lock-ups is inversely correlated to the size of the float and directly correlated with the risk absorption capacity of the market. Lock-ups are contractual commitments by the issuer to hold its shares for a period (normally six months) in order to prevent rent extraction from underwriters, signal firm quality, and alleviate moral hazard problems. In recent years, lock-up clauses have become an industry standard affecting over 80 percent of IPOs in industrial countries.

11. There were practically no significant IPOs during 2003 and 2004. Thus, the weighted effect of the IPO underpricing policy on the ADSM and DFM price indices during 2002–05 could be estimated to be up to 30 percent and 4 percent for the ADSM and DFM, respectively.

12. Loughran, Ritter, and Rydqvist (1994) updated their information in the Pacific-Basin Finance Journal article in May 2004 and found that the average initial returns for 38 countries are as low as 5.4 percent for Canada and as high as 256.9 percent for China. The figure stands at 594.8 percent for the United Arab Emirates.

13. See footnote 41.

14. Although the authorities made significant efforts to improve the dissemination of market information, the market is in need of more transparency through the promotion of timely disclosure and dissemination of information to the public, so as to allow investors to analyze the data and make their investment decisions based on these data.

15. The PERs for the ADSM and DFM were above 35 and 40 times at the peak date of each index, respectively.

16. In fact, the PER can be considered as the inverse of domestic long bond yields (around 6 percent on five-year government bonds in the UAE) plus a 2 percent risk premium. This translates to 18 (16 percent plus 2 percent). PBV, which is the most important indicator for financial institutions, exceeds 5 for the UAE and is well above the acceptable averages worldwide of around 2.

17. Excluding negative earnings (Ned Davis Research, Inc., 2005).

18. Until November 2005.

19. The coefficient of variation of both the ADSM and the DFM indices increased from 0.008 and 0.011 in March 2003 to 0.035 and 0.044 in December 2005, respectively.

20. This argument is based on the assumption that stock price changes may reduce consumption more than they increase it (Shirvani and Wilbratte, 2000).

21. Mishkin and White (2003).

22. In April 2005, the Central Bank introduced new rules aiming to strengthen its policies on "loans extended to finance the purchase of company shares" (Circular 25/2005). The new rules stipulated that: (a) loans extended against shares of companies that have been in operation for more than five years could not exceed 70 percent of the market value of these shares (this limit was eased to 80 percent in 2006); (b) loans could only be issued against tangible securities; and (c) loans extended in the case of IPOs cannot exceed five times the amount contributed by the subscriber. Moreover, in May 2006 the Central Bank issued new rules requiring banks and investment companies to report their "direct and indirect exposure to local shares" on a quarterly basis (Notice No. 2134/2006). As such, these institutions were required to disclose the loans and/or guarantees on their books that are secured by shares or issued to, among others, stock brokers, fund managers/advisors and businesses used for share trading. They are also required to report their own investment position in securities and investment funds.

23. Established in 2000, ESCA is a public establishment, which enjoys a separate corporate identity. It is financially and administratively autonomous, having all the necessary control and executive powers to exercise its tasks. It is based in Abu Dhabi, the capital of the United Arab Emirates, and is chaired by the Minister of Economy.

REFERENCES

Barry, E. and Tong, H., (2003). "Stock Market Volatility and Monetary Policy: What the Historical Record Shows," Asset Prices and Monetary Policy Conference, Federal Reserve Bank of Australia.

Fernández, P., (2002). *Valuation Methods and Shareholder Value Creation*, Academic Press (San Diego: CA).

Fortune, P., (2001). "Perspective: Is Margin Lending Marginal?" *Regional Review, Federal Reserve Bank of Boston*.

Hong, H., Sheinkman, J., and Xiong, W., (2005). "Asset Float and Speculative Bubbles," Working Paper 11367, National Bureau of Economic Research.

Loughran, T., Ritter, J.R., and Rydqvist, (1994). "Initial Public Offerings: International Insights," *Pacific-Basin Finance Journal*, 2, 165–99.

Mishkin, F., and White, E., (2003). "U.S. Stock Market Crashes and Their Aftermath: Implications for Monetary Policy," in Hunter, W., Kaufman, G., and Pormerleano, M., eds., *Asset Price Bubbles: The Implications for Monetary, Regulatory and International Policies* (MIT Press, Cambridge Mass), 53–79.

Ned Davis Research, Inc., (2005). "NASDAQ Composite Price/Earnings Ratio vs. Margin Debt," Ned Davis Research, Inc.

Shirvani, H., and Wilbratte, B., (2000). "Does Consumption Respond More Strongly to Stock Market Declines than to Increases?" *International Economic Journal*, 14 (3), 41–49.

CHAPTER 8

Institutional and Legal Aspects of Capital Markets in the GCC Countries

Mitra Farahbaksh

8.1 INTRODUCTION

The strengths and vulnerabilities of capital markets depend critically on the design and implementation of regulatory framework. Well-designed and properly enforced securities regulations help create deep and liquid markets, stimulate competition between intermediaries, and reduce the cost of capital for issuers. By increasing transparency and investor confidence, regulations alleviate concerns about the functioning of the markets through the provision of adequate information and promotion of fair trading practices. As financial systems become increasingly globalized, capital moves not only in response to countries' monetary policies, but also to competing financial systems. Weak and inefficient financial systems are therefore likely to be increasingly penalized.

The capital markets of the Gulf Cooperation Council (GCC) countries have developed under a diversified set of institutional arrangements and regulatory structures, and are not uniform in terms of strengths and weaknesses. A few GCC countries enforce best international practices, as set out by the International Organization of Securities Commission (IOSCO).[1] Others are working on updating their regulatory frameworks and institutional settings to meet the significant growth that has occurred in their capital markets over the last couple of years.

This chapter reviews the regulatory and institutional frameworks of capital markets in GCC countries.[2] Section 8.2 discusses briefly the evolution of the securities regulatory framework across the region over the last few years. Section 8.3 identifies the similarities and differences between the institutional set-ups and regulatory frameworks in GCC countries, with the IOSCO's best practices taken as benchmarks. Finally, the chapter provides a number of recommendations for future reform.

8.2   RECENT DEVELOPMENTS IN LEGAL AND INSTITUTIONAL FRAMEWORKS

Traditionally, legal norms in most of the GCC countries were designed for a business culture primarily based on personal and family relationships. For example, prior to the recent tightening of laws in many countries, regulatory frameworks paid little attention to primary markets. Initial Public Offerings (IPOs) of equities were not regulated by a standardized and detailed set of prudential rules.[3] Regulations for the secondary markets were also scant, and due to the multiplicity of laws and agencies, regulatory bodies were not able to effectively ensure market efficiency or fairness. Information and transparency were inadequate, contributing to high transaction costs. In addition, public financial institutions were prevalent in the stock markets. In Saudi Arabia, for example, approximately 40 percent of listed shares were owned by the state's autonomous government institutions in 2000. In addition, governments had major influence on domestic capital markets, either through public sector pension funds supporting the government's divestment programs, and/or through the underpricing of IPOs in relation to their list price.

Over the last few years, the legal frameworks and institutions underpinning the capital markets of most GCC countries underwent a major transformation. Table 8.1 outlines the key regulations governing capital markets in the region and their date of implementation. These changes took place either because of the authorities' desire to deepen capital markets in order to diversify the economy (Bahrain), or as responses to market booms and subsequent crashes (Oman). In some cases, legal and institutional enhancements came either as a response to or in conjunction with the rapid and substantial growth in stock markets. Both Saudi Arabia and the United Arab Emirates, for example, introduced significant changes to their regulatory frameworks at a time when their markets were beginning to witness considerable growth in both prices and turnover ratios – mainly since 2003.

The rapid rise in equity price indices across the region, combined with strong growth in both the money supply and credit to the private sector over the last few years, have prompted some GCC authorities to tighten prudential norms.[4] Concerned that an important part of the increase in private sector credit might be channeled to finance speculative demand in the stock market, Kuwait, for example, introduced in 2004 an 80 percent ceiling on the ratio of credit (net of provisions) to deposits. This move was designed to address the rapid expansion of credit, which had not been accompanied by a parallel increase in bank deposits. Qatar reduced the loans-to-deposits ratio from 95 percent to 85 percent. Bahrain introduced a 50 percent ceiling on the ratio of borrowers' total debt to income in 2004. Also in 2004, Saudi Arabia set up a ceiling per customer to finance IPO purchases. Consumer loan terms were cut to five years from ten and the amount of debt service was capped at one-third of the borrower's net monthly salary.

Following the wave of market corrections that began in late 2005, some regulatory authorities introduced new measures to boost investor confidence. In Saudi Arabia, for example, companies were required to split their stocks to make it easier for individuals with modest amounts of capital to participate in the market. Also, foreign residents were allowed to invest in the stock market, and daily fluctuation limits for stock prices were set at 10 percent. Oman, Qatar, and the United Arab Emirates allowed companies listed on the securities markets to buy back their own listed shares.

The GCC countries have introduced diverse rules on margin lending. Margin lending refers to loans specifically provided to buy stocks, where the borrowed money is collateralized by the purchased stocks. If the value of the collateral stock drops, the borrower will be asked to increase its collateral, repay part of the loan, or sell some of the stock. Margin lending is not permitted in Bahrain and Oman. In Saudi Arabia, margin trading collateralization has been tightened and the maximum margin trade loan amount and the loan tenor have been reduced in order to avoid an increase in banks' exposure through the channeling of personal loans to the stock market. In the United Arab Emirates, there are multiple margin rates for the same publicly traded security depending on the nature of the loan, including borrowing for purchases of IPOs (5 to 1 ratio) and for purchases of shares of already established companies (80 percent of the book value of shares).

The regulations regarding foreigners' access to capital markets have become less restrictive in some countries. By allowing non-GCC investors to purchase up to 25 percent of a listed company, Qatar has joined the rest of the region in permitting foreigners to participate in the domestic capital market. As noted above, in the aftermath of a sharp market correction in March 2006, Saudi Arabia opened the stock market to non-Saudi resident investors. Non-resident, non-Saudi investors, however, are only allowed to invest through a special mutual fund established in London. Foreign investors are permitted to hold up to 49 percent of the outstanding shares of public joint stock companies in Bahrain and the United Arab Emirates Nonetheless, in the United Arab Emirates, the articles of association of a vast majority of companies restrict ownership exclusively to nationals. In Oman, foreign investors are allowed to hold up to 70 percent of the outstanding shares of public joint stock companies. Non-GCC nationals are permitted to participate in the primary markets in Bahrain, Oman, and the United Arab Emirates.

8.3   KEY CHARACTERISTICS OF THE GCC REGULATORY FRAMEWORK

To provide guidance on implementing best international practices, in 1998 IOSCO established 30 Principles to help limit weaknesses in securities markets (Box 8.1). These Principles seek to ensure that (a) investors are well protected; (b) markets are fair, efficient, and transparent; and (c) systemic risks are reduced. The Principles set minimum standards for regulation and supervision of securities markets. They address the role of regulators, enforcement of securities regulation and self-regulation, disclosure requirements for issuers of securities and for secondary markets, and prudential requirements for market intermediaries.

This section will review the institutional set-ups and regulatory frameworks of the GCC countries, taking into account the best practices set out by IOSCO. It is important to bear in mind that the assessment discussed in this section is subjective in nature. Regulations are not directly comparable across countries, and the Principles were developed by IOSCO mainly to set standards against which a country's practices can be assessed. Moreover, even the best regulatory framework requires sufficient implementation capacity, which entails considerable time and resources.

The section is divided into three parts.[5] The first part deals with regulatory governance, including the capacity of regulatory bodies to make decisions and formulate, implement, and enforce sound policies and practices. The second part deals with cross-cutting themes relating to prudential frameworks, which comprise rules, directives, and regulatory requirements aimed at minimizing risks and vulnerabilities in capital markets. This part also discusses the practical implications of prudential frameworks, including issues related to licensing, inspection, and supervision. The third part discusses financial integrity and safety nets. It deals with regulations that promote fairness and integrity in the operation of markets, and the provision of safeguards for investors and consumers, particularly during times of financial distress and crisis.

Box 8.1   IOSCO Objectives and Principles of Securities Regulation

Objectives

The three core objectives of securities regulations are protecting investors; ensuring that markets are fair; and reducing systemic risk.

Principles

Principles relating to the regulator

- The responsibilities of the regulator should be clear and objectively stated.

- The regulator should be operationally independent and accountable in the exercise of its functions and powers.

- The regulator should have adequate powers, proper resources, and the capacity to perform its functions and exercise its powers.

- The regulator should adopt clear and consistent regulatory processes.

- The regulator's staff should observe the highest professional standards, including appropriate standards of confidentiality.

Principles of self-regulation

- The regulatory regime should make appropriate use of Self-Regulatory Organizations (SROs) that exercise direct oversight responsibility for their respective areas of competence, to the extent appropriate, to the size and complexity of the markets.

- SROs should be subject to the oversight of the regulator and should observe standards of fairness and confidentiality when exercising powers and delegating responsibilities.

Principles for the enforcement of securities regulation

- The regulator should have comprehensive inspection, investigation, and surveillance powers.

- The regulator should have comprehensive enforcement powers.

▶

■ The regulatory system should ensure an effective and credible use of inspection, investigation, surveillance, and enforcement powers, and implementation of an effective compliance program.

Principles for cooperation in regulation

■ The regulator should have the power to share both public and nonpublic information with domestic and foreign counterparts.

■ Regulators should institute information-sharing mechanisms that establish when and how they will share both public and nonpublic information with domestic and foreign counterparts.

■ The regulatory system should allow for assistance to be provided to foreign regulators who need to make enquiries in the discharge of their functions and exercise of their powers.

Principles for issuers

■ There should be full, timely, and accurate disclosure of financial results and other information that is material to investors' decisions.

■ Holders of securities in a company should be treated in a fair and equitable manner.

■ Accounting and auditing standards should be of a high and internationally acceptable quality.

Principles for Collective Investment Schemes (CISs)

■ The regulatory system should set standards for the licensing and regulation of those who wish to market or operate a CIS.

■ The regulatory system should provide rules for governing the legal form and structure of CISs and the segregation and protection of client assets.

■ Regulation should require disclosure, as set forth under the principles of issuers, which is necessary to evaluate the suitability of a CIS for a particular investor and the value of the investor's interest in the scheme.

■ Regulation should ensure that there is a proper and disclosed basis for asset valuation and pricing and the redemption of units in a CIS.

Principles for market intermediaries

■ Regulations should provide for minimum entry standards for market intermediaries.

►

- There should be initial and ongoing capital and other prudential requirements for market intermediaries.

- Market intermediaries should be required to comply with standards for internal organization and operational conduct that aim to protect client interests, ensure proper risk management, and under which management of the intermediary accepts primary responsibility for these matters.

- There should be procedures for dealing with the failure of a market intermediary in order to minimize damage and loss to investors, and to contain systemic risk.

Principles for the secondary market

- The establishment of trading systems, including securities exchanges, should be subject to regulatory authorization and oversight.

- There should be ongoing regulatory supervision of exchanges and trading systems, which should aim at ensuring that the integrity of trading is maintained through fair and equitable rules that strike an appropriate balance between the demands of different market participants.

- Regulations should promote transparent trading.

- Regulations should be designed to detect and deter manipulation and other unfair trading practices.

- Regulations should ensure the proper management of large exposures, default risk, and market disruption.

- The system for clearing and settlement of securities transactions should be subject to regulatory oversight and should be designed to ensure that it is fair, effective, and efficient, and that it reduces systemic risk.

8.3.1   Regulatory governance[6]

The GCC countries have adopted a diversified set of institutional arrangements for regulating their capital markets. In Saudi Arabia and Oman, the regulatory and supervisory functions are under the jurisdiction of a Capital Market Authority (CMA), while the day-to-day operational responsibilities are with the stock exchanges. Bahrain, however, has adopted a single regulatory model. The Central Bank of Bahrain (CBB) is responsible for cross-sector regulation and supervision of the banking system, the capital markets, the insurance sector, and all institutions working with these sectors. There are no capital market authorities in Kuwait and Qatar.[7] The securities markets in these countries are regulated by a number of regulatory bodies, including a Market Committee (MC) of the securities exchange itself, the central bank, and the Ministry of Commerce and Industry. In the United Arab Emirates, capital markets are also regulated by a number of entities. The central bank is responsible for licensing and authorizing all non-bank financial intermediaries, including brokers and investment companies, while the Ministry of Economy (MOE) is responsible for implementing the company law, corporate governance standards for issuers, prospectus disclosure requirements, and the pricing of IPOs. The Emirates Securities and Commodities Authority (ESCA) licenses intermediaries to trade on the two stock exchanges, Abu Dhabi Securities Market (ADSM) and Dubai Financial Market (DFM), and the Dubai Gold and Commodity Exchange (DGCX).

Some countries have adopted comprehensive capital market laws (Bahrain, Oman, and Saudi Arabia). In these countries, the responsibilities and powers of the regulators are stated clearly in the laws, which also establish the supervisory authorities, the exchange markets, and the security clearing and deposit centers. In some countries, regulations governing capital markets are contained in other laws as well, including the company law and the banking law (Oman and the United Arab Emirates). In Kuwait, a draft capital market law, which would create a single, independent and accountable authority with full powers to develop and regulate the securities market, is under review by the Ministry of Finance before its submission to parliament. Until its passage by Parliament, Kuwait's capital market will continue to be regulated by the Amiri Decree of 1983 and regulations promulgated subsequently.

To ensure operational independence and accountability, the regulators appear to exercise their authority without interference from either the government or the business community. In principle, the regulators should be autonomous bodies accountable to governments. In some countries, members of the regulatory authorities may be market participants themselves (Kuwait and Oman), which could potentially create a conflict of interest. In Bahrain, the prime minister and the finance minister act as the chairman and deputy chairman of the Bahrain Monetary Agency (BMA). In Kuwait, the minister of the economy is the chairman of the MC. In almost all countries, regulators report to either the Ministry of Finance or other government agencies, such as the Ministry of Commerce and Industry. Almost none of the regulatory agencies are funded through the government budget (in the United Arab Emirates, the federal government allocates some funds to the regulatory agency); funding comes from membership and subscription fees. In Kuwait, the MC is also funded through proceeds from services rendered by the stock exchange and returns from the exchange's investments.

The security exchanges of Bahrain, Saudi Arabia, and the United Arab Emirates function as Self-Regulatory Organizations (SROs). These exchanges are empowered to make rules and regulations for their members. Conflict of interest is avoided because the exchanges are not owned or managed by members who enjoy trading rights in their exchanges. In Oman, while the laws provide for the establishment of the exchange as an SRO, the exchange does not function as such. The two stock markets in the United Arab Emirates act as quasi-SROs; they authorize firms to trade on their respective exchanges, set listing standards, and accept listings of public companies and investment fund securities. The stock markets, however, are not subject to the oversight of a regulatory authority.

8.3.2   Prudential regulations[8]

In general, prudential regulations aim to contain risk and protect the interests of investors. These regulations cover a number of areas, including risk management, risk concentration, corporate governance, capital requirements, and internal control. They are put in place in order to deter and detect unlawful and fraudulent practices, such as insider trading and market manipulation. Best international practices require that entry standards for all types of market intermediaries be well-defined and prudential regulations governing their licensing, supervision, and performance be in place. Owners and officers of licensed intermediaries should be subject to fit and proper conditions. The regulator should have the capacity to enforce disclosure requirements and to examine the compliance of auditors and audited companies with internationally acceptable accounting and auditing standards.

Despite some increase in mutual funds in the region in recent years, comprehensive standards for eligibility and the regulation of Collective Investment Schemes (CISs) are in place in only a few countries. The strength of the equity markets across the region has prompted a number of commercial banks to launch mutual funds. Banks have been able to significantly increase their earnings from these mutual funds through performance, subscription, and management fees. Investment funds are becoming important players in the capital markets of Bahrain, Kuwait, Saudi Arabia, and the United Arab Emirates. Only Bahrain and Saudi Arabia, however, have established specific eligibility criteria in terms of net worth, track record, and internal management procedures. These regulations lay down disclosure requirements, procedures for calculating and declaring Net Asset Values (NAV), and accounting standards.

Detailed regulations regarding market intermediaries, such as brokerage firms, have been established in Bahrain, Oman, and Saudi Arabia. In these countries, the regulators have powers to carry out routine inspections of market intermediaries to ensure compliance with prescribed standards. The regulators' enforcement powers include the issuance of directions, imposition of monetary penalties, cancellation of registration, and even prosecution of market intermediaries. While minimum entry standards and capital adequacy requirements are also in place in other countries, standards for internal organization and procedures for dealing with the failure of market intermediaries need to be significantly strengthened. In Kuwait and Qatar, rules regarding comprehensive inspection and investigation of brokerage companies need to be strengthened significantly. Each country's central bank inspects brokerage firms only in cases of trading rules' violations. The lack of skilled staff hampers the authorities' ability to efficiently undertake market surveillance. The effectiveness of the oversight process can also be limited if regulators have few sanctions at their disposal.

In Saudi Arabia and the United Arab Emirates provisions in the law specify that the regulators should share information with other domestic and foreign regulatory bodies. Such provisions are deemed important by IOSCO because of the linkages between domestic and international capital markets – regulatory interventions, or the lack thereof, in one market tend to have repercussions in other markets. Also, there are increasing instances of the same market intermediary coming under the purview of multiple regulatory bodies as financial transactions become more complex. Therefore, the potential for regulatory gaps, as well as regulatory overlaps, underlines the need for greater cooperation among the various regulators. Bahrain, Kuwait, and Oman do not have clear rules allowing the authorities to share nonpublic information with domestic or foreign counterparts.

8.3.3   Financial integrity and safety nets[9]

Financial integrity and safety nets refer to the regulatory policies and instruments that are designed to promote fairness and integrity in the operations of financial institutions and exchanges. They also provide safeguards for depositors, investors, and policyholders, particularly during times of financial distress and crisis. Appropriate policies require regulations regarding transparency and disclosure practices, stock exchanges, and customer protection.

Over the past few years, most GCC countries have put in place comprehensive and explicit regulations regarding transparency and disclosure practices. Financial reporting requirements have been established and are being enforced. Listed companies are required to disclose their annual and quarterly financial statements in accordance with International Financial Reporting Standards (IFRS) in a timely manner.

Disclosure requirements and pricing of IPOs do not meet international standards in most GCC countries. Bahrain and Oman have put in place disclosure requirements for IPOs that are elaborate enough to allow investors to make informed investment decisions. In Kuwait, Qatar, and the United Arab Emirates, however, the requirements governing disclosure by public issuers are broad and allow the issuer much latitude in determining what information is included in the prospectus and other disclosure documents. In these countries, the use of a prospectus is only a listing requirement, which should be observed by companies seeking listing on the exchanges. In the United Arab Emirates, the company law requires the MOE to set the prices of IPOs for both state-owned and private companies at a nominal value of the company's shares, rather than through accurate assessment of the fair market value. The MOE is also involved in the pricing of subsequent offerings by public companies, usually at a substantial discount. As a result, share prices are set artificially low, leading to substantial over-subscription of IPOs and considerable market volatility.[10] Underpricing IPOs also deprives enterprises of the full value they should receive for their shares.

Company laws address the rights of minority shareholders in almost all GCC countries. Oman, however, is the only country that has a comprehensive code of corporate governance. The code aims to protect minority shareholders' interests and ensure that all holders of securities in a company are treated in a fair and equitable manner.[11] The other countries require that issuers and stockholders disclose share-ownership levels that exceed specified thresholds.

Best international practices require that marketplaces, including stock exchanges, dealer markets, organized over-the-counter markets, and clearing and settlement systems be subject to regulations that prohibit price manipulation, misleading statements, insider trading, and other market abuses. Effective monitoring of these organizations would ensure that large exposures and default risks are properly managed. While the regulation of organized and off-exchange markets is generally in place, the detection and prosecution of manipulation and other unfair trading practices must be more effectively enforced. Identification of illicit trading activities is potentially compromised by the limited integration of the surveillance function between the exchanges and the regulators (Kuwait and Oman). Insider trading laws that specifically define and prohibit price manipulation, misleading statements, insider trading, and other market abuses are needed in the majority of the countries. In Saudi Arabia, the CMA took strong actions to stop price manipulations, leading to the suspension of some traders' operations. Subsequent to the sharp market correction of March 2006, the United Arab Emirates imposed intra-day trading limits to control exposure and volatility during a single day.

Accounting rules are well-established in some countries. For example, the IFRS were adopted in Oman as early as 1986. All companies, public and private, are required to use these standards, and the CMA closely examines the financial statements of listed companies. In Kuwait and Qatar, however, there is a need to strengthen the enforcement of internationally accepted accounting and auditing standards.

8.4   ISSUES GOING FORWARD

This chapter provided a preliminary analysis of the regulatory and institutional frameworks of securities markets in the GCC countries. A more refined evaluation based on a formal IOSCO assessment is needed to draw more definite conclusions about the institutional arrangements and regulatory structures. By dividing the main regulatory issues into three general areas, the paper discussed the level of implementation of various regulatory standards in the GCC countries, based on the available information. The analysis points to the following broad conclusions.

a.   Considerable progress has been made in recent years toward strengthening the regulatory and institutional aspects of securities markets, which has led to increased transparency and market resiliency. Some countries (Bahrain, Oman, and Saudi Arabia) have enacted comprehensive capital market laws that provided the legal basis for subsequent regulations governing the markets. They have also established capital market authorities that promulgate regulations and conduct supervision. Available information suggests that considerable work is still needed in Kuwait and Qatar in order to bring their regulatory frameworks and supervision of capital markets up to international standards. In the United Arab Emirates, there is a need to define the responsibilities of each authority involved in regulating the capital market and its participants, and to address gaps in the regulations in order to safeguard the investors' interest. Prudential regulations and financial integrity and safety net arrangements require strengthening in almost all countries.

b.   Most countries need to establish an appropriate legal framework for CISs and strengthen their supervision. While specific governance requirements for CISs vary across countries, laws are not generally comprehensive regarding distribution, disclosure, management, and custody of mutual fund assets. In particular, laws should give the regulatory authorities clear powers to set and enforce comprehensive prospectus requirements and corporate governance standards for public companies. The responsibility for licensing investment companies and brokers should be consolidated in one authority, which should also be responsible for establishing and enforcing initial (prospectus) rules and continuous disclosure requirements for public companies. Finally, given rapid capital market developments, the regulatory authorities need to build capacity to ensure that their staff have the right skills to carry out their mandate effectively.

c.   IPOs should be priced at fair market value in order to reduce excessive market volatility and allow firms to receive full value for their shares. Subscription prices for new offerings should be set by the market through professional underwriters based on an appropriate valuation of the company. IPOs should be permitted only for companies that have had audited balance sheets for at least two years.

d.   Governments should refrain from influencing the stock markets. In the aftermath of the sharp price correction in March 2006, the GCC governments generally refrained from direct interference in the markets. Nevertheless, some governments took new measures to support the markets. In Saudi Arabia, the authorities allowed non-GCC residents to participate in the markets, and required all companies to split their shares 5 to 1. In Kuwait, the government announced that it would provide liquidity to the markets through the Kuwait Investment Fund to stabilize the market. Some of these measures may create moral hazard and prevent investors from assessing risks in a manner consistent with the functioning of a competitive market.

e.   Public floating of securities should be increased in order to create deep and liquid markets. In a deep market, large blocks of stocks can be traded quickly without unduly affecting market prices. Moreover, a wide distribution of shares among a large number of active traders helps increase liquidity. The large proportion of shares of public companies owned by the governments in many GCC countries has resulted in fewer shares being available for trading in the market. Also, requirements that force the founding shareholders to subscribe to a significant portion of a company's equity for long periods of time have resulted in few shareholders holding a significant number of outstanding shares.

f.   Licensing rules establishing minimum entry standards for market intermediaries appear to be in place in most countries. Regulations in several other areas need sharpening. In particular, regulations regarding risk management and the internal organization of firms, capital adequacy, and other prudential controls and procedures in case of the failure of an intermediary require substantial strengthening. This issue will become even more important as markets develop further. Regulatory shortcomings in these areas may have implications for public confidence in the securities market and, in case of inadequate mechanisms to address the failure of a firm, could entail potential systemic risks.

g.   Institutional investors should be encouraged to participate in the markets to reduce excessive volatility. In a number of countries, some key capital market activities, such as investment advice, fund management, placement and underwriting, are left either largely unregulated or outside the jurisdiction of the securities market regulators. Detailed prudential rules and disclosure requirements for investment funds are needed in most countries. Fit and proper assessments need to be strengthened and guidelines and regulations should be enforced. In addition, the markets would benefit from the introduction of market stabilization mechanisms, such as hedging instruments that can provide liquidity and allow investors to manage their risks more effectively.

The regulatory standards discussed in this chapter represent the minimum requirements for a good regulatory system. An appropriate legal framework for effective securities regulation should also include commercial code/contract laws (property rights, private right of contract, etc.); bankruptcy and insolvency laws; a competition law; a modern banking law; consistent taxation laws; and an appropriate dispute resolution mechanism.

Finally, the planned GCC monetary union by 2010 will require the countries' economic and financial markets to integrate at an accelerated pace. Important steps have already been taken with respect to economic integration, including the harmonization of customs tariffs and the lifting of formal impediments to the free movement of goods and services, as well as labor and capital within the GCC. However, considerable work is still needed to harmonize the region's capital market regulations, structures, and practices. Harmonization requires two layers of legislation: basic principles to set out an adequate framework and more detailed technical measures consistent with this framework.

Table 8.1 Capital market regulations in the GCC

Capital market authority	Capital market law	Disclosure & transparency rules	CIS regulations	Regulation of market intermediaries	Regulatory oversight of secondary markets	Code of corporate governance	Money laundering law
Bahrain: Bahrain's Monetary Authority (BMA) was established in 1987, and was given authority to regulate and supervise the entire financial sector in 2002. BMA is responsible for securities regulation, but the Ministry of Industry and Commerce shares some responsibilities. The Bahrain Stock Exchange is a self-regulatory organization.	Issued in 2002. Securities and Exchange Regulations were passed in 2006, which further clarified the responsibilities of the supervisory authorities.	Issued in 2003. Provide for timely, comprehensive, and specific disclosure requirements. Rights and equitable treatment of shareholders are fully addressed. Accounting and auditing practices are of high standards.	Comprehensive regulations issued in 1992, 1995, and 2003. They set comprehensive standards for eligibility regulation of CIS. Rules provide for legal form and structure of CIS, segregation and protection of client assets, and full disclosure. Proper and disclosed basis for asset valuation and pricing and redemption of units in a CIS are required.	Comprehensive rules issued in 1995 and 2000. They set minimum entry standards and clearly defined capital requirements and trading caps for brokers. Intermediaries are required to comply with standards of internal organization and operational conduct; and risk management systems are properly in place.	Security exchange is fully subject to regulatory authority and oversight of the BMA. Ongoing regulatory supervision takes place on a daily basis. Regulations promote full transparency of trading and ensure proper management of large exposures, default risk, and market disruptions. Systems for clearing and settlement of transactions are subject to regulatory oversight; and systems are broadly designed to reduce systemic risk.	None. However, various provisions in the existing Commercial Companies' Law and its implementing regulations control corporate governance.	Issued in 2001.

Table 8.1 Continued

Capital market authority	Capital market law	Disclosure & transparency rules	CIS regulations	Regulation of market intermediaries	Regulatory oversight of secondary markets	Code of corporate governance	Money laundering law
Kuwait:							
None. Securities market is regulated by several agencies, including the Kuwait Stock Exchange (KSE), which oversees the securities secondary market, and the Central Bank of Kuwait, which regulates investment companies. The Ministry of Commerce and Industry regulates the primary securities market.	Amiri Decree-Law of 1983 governs the operations of the securities market.	Disclosure requirements are broad. Public offerings of securities need to be fully organized and clear regulations need to be established. There are discrepancies between Securities Law and Company Law regarding IPO regulations. The application of accounting and auditing standards is a legal requirement; however, supervisors rely	Issued in 1990, 1992, and 2005. Supervision is segmented between different agencies. Prudential rules are required to ensure the solvency of mutual funds. Regulations regarding investment policy need to be announced and strictly adhered to.	Rules on investment funds issued in 2005. Licensing requirements for market intermediaries are broad. Intermediaries are supervised by different agencies. Detailed prudential rules are needed, including rules for intermediaries on standards of internal organization and operational conduct.	Regulations provide for the oversight and supervision of the KSE by a Market Committee (MC) through reporting. No inspection or surveillance is conducted. Conduct of brokers is not directly supervised by the MC. The reporting system followed by the KSE is the MC's main supervision tool. There are no specific regulations on insider trading. Regulations should be strengthened to fully promote transparent trading and ensure proper management of large exposures, default risk, and market disruptions. Systems for clearing and settlement of transactions are not formally subject to oversight; systems	None.	Issued in 2003.

Oman: Established in 1998. Responsible for issuing rules related to securities trading, inspection, investigation, and surveillance over issuers, listed companies, brokers and insurance companies.	Issued in 1998. Some regulations overlap with Company Law and Competition Law.	Issued in 2000 and 2001. Clearly spells out disclosure requirements. Needs to differentiate between public offerings and private placements and enhance the disclosure of product information.	General regulations regarding closed-end funds issued in 1994.	Regulations on investment funds were issued in 2004. Licensing requirements for all intermediaries are clearly spelled out. Capital adequacy requirements for all market intermediaries are in place as of 2003. Procedures for dealing with the failure of a market intermediary are not yet in place. There are no risk management procedures.	Security exchange is fully subject to CMA regulatory authorization and oversight. Ongoing regulatory supervision takes place on a daily basis. Regulations promote full transparency of trading and ensure proper management of large exposures, default risk, and market disruptions. Systems for clearing and settlement of transactions are subject to regulatory oversight; systems are broadly designed to reduce systemic risk.	Comprehensive rules issued in 2002 and 2003.	Issued in 2004.
		only on external auditors to monitor compliance.			need to be designed in such a way as to reduce systemic risk.		

Continued

Table 8.1 Continued

Capital market authority	Capital market law	Disclosure & transparency rules	CIS regulations	Regulation of market intermediaries	Regulatory oversight of secondary markets	Code of corporate governance	Money laundering law
Qatar: None. Regulation and supervision of the market are mainly the responsibilities of both the Qatar Central Bank (QCB) and the Doha Securities Market (DSM). Fragmentation of responsibilities between the two organizations. Neither the QCB nor the DSM have operational independence from the government. Need strengthening of transparency. The DSM is both regulator and market operator. The authorities	Decree Law of 1997.	Issued in 2003. It includes broad provisions for disclosure requirements. Disclosure requirements and corporate governance regulations are limited. Review of the information submitted by issuer is limited and issuer's compliance with disclosure requirements appears low. Rights and equitable treatment of shareholders are not fully addressed; no	Regulations do not distinguish between the responsibilities of the founder, the custodian, and the manager. Provisions related to the structure of CIS and investor protection need to be strengthened. Reasonable mechanisms for off-site and on-site supervision of CIS need to be put in place.	Investment fund law issued in 2002. Market intermediaries are subject to minimum capital requirements. The QCB conducts off-site and on-site supervision of investment companies. Off-site supervision of brokerage houses by the DSM need to be strengthened. Market conduct regulations, such as suitability requirements, should be developed.	Regulations ensure the oversight and supervision of the DSM. The DSM is not subject to licensing in its function of market operator nor does the law provide for the licensing of other market operators. There are no specific regulations on insider trading. Regulations need to be strengthened to promote transparency of trading, and ensure proper management of large exposures, default risk, and market disruptions. Systems for clearing and settlement of transactions are not formally subject to oversight; systems need to be designed in such a way as to reduce systemic risk. Need to strengthen supervisory capabilities.	None.	Issued in 2002, as amended in 2003 and 2004.

are in the process of establishing a new Qatar Financial Market Authority Law that, if effectively implemented, would fully meet the IOSCO requirements.	provisions for accounting and auditing standards.	Issued in 2003.	General provisions included in the Capital Market Law.	None.
Saudi Arabia: Established in 2004. Responsible for issuing rules related to securities trading, inspection, investigation, and surveillance over issuers, listed companies, and brokers.	Issued in 2004. Provides for timely, comprehensive, and specific disclosure requirements. Rights and equitable treatment of shareholders are fully addressed. There are broad provisions for accounting and auditing standards.	Comprehensive rules issued in 2005. They set minimum entry standards, capital requirements for brokers, and broad rules for intermediaries on standards of internal organization and operational control. There are no procedures for dealing with the failure of an intermediary. Also, no risk management procedures exist.	The exchange has the power to conduct ongoing regulatory supervision on a daily basis. Regulations promote transparency of trading. Further regulations are needed to ensure proper management of large exposures, default risk, and market disruptions. Securities deposit center is under the jurisdiction of the securities exchange.	Issued in 2004.

Continued

Table 8.1 Continued

Capital market authority	Capital market law	Disclosure & transparency rules	CIS regulations	Regulation of market intermediaries	Regulatory oversight of secondary markets	Code of corporate governance	Money laundering law
United Arab Emirates:							
Emirates Securities and Commodities Authority (ESCA) was established in 2000. ESCA is responsible for supervising the Abu Dhabi Securities Market (ADSM) and the Dubai Financial Market (DFM); It also licenses brokers, establishes disclosure requirements, and issues rules related to securities trading.	Issued in 2000. Lacks provisions on investment funds, advisors, and collective investment schemes, manipulation, and insider trading; requires further provisions on clearing and settlement. A new draft securities law is currently being finalized.	Issued in 2000. Provides for timely, comprehensive, and specific disclosure requirements; rights and equitable treatment of shareholders are addressed. There are no provisions for accounting and auditing standards.	Central Bank resolution dates back to 1994.	Issued in 2000 and 2005. They set minimum entry standards and capital requirements for brokers. Broad rules are in place for intermediaries to comply with standards of internal organization and operational control. Procedures for dealing with the failure of an intermediary are broad. There are no risk management procedures. Regulations on investment funds date from 1994.	Issued in 2001 and 2005. Exchanges are not fully subject to regulatory authorization and oversight of ESCA. Ongoing regulatory supervision takes place on a daily basis. Regulations promote full transparency of trading. Systems for clearing and settlement of transactions are subject to regulatory oversight. Further regulations are needed to ensure proper management of large exposures, default risk and market disruptions.	Issued and promulgated in 2007.	Issued in 2002.

Source: GCC country authorities.

NOTES

1. IOSCO is an international forum for securities' regulators with over 170 members (securities regulatory agencies, self-regulatory organizations, and international institutions), representing about 100 jurisdictions.
2. This chapter describes the legal and institutional developments as of mid-2006. Some changes that have taken place since then are also reflected.
3. Historically, there have been few IPOs because of the limited number of privatizations and families' lack of interest in taking their businesses public.
4. Consumer loans in all the countries in the region are secured by salaries. The limits on lending in the United Arab Emirates and Saudi Arabia are 40 times and 30 times individuals' salaries, respectively. Oman has had in place, for many years, a ceiling on personal credit, currently set at 40 percent of banks' total credit outstanding.
5. This grouping is broadly based on the Bank for International Settlements Joint Forum, Basel Committee on Banking Supervision, November 2001.
6. Includes Principles 1 to 7.
7. In July 2007, the Qatari authorities announced the merger of the entire domestic financial center into a single financial market, which would have the legal mandate and a governance structure to conduct activities in both the on-shore Qatar Financial Center (QFC) and Qatari institutions. A unified independent financial services regulatory body, which will consist of the QFC Regulatory Authority (QFCRA), QCB's banking supervision department and the Doha stock market regulator, is scheduled to begin operations in 2008. This regulatory body will have a broad range of powers to authorize, supervise and, where necessary, discipline all regulated financial institutions, firms, and individuals.
8. Includes Principles 8 to 13, 17 to 18, 20 to 23, 25, 27, and 29.
9. Includes Principles 14 to 16, 19, 24, 26, 28, and 30.
10. The two IPOs issued in March 2006 were oversubscribed by 500 times and 167 times the shares offered, raising $74 billion (60 percent of GDP), and $109 billion (80 percent of GDP), respectively. The liquidation of existing positions to fund the subscriptions for the IPOs created a liquidity crunch that helped trigger a sharp correction in the DFM of almost 12 percent on March 14, 2006.
11. Bahrain plans to issue a comprehensive code of governance in 2006.

Index